D. H. Lawrence: A Centenary Con-sideration will be rewarding reading both for Lawrencian specialists and for others interested in modern literature.

D. H. LAWRENCE

D. H. LAWRENCE

A Centenary Consideration

EDITED BY PETER BALBERT

AND PHILLIP L. MARCUS

CORNELL UNIVERSITY PRESS

ITHACA AND LONDON

First published 1985 by Cornell University Press.

International Standard Book Number 0-8014-1596-9
Library of Congress Catalog Card Number 84-45800
Printed in the United States of America
*Librarians: Library of Congress cataloging information
appears on the last page of the book.*

*The paper in this book is acid-free and meets the guidelines for
permanence and durability of the Committee on Production Guidelines
for Book Longevity of the Council on Library Resources.*

TO THE MEMORY OF OUR FATHERS

Bert Balbert (1911–1978)

Ben C. Marcus (1904–1983)

CONTENTS

[7]

CONTENTS

PREFACE

Although this collection appears in the centenary year of D. H. Lawrence's birth, it is not intended as a celebration. The outstanding fact about the man and his work is the way they continue to *engage* us, to challenge us to understand them and to evaluate them justly. The contributors to this volume were charged with meeting that challenge. To ensure fresh perspectives, we sought a combination of "Lawrencians" and critics whose reputations rest primarily on other work. Nine of the essays are entirely new, the others significant revisions of published pieces. The order of the essays follows the chronology of Lawrence's career, and together they cover the full range of Lawrence's creative achievement, from analyses of major novels and short fiction to reassessments of his poetry and visionary thought.

Our greatest concern, however, was to allow the contributors to explore as freely as possible whatever aspects of the life and work they found most compelling, and we did not assign or commission essays systematically covering every major topic and text. Thus *The Lost Girl* and *Lady Chatterley's Lover,* for example, are considered only briefly. Nor was there any desire on our part to obtain ideological or methodological uniformity such as might characterize, say, a volume of Marxist or psychoanalytic studies. The essays included range from traditional humanistic studies and formalist readings to feminist approaches and analyses that reflect current poststructuralist thought. Such eclecticism offers the greatest promise of doing justice to the multifaceted nature of Lawrence's achievement. On the other hand, it brings a concomitant likelihood that even the most open-minded readers will not be equally sympathetic to *all* of the essays. Some of the pieces implicitly challenge the validity of others; some may become quite controversial. But the volume as a whole should both under-

[9]

score the richness of the subject and stimulate further engagement in its light.

In the first essay, A. Walton Litz sees the tensions between Lawrence and his supporter-turned-antagonist Ezra Pound as epitomizing the polarities characteristic of literary modernism in general. Mark Spilka expands his consideration of Mark Schorer's facsimile edition of the manuscript of *Sons and Lovers* into a critical reevaluation of Lawrence and shows how the manuscript reveals Lawrence discovering the techniques and values of his great "psychic dramas." That major fiction itself is the subject of the next three studies. Peter Balbert isolates a pattern of instinctual emphasis, a "logic of the soul," as he uses the sexual dialectics of Lawrence and Norman Mailer to argue for the presence of a radical conservatism in *The Rainbow*. Maria DiBattista, viewing *Women in Love* as Lawrence's "judgment book," explores ways in which such concepts as totemism, natural language, and spiritual determinism inform the text. Robert Kiely, focusing upon the same novel, examines the issue of "bad form" in the fiction, suggesting that ostensible flaws may reflect Lawrence's feeling that "the greatest artistic masterpieces pay homage to nature by acknowledging their own defects" and demonstrating the subtleties in several scenes involving "purposeful accidents."

Not surprisingly, several of the contributors concern themselves with the problematical works of the transitional period after the Great War. In a revisionist essay based mainly on *Birds, Beasts and Flowers,* Marjorie Perloff argues that the "performative stance" characteristic of Lawrence's poetry is closer to Futurist tendencies than to Romantic paradigms and thus looks ahead to the poetic discourse of our own time; and Sandra Gilbert places "The Ladybird" within the context of mythic patterns involving "the Great Mother," highlighting both Lawrence's awareness of the reasserted primacy of the maternal and the anxieties such awareness created in him. Avrom Fleishman employs the narratological categories of Bakhtin to reveal the subtleties of Lawrence's later prose style, with particular attention to *St. Mawr.* And Charles Rossman closely examines Lawrencian biography in tracing the ways in which his personal experiences of Mexico affected the preoccupations of *The Plumed Serpent* and *Mornings in Mexico.*

The last two essays help complete the picture and integrate the collection. Balancing Litz's study, which concentrates on the early career, Phillip L. Marcus's essay explores Lawrence's relationship to Yeats, using a comparison between the late novella *The Escaped Cock* and Yeats's play *Calvary* to suggest both the significant similarities in vision of the two writers and the irreconcilable differences between them. George Zytaruk extracts from Lawrence's oeuvre the elements of a coherent "metaphysic" of individuality. In doing so Zytaruk necessarily touches at various points upon the concerns of many of the preceding pieces and thus provides an appropriate conclusion to the volume.

The texts of Lawrence's work are currently in a transitional state from embarrassing conditions of disorder and corruption to the unity and authority promised by the new Cambridge Edition. Unfortunately, that project was not far enough advanced to be of extensive use to the contributors to this volume. The first two volumes of the Cambridge Edition of the *Letters* and a few other Cambridge texts have been used, but otherwise no effort has been made to achieve uniformity in the citation of editions.

For permission to quote from the works of D. H. Lawrence, as published in the list of titles below, we gratefully acknowledge the estate of D. H. Lawrence, the estate of Mrs. Frieda Lawrence Ravagli, and Lawrence Pollinger, Ltd. Permission to reproduce the "phoenix" embroidery design worked by D. H. Lawrence and Frieda Lawrence and used as part of the design of the dust jacket of this volume has been granted by the same parties; the photograph is by John Zytaruk.

Black Sparrow Press: *The Escaped Cock*
Cambridge University Press: *The Letters of D. H. Lawrence*, vols. 1 and 2; *The Lost Girl; St. Mawr and Other Stories*
William Heinemann, Ltd.: *Mornings in Mexico*
Indiana University Press: *Reflections on the Death of a Porcupine*
Penguin Books: *Women in Love*
Random House: *Lady Chatterley's Lover; The Plumed Serpent*
Thomas Seltzer: *Fantasia of the Unconscious*
University of California Press: *Sons and Lovers: A Facsimile of the Manuscript*
The Viking Press, Inc.: *Aaron's Rod; Apocalypse; The Collected Letters of D. H. Lawrence; The Complete Poems of D. H. Lawrence; The Complete Short Stories; Four Short Novels; Phoenix; Phoenix II; Psychoanalysis and the Unconscious* and *Fantasia of the Unconscious; The Rainbow; Sea and Sardinia; Selected Literary Criticism; Sons and Lovers; Studies in Classic American Literature; Women in Love*

"Crazy Jane Talks with the Bishop" is reprinted with permission of Macmillan Publishing Company, Inc., from *The Variorum Edition of the Poems of W. B. Yeats*, by W. B. Yeats, ed. Peter Allt and Russell K. Alspach, 3d printing, with corrections (New York: Macmillan, 1973). Copyright 1933 by Macmillan Publishing Company, Inc., renewed 1961 by Bertha Georgie Yeats.

Lines from "The Tower" are quoted with permission of Macmillan

Publishing Company, Inc., from *The Variorum Edition of the Poems of W. B. Yeats*, by W. B. Yeats, ed. Peter Allt and Russell K. Alspach, 3d printing, with corrections (New York: Macmillan, 1973). Copyright 1928 by Macmillan Publishing Company, Inc., renewed 1956 by Georgie Yeats.

Passages from the plays of W. B. Yeats are quoted with permission of Macmillan Publishing Company, Inc., from *The Variorum Edition of the Plays of W. B. Yeats,* by W. B. Yeats, ed. Russell K. Alspach, assisted by Catharine C. Alspach (New York: Macmillan, 1966). Copyright © Russell K. Alspach and Bertha Georgie Yeats 1966. Copyright © Macmillan & Co. Ltd 1965.

Passages from the work of W. B. Yeats are also quoted by permission of Senator Michael B. Yeats, Miss Anne Yeats, A. P. Watt & Son, Ltd., and the Macmillan Press, Ltd.

Lines from "The Fish" by Elizabeth Bishop are quoted by permission of Farrar, Straus & Giroux.

Mark Spilka's essay in an earlier form appeared in *Review* 3 (1981), 129–47, and is reprinted with the permission of the editor.

Peter Balbert's essay in an earlier form appeared in *Papers on Language and Literature* 19 (1983), 309–25, and is reprinted with the permission of the Board of Trustees of Southern Illinois University.

Individuals who have aided us in various ways include Lynne Balbert, Marcia Brubeck, Valorie J. Eamer, Maria Hyland, Gerald Lacy, Elizabeth Mansfield, Sarah J. Marcus, Phyllis Molock, Gerald Pollinger, Warren Roberts, Keith Sagar, Lindeth Vasey, Lydia Zelaya, and the staff of Cornell University Press, especially Carol Betsch, Bernhard Kendler, and Marilyn Sale.

PETER BALBERT
PHILLIP L. MARCUS

Ithaca, New York

D. H. LAWRENCE

[1]

Lawrence, Pound, and
Early Modernism

A. Walton Litz

In a memorable chapter of *Everyman Remembers* (1931), Ernest Rhys recalls the "gathering of young poets" at his home in the years just before the First World War, "informally resuming the nights at the old Cheshire Cheese of the Rhymers' Club," and especially an evening in 1909 when Ford Madox Hueffer brought his latest discovery, D. H. Lawrence, to join a group dominated by W. B. Yeats and Ezra Pound. The account has become an essential part of the mythology of literary modernism.

> During the supper, Willie Yeats, always a good monologuer, held forth at length on this new art of bringing music and poetry together, and possibly Ezra Pound, who could also be vocal on occasion, may have felt he was not getting a fair share of the festivity. So, in order to pass the time perhaps, and seeing the supper table dressed with red tulips in glasses, he presently took one of the flowers and proceeded to munch it up. As Yeats, absorbed in his monologue, did not observe this strange behavior, and the rest of us were too well-bred to take any notice, Ezra, having found the tulip to his taste, did likewise with a second flower. Now, memory I admit is an artist, but not always to be trusted, and may have deceived me into recalling that by the end of supper all the tulips had been consumed. It was not until after the Rhymers' program had run half its course that the tulip-eater recovered his insouciance and was able to join freely in the performances. . . .
>
> In his turn, Ford Madox Ford read us a witty burlesque, after which we persuaded D. H. Lawrence, who had been sitting silent in a corner, to read us some of his verse. He rose nervously but very deliberately, walked across to a writing desk whose lid was closed, opened it, produced a mysterious book out of his pocket, and sat down, his back to the com-

pany, and began to read in an expressive, not very audible voice. One could not hear every word or every line clearly, but what was heard left an impression of a set of love-poems, written with sincerity and not a little passion, interspersed with others written in dialect not easy to follow. . . .

Lawrence's reading went on and on, seemed as if it might go on the whole evening, and the other poets became restive, and chattered *sotto voce*. At the end of half an hour, these murmurings had increased, and one murmurer, with nod and gesture, seemed to ask his hostess to intervene. She appealed to me, and I whispered: "What am I to do?"

"Tell him he must want a little rest."

This I did, adding that if so inclined he might resume at midnight! He took it in good part, and getting up with an awkward little bow shut up book and desk, and retired to his corner. And now Ezra Pound, fortified, if anything, by the tulips, started up, asking if we minded "having the roof taken off the house." He went on to declaim in a resonant, histrionic voice, a little like Henry Irving with an American accent, his imaginative "Ballad of the Goodly Fere". . . .

As the evening wound to a close with other readings and Florence Farr's performance on her psaltery, the company "tried to get Lawrence to give us one more lyric out of his black book, and impressed it on him that one only would satisfy our ritual needs; but Madox Ford took him under his arm and marched him off murmuring wickedly, 'Nunc, nunc dimittis.'"[1]

Unfortunately, Rhys's colorful account is shot through with errors in fact. Pound is described as a former member of the Rhymers' Club (Rhys probably had in mind the Poets' Club of 1909); Florence Farr (Mrs. Edward Emery) is called Winifred Emery; and if the event took place in December 1909, as Kim Herzinger has persuasively argued, then John Davidson (who "came very late") was indeed a shadowy guest, since he had drowned himself a few months before. What we have at work are the usual lapses of memory and conflations of different incidents from the past, but it also seems likely that the characterizations of Lawrence and Pound were affected by Rhys's knowledge of their later attitudes. Pound is the "mountebank" of Lawrence's 1929

[1] Ernest Rhys, *Everyman Remembers* (New York: Cosmopolitan, 1931), 243–49. For evidence concerning the date of the incident, see Kim A. Herzinger, *D. H. Lawrence in His Time: 1908–1915* (Lewisburg: Bucknell University Press, 1982), 183–85. Herzinger's study (especially pp. 140–57) contains an excellent account of the early artistic relationship between Pound and Lawrence. For a summary of biographical information, see Warren Roberts, "London 1908: Lawrence and Pound," *Helix* (Australia), nos. 13/14 (1983), 45–49.

comments to Glenn Hughes,[2] Lawrence the boring and disagreeable person who emerges from Pound's later letters.

An even sharper example of retrospective reshaping is found in Jessie Chambers's memoir, where she recalls after a quarter century a visit to the home of Ford Madox Hueffer and Violet Hunt in November 1909. Pound is described as "an amiable buffoon," moving with "the stiff precision of a mechanical toy," like one of the clockwork quatrains in *Hugh Selwyn Mauberley*. As in most reminiscences of Lawrence's early life, questions of class and social behavior hang heavily in the air.

> The American poet continued to rattle off his questions like a succession of squibs. Finally he put a question to Hueffer that electrified me.
>
> "How would *you* speak to a working man?" he asked. "Would you speak to him just the same as to any other man, or would you make a difference?" I nearly held my breath for the answer. Perhaps Hueffer found my gaze embarrassing, because he hesitated a moment and glanced at me before he said:
>
> "I should speak to a working man in exactly the same way that I should speak to any other man, because I don't think there is any difference."[3]

It is instructive to read these and other retrospective accounts against this passage from Lawrence's letter to Louie Burrows of 20 November 1909.

> I went on Tuesday to Violet Hunts "at home" at the Reform Club in Adelphi Terrace, on the Embankment. It was very jolly. Elizabeth Martindale and Ellaline Terriss and Mary Cholmondeley were there—and Ezra Pound. He is a well-known American poet—a good one. He is 24, like me,—but his god is beauty, mine, life. He is jolly nice: took me to supper at Pagnani's, and afterwards we went down to his room at Kensington. He lives in an attic, like a traditional poet—but the attic is a comfortable well furnished one. He is an American Master of Arts and a professor of the Provençal group of languages, and he lectures once a week on the minstrels [at] the London polytechnic. He is rather remarkable—a good bit of a genius, and with not the least self consciousness.[4]

[2]See Glenn Hughes, *Imagism and the Imagists* (Stanford: Stanford University Press, 1931), 170.

[3]Jessie Chambers ["E.T."], *D. H. Lawrence: A Personal Record* (London: Jonathan Cape, 1935), 171–74.

[4]*The Letters of D. H. Lawrence*, vol. 1, ed. James T. Boulton (Cambridge: Cambridge University Press, 1979), 144–45.

This letter would seem to confirm the recollection of Grace Lovat Fraser (Grace Crawford) that in the early months of their acquaintanceship Lawrence and Pound were on friendly terms, in spite of their "wildly dissimilar" temperaments: "The atmosphere between them was sometimes rather strained and disturbing, but this was a rare occurrence and for the most part they seemed attracted to each other because of their very dissimilarity. It was always clear that they liked and respected each other's work."[5]

But although retrospective accounts of the early relationship between Lawrence and Pound may have been distorted by later events and later biases, they do reflect the deep divisions in personality and artistic ideals that would gradually separate the two writers, and that would come to symbolize the most fundamental divisions in modernist literature. As each writer began to draw away from the other, in the years after Pound's visit to America in 1910–11, he did so in a characteristic way, one following the god of "beauty," the other the god of "life." It is typical of Pound's absorption in the craft of literature that most of his comments on Lawrence refer to the personality in the works; even when he says that Lawrence is "boring" or "disagreeable," he usually has the form of the writings in mind. By contrast, Lawrence treats Pound novelistically, as a character in an evolving narrative that is the life of D. H. Lawrence. Already by June 1910 he feels self-confident enough to distance Pound through this brilliant portrait of the American dandy:

> Pound was at Hueffer's when I called on Sunday week. He was just back from Sermione which he announces as the earthly paradise. Perhaps the tree of wisdom is there, always in blossom, like a gorse bush. At any rate Pound's David Copperfield curls—perhaps you never saw them—like bunches of hop leaves over his ears—they were cut. They used to make me quote to myself: "Good wine needs no bush". His great grandfather's black satin stock, which would throw into relief the contour of his chin four months ago, had given way to a tie of peach-bloom tint and texture. He wore a dark cotton shirt, no vest and a Panama hat. What is this guise?—sort of latest edition of Jongleur? Italy had improved his health: I was glad of that. It had not improved his temper: he was irascible. He discussed with much pursing of lips and removing of frown-shaken eyeglasses, his projection of writing an account of the mystic cult of love—the Dionysian rites and so on—from earliest days to the present. The great difficulty was that no damned publisher in London would dare publish it. It would have to be published in Paris. Then how about

[5]Grace Lovat Fraser, *In the Days of My Youth* (London: Cassell, 1970), 137.

the sales. I suggested its being written in French like Vathek or Salomé: impertinence on my part. But how was this matter of publishers to be arranged... ? It was a knot. At the crowing of the cock we saw the ground illuminated with a golden race of chickens: the offspring of the crow.

Pound, as perhaps you know, was returning to America by last Saturday's boat. Having had all the experience possible for a poor man, he will now proceed to conquer riches, and explore the hemisphere, he will sell boots—there is nothing in that blown egg, literature. I ventured that he should run a cinematograph! a dazzling picture palace; for which valuable suggestion he tendered me a frown.[6]

Here Pound is assigned the part he would subsequently play in Lawrence's life drama. After 1910 Lawrence seems to have paid little attention to Pound's poetry or criticism, and there is no convincing evidence that he was affected by it. Pound, on the other hand, tried for a time in 1912–14 to gather Lawrence into "the movement" and in ways that tell us a great deal about the two poets and their roles in the shaping of early modernism.

Writing to Harriet Monroe in March 1913 in his new capacity as "foreign correspondent" for *Poetry* (Chicago), Pound reported that "Lawrence has brought out a vol." (*Love Poems and Others*).

He is clever; I don't know whether to send in a review or not. We seem pretty well stuffed up with matter at the moment. (D. H. Lawrence, whom I mentioned in my note on the *Georgian Anthology*.) Detestable person but needs watching. I think he learned the proper treatment of modern subjects before I did. That was in some poems in *The Eng. Rev.*; can't tell whether he has progressed or retrograded as I haven't seen the book yet. He may have published merely on his prose rep.[7]

Pound's interest in Lawrence's poetry had probably been sharpened by their joint appearance in the *English Review* for June 1912, where "The Return" and "Apparuit" were printed next to Lawrence's long poem "Snap-Dragon." Six months later "Snap-Dragon" was included in *Georgian Poetry, 1911–1912*, where it might well have been paired again with poems by Pound. Edward Marsh had asked Pound to contribute to the anthology, but Pound was cautious about the "gallery" he would be joining and felt that his "modern" work was already

---

[6]Ibid., 142–43. Lawrence to Grace Crawford, 24 June 1910.

[7]*The Letters of Ezra Pound, 1907–1941*, ed. D. D. Paige (New York: Harcourt, Brace, 1950), no. 15. Since the American and English editions of the *Letters* differ in pagination, I cite letter numbers.

committed to *Ripostes* (published in October 1912).[8] When *Georgian Poetry* was published in December 1912, Pound must have congratulated himself on his caution, since he sent a scathing brief review to Harriet Monroe (the "note" mentioned in his letter of March 1913). Written in great haste (Pound first headed it "An Anthology of Gregorian Verse," then substituted "Georgian"), the "note" was never printed, and is interesting chiefly for its mention of Lawrence and its revelation of Pound's growing contempt for the Georgians.

> This collection of verse printed since 1910 will reveal to the American reader about all the younger London points of view in poetry which are likely to be unrepresented in my notes.
> The work of Lascelles Abercrombie is about the best in the book, though the poem by D. H. Lawrence stands in pleasing contrast to its neighbors.
> Those who have read the *Lyric Year* with interest will peruse this anthology with deepest admiration.[9]

The ironic last sentence refers to *The Lyric Year: One Hundred Poems*, edited by Ferdinand Earle (1912), described in the preface as "a selection from one year's work of a hundred American poets. . . . Ten thousand poems by nearly two thousand writers of verse have been personally examined by the Editor for this competition."

Pound may well have been impressed by the technique of "Snap-Dragon" and especially by Lawrence's skillful variations on a basic rhyme pattern, which match well with his own experiment in "The Return" and "Apparuit"; but to gain a context for his appreciation we should look back to the poems in the *English Review* that show what Pound meant when he said that Lawrence "learned the proper treatment of modern subjects before I did." Two of Pound's strongest poems in his early mode of pseudotranslation, "Sestina: Altaforte" and "Ballad of the Goodly Fere," appeared in the *English Review* in June and October 1909, and Lawrence would certainly have admired their vigor and direct narrative force. But the other two poems grouped with the "Ballad of the Goodly Fere" in the October issue, "Nils Lykke" and "Un Retrato" (later "Portrait from 'La mère incon-

---

[8]Christopher Hassall, *Edward Marsh: Patron of the Arts* (London: Longmans, 1959), 193.

[9]From the papers of *Poetry* magazine, Department of Special Collections, University of Chicago Library. First printed in *Ezra Pound and Dorothy Shakespear: Their Letters, 1909–1914*, ed. Omar Pound and A. Walton Litz (New York: New Directions, 1984), 168.

nue'") hark back to the weaker academic romanticism of *A Lume Spento*. Neither made it through to *Personae: The Collected Poems*, and although Pound retained the "Ballad of the Goodly Fere," he would not allow Edward Marsh to consider it for *Georgian Poetry*, since the poem did not "illustrate any *modern* poetic tendency."[10] "Nils Lykke" is an especially good example of how far Pound had to go to achieve the styles of *Ripostes* and *Lustra*.

> Beautiful, infinite memories,
> That are a-plucking at my heart,
> Why will you be ever calling and a-calling
> And a-murmuring in the dark there,
> And a-stretching out your long hands
> Between me and my beloved?
>
> And why will you be ever a-casting
> The black shadow of your beauty
> On the white face of my beloved,
> And a-glinting in the pools of her eyes?

In contrast to Pound's *English Review* poems of 1909, Lawrence's sequence "A Still Afternoon" in the November issue seems more "modern" by any standard. In "Dreams Old and Nascent," the deliberate style of a "nineties" reverie in "Dreams Old" gives way in "Dreams Nascent" to the cadences of Whitman:

> Through the wakened afternoon, riding down my dreams
> Fluent active figures of men pass along the railway.
> There is something stirs in me from the flow of their limbs as they move
> Out of the distance, nearer.

And as Sandra Gilbert has noted, the two poems of "Baby-Movements" have many affinities with the programmatic Imagist poems written by Pound and others a few years later.[11] The first, "Running Barefoot," which ends with the following lines, could easily have been included in Pound's anthology *Des Imagistes* on the ground that it exhibited, like Joyce's "I Hear an Army," pre-Imagist tendencies.

---

[10]Hassall, 193.

[11]Sandra M. Gilbert, *Acts of Attention: The Poetry of D. H. Lawrence* (Ithaca: Cornell University Press, 1972), 36–38. Gilbert points out that the two poems were regularized considerably, with the addition of new rhymes, before their appearance in the 1928 *Collected Poems*.

I wait for the baby to wander hither to me,
Like a wind-shadow wandering over the water,
So she may stand on my knee
With her two bare feet on my hands
Cool as syringa buds
Cool and firm and silken as pink young peony flowers.

In the April 1910 issue of the *English Review,* perhaps the last to show the influence of Hueffer's editorial policy, Hardy's memorial tribute to Swinburne ("A Singer Asleep") is followed by Lawrence's "Night Songs," a suite of five poems, and two poems by Ezra Pound. Pound's contributions, "Canzon: Of Incense" and "Thersites: On the Surviving Zeus," are extreme examples of the imitative medievalism that informs so many of the poems in *Canzoni* (1911). "Canzon: Of Incense" did not survive beyond that volume, and "Thersites" was never reprinted during Pound's lifetime. They are exactly the sort of stilted performances that caused Ford Madox Hueffer to roll on the floor when Pound visited him at Giessen in 1911, a roll that Pound believed saved him "at least two years, perhaps more. It sent me back to my own proper effort, namely, toward using the living tongue (with younger men after me), though none of us has found a more natural language than Ford did."[12] Lawrence's "Night Songs" are not free of academic romanticism, but they flare with occasional Imagist effects, and the two poems of "Workday Evenings" (later published in *New Poems* as "Hyde Park at Night: Clerks" and "Piccadilly Circus at Night: Street Walkers") have a base in realistic observation. They read, as Kim Herzinger has said, "a bit like the Eliot of 'Preludes' suffering a severe attack of Swinburne," and I am sure Herzinger is right in singling out Lawrence's "unembarrassed evocations of lower-class life" as the quality that Pound found most "modern" in the *English Review* poems.[13] By the time Pound began to exhibit a renewed interest in Lawrence's poetry in 1913–14 he had decided to make Hueffer's notion of the prose tradition in verse a central principle of the "new poetry," and Lawrence was the best example at hand of a distinguished contemporary prose writer whose poetry reflected some of the qualities of his fiction. Looking at the *English Review* poems and the contents of *Love Poems and Others* (February 1913) for signs of the "modern," Pound could have seized on Lawrence's early

[12]Ezra Pound, *Selected Prose, 1909–1965,* ed. William Cookson (London: Faber & Faber, 1973), 432. From Pound, "Ford Madox (Hueffer) Ford: Obit," *Nineteenth Century and After,* August 1939.
[13]Herzinger, 145–46.

use of vers libre or his pre-Imagist effects, but he needed a poet-novelist for his movement and chose to stress the novelistic aspects of Lawrence's poetry. Writing to Harriet Monroe on 23 September 1913, he acknowledged the programmatic nature of his interest, which went against the grain of his personal feelings. "Lawrence, as you know, gives me no particular pleasure. Nevertheless we are lucky to get him. Hueffer, as you know, thinks highly of him. I *recognize* certain qualities of his work. . . . As a prose writer I grant him first place among the younger men."[14]

Pound's two reviews of *Love Poems and Others* (*Poetry*, July 1913, and *New Freewoman*, 1 September 1913) make sense only when read against the background of his general critical activities at that time. Since the two reviews make the same argument and cite the same works, I shall quote the less familiar comments from the *New Freewoman*, which are part of a longer notice that includes Walter de la Mare's *Peacock Pie* and Frost's *A Boy's Will* ("His language is for the most part natural and simple").

The disagreeable qualities of Mr. Lawrence's work are apparent to the most casual reader, and may be summed up in the emotion which one gets from the line of parody:
"Her lips still mealy with the last potato."
Love consisteth (at least we presume that it consisteth) not so much in the perception of certain stimuli, certain sensations, whereof many would seem—if we are to believe Mr. Lawrence—rather disagreeable, but in a certain sort of enthusiasm which renders us oblivious, or at least willing to be oblivious, of such sensuous perceptions as we deem derogatory to the much derided pleasures of romance.

Having registered my personal distastes let me say without further preamble that Mr. Lawrence's book is the most important book of poems of the season. With the appearance of "Violets" and "Whether or Not" the Mansfield [that is, Masefield] boom may be declared officially and potentially over.

Mr. Lawrence, almost alone among the younger poets, has realized that contemporary poetry must be as good as contemporary prose if it is to justify its publication. In most places Mr. Lawrence's poetry is not quite as good as his own prose, but, despite his (to me) offensive manners of rhyming and of inverting and of choosing half of his words, his verse is considerably better than what we call "contemporary" verse.

I know of no one else who could have presented the sordid tragedy of "Whether or Not" with such vigour and economy. "Violets" at the pen of any of the other younger men would have descended into music-hall

[14]Pound, *Letters*, no. 23.

sentiment. As it is both poems are great art. The poems are narrative and quotation in fragments is therefore worse than useless. It is for this narrative verse that I think Mr. Lawrence is to be esteemed almost as much as we esteem him for his prose. He is less happy in impressions—I suppose he classifies himself as an "Impressionist"—and the following composition shows his good as well as his bad:—

MORNING WORK.

A gang of labourers on the piled wet timber
That shines blood-red beside the railway siding
Seem to be making out of the blue of the morning
Something faery and fine, the shuttles sliding,

The red-gold spools of their hands and faces shuttling
Hither and thither across the morn's crystaline frame
Of blue: trolls at the cave of ringing cerulean mining,
And laughing with work, living their work like a game.

To the first five lines one can make little objection beyond stating that they are not particularly musical, but when it comes to "Morn's crystaline frame of blue," "ringing cerulean mining" we are back in the ancient kingdom of ornaments and block phrases and ready, quite ready, to forget that Mr. Lawrence is a distinguished writer of prose.

Both reviews begin with an attack on the "disagreeable" aspects of the "Love Poems," which are—Pound says in the *Poetry* notice—"a sort of preraphaelitish slush, disgusting or very nearly so," in which Lawrence is indulging "his own disagreeable sensations."[15] This judgment is not surprising, since the "Love Poems" go against not only Pound's temperament but his newfound insistence on ironic or pseudoscientific objectivity. His interest lies in the "Others" of the volume's title, especially the narrative verse. The reviews of *Love Poems and Others* are thus an important stage in the critical argument that begins with "Prolegomena" (*Poetry Review*, February 1912), runs through the Imagist documents of early 1913 and the "Approach to Paris" essays of later that year (*New Age*, September–October 1913), and culminates in "Mr. Hueffer and the Prose Tradition in Verse" (*Poetry*, June 1914)—an argument that developed around Hueffer's dictum that "poetry should be written at least as well as prose."[16]

[15]*Literary Essays of Ezra Pound*, ed. T. S. Eliot (Norfolk: New Directions, 1954), 387. The entire *Poetry* review appears on pp. 387–88.
[16]Ibid., 373. The entire essay from the June 1914 issue of *Poetry* appears on pp. 371–77 as "The Prose Tradition in Verse."

"Contemporary poetry must be as good as contemporary prose," and it is in his vigorous and economical narrative verse that Lawrence declares himself a "modern." It is interesting to note that one of the two poems that are—in Pound's view—"great art" is "Whether or Not," the long dialect poem that Ernest Rhys remembered Lawrence reading at that famous evening in December 1909.

The special focus of Pound's reviews becomes clear if we place them beside the comments on "The Poetry of D. H. Lawrence" that Olivia Shakespear contributed to the *Egoist* (successor to the *New Freewoman*) of 1 May 1915. (Olivia Shakespear was a close friend of Yeats and a talented minor novelist; Pound married her daughter, Dorothy, in April 1914). Like Pound, Olivia Shakespear thinks the dialect poems are the finest in the collection:"'The Drained Cup' is a masterpiece of passion and understanding; it is written with straight naked simplicity, and is realistic in a true sense—that is to say, it does not deal with external realities only. I cannot quote from "The Drained Cup," "Whether or Not," or "A Collier's Wife" without spoiling them as a whole, for each is a little drama in itself, tragic and full of irony." Olivia Shakespear's responses are, not surprisingly, close to those of Pound, but she is more balanced and generous in her assessment of the entire volume and is sensitive to "modern" tendencies that Pound chose to ignore.

> There are three little poems which I do not think I am wrong in calling "imagist," for they each contain two "images," one superimposed upon the other. I have only space to quote "Aware," which is perfect from beginning to end. "Reminiscence" and "A White Blossom" both lapse into a banalité in the last line: "A tear which I had hoped even hell held not in store"; and "She shines, the one white love of my youth, which all sin cannot stain."

AWARE

> "Slowly the moon is rising out of the ruddy haze,
> Divesting herself of her golden shift, and so
> Emerging white and exquisite; and I in amaze
> See in the sky before me a woman I did not know
> I loved; but there she goes and her beauty hurts my heart;
> I follow her down the night, begging her not to depart."

Judging from his review in the *New Freewoman,* Pound would have excluded Lawrence from the inner circle of Imagism; he would probably have called these poems "impressions," already a pejorative term in his critical vocabulary and one that anticipates his later strictures on the looseness of "Amygism." By the time of his "Vorticism" essay (*Fortnightly Review*, 1 September 1914) he could declare dogmatically that "Imagisme is not Impressionism, though one borrows, or could borrow, much from the impressionist method of presentation."

Pound was soon released from his need to "recognize" Lawrence's qualities, and Lawrence from his role as hostage to a movement he found basically uninteresting, by the advent of James Joyce. Pound learned of Joyce's work from Yeats during their first winter together at Stone Cottage (1913–14) and decided to include the last poem from Joyce's *Chamber Music* (1907), "I Hear an Army," in his anthology *Des Imagistes,* published in February–March 1914. Soon Pound realized that he had discovered a writer closer to his—and Hueffer's—notion of the prose tradition than D. H. Lawrence, and one he could support without reluctance or qualification. *A Portrait of the Artist* began to appear serially in the *Egoist* in February 1914, and *Dubliners* was published the following June. In March 1914, writing to Amy Lowell, Pound could group Joyce with Hueffer, Lawrence, F. S. Flint, and himself as potential staff for a new avant-garde magazine,[17] but four months later in his review of *Dubliners* (*Egoist*, 15 July 1914) he relegated Lawrence to a minor position, bracketing him with the French writers Francis Jammes and Charles Vildrac as poets who "have written short narratives in verse, trying, it would seem, to present situations as clearly as prose writers have done."[18] Pound divides impressionist writers into two schools, those who follow Flaubert in "exact presentation" and those who "write in imitation of Monet's softness instead of writing in imitation of Flaubert's definiteness."[19] Clearly Pound thought Joyce was more "rigorous" than Lawrence, who was drawn too much toward the weaker impressionism. In Joyce he had found, at last, the master of symbolic realism who would enable English writers to catch up with the French. Within a few months his quarrel with Amy Lowell over her anthology *Some Imagist Poets* (1915), which included poems by Lawrence, would give Pound a convenient way to temper his earlier praise, since he could group Lawrence with the other apostates. Henceforth Lawrence would be an "*Amy*gist."[20]

But even if Joyce had not arrived on the scene so dramatically in

[17]Pound, *Letters*, no. 41.
[18]Pound, *Literary Essays*, 401. "*Dubliners* and Mr. James Joyce" is reprinted on pp. 399–402.
[19]Ibid., 399, 400.
[20]Pound, *Letters*, no. 227. Pound to Glenn Hughes, 26 September 1927.

early 1914, it is doubtful if Pound could have sustained his enthusiasm for Lawrence's fiction and narrative verse much longer. I suspect that his admiration for the early stories stemmed primarily from Hueffer's praise, although the earlier versions of the *Prussian Officer* stories that appeared in the *English Review* in 1910–11 ("Goose Fair" and "Odour of Chrysanthemums") could have been located in the Flaubertian tradition. Certainly Lawrence's fiction after *Sons and Lovers* (May 1913) would have struck Pound as perverse and misdirected. As Keith Cushman has demonstrated, the "great watershed in Lawrence's career falls between *Sons and Lovers* and *The Rainbow*," where he "leaves behind traditional notions of form and conventional representations of scene, character, and story."[21] By late 1915 the divergence between the two writers was radical and permanent, ready to be processed into the history of modernism. In the years immediately following, while Pound and Eliot were plotting a reaction against "the dilutation of *vers libre,* Amygism, Lee Masterism, general floppiness"[22] that issued in the controlled quatrains of *Hugh Selwyn Mauberley* and Eliot's *Poems* (1920), Lawrence was moving in his own poetry toward the position announced in "Poetry of the Present" (1919), where vers libre is exalted into a mode of vision, of belief. In contrast to Eliot's cautious and academic "Reflections on Vers Libre" of two years before, Lawrence's introduction to the American edition of *New Poems* is a lyrical celebration in which "finished crystallisation" and "the rhythm which returns upon itself like a dance" are rejected in favor of "another kind of poetry: the poetry of that which is at hand: the immediate present. In the immediate present there is no perfection, no consummation, nothing finished. The strands are all flying, quivering, intermingling into the web, the waters are shaking the moon. There is no round, consummate moon on the face of running water, nor on the face of the unfinished tide. There are no gems of the living plasm."[23] When this manifesto and the poems of *Look! We Have Come Through!* are read against the poetry and criticism Pound and Eliot were writing at the time, a series of either/or choices emerges that has determined the shape of later criticism, not only of Lawrence but of modernist literature in general: either openness or closure, either the temporal sequence or the spatial image, either expressive form or the rational imagination, either the confessional

---

[21]Keith Cushman, *D. H. Lawrence at Work: The Emergence of the "Prussian Officer" Stories* (Charlottesville: University Press of Virginia, 1978), 15.

[22]From Ezra Pound's memorial essay on Harold Monro, *Criterion* 11 (July 1932), 590.

[23]*The Complete Poems of D. H. Lawrence*, ed. Vivian de Sola Pinto and Warren Roberts (New York: Viking, 1964), I, 182.

mode or a poetry of "impersonality." Whether the critic is attacking Lawrence's poetry or defending it, the terms have remained the same, and they have led to some of the bloodiest ritual sacrifices in the history of twentieth-century literary criticism.[24] The debate, which shows no signs of subsiding, had its origins in the development of Romantic and post-Romantic literature, but the particular form it took owed a great deal to the accidents of literary history and the personal relationship between two young poets from the provinces in the London of 1909–15.

[24]See, for example, R. P. Blackmur's criticisms in "D. H. Lawrence and Expressive Form" (1935) and "Lord Tennyson's Scissors: 1912–1950" (1951), both collected in *Language as Gesture* (New York: Harcourt, Brace, 1952); and Harold Bloom's response, "Lawrence, Blackmur, Eliot, and the Tortoise," in *A D. H. Lawrence Miscellany,* ed. Harry T. Moore (Carbondale: Southern Illinois University Press, 1959).

[2]

For Mark Schorer with Combative Love: The *Sons and Lovers* Manuscript

MARK SPILKA

The publication within recent years of the *Sons and Lovers* manuscript was a happy event for Lawrence scholars, who are in a better position now to assess the novel's value and its seminal place within the Lawrence canon.[1] It was a moving event as well for those who have followed the shifting views of a great modern critic toward the author's work and world. The editing of this volume was Mark Schorer's last scholarly task before his death on 11 August 1977. As his final remark in the introduction suggests—"I have a journey, sir, shortly to go" (p. 9)—he had a strong sense of the fitness of this ending. In the famous essay "Technique as Discovery," with which he launched his own critical career in 1948, Schorer had condemned *Sons and Lovers* as a modern example of technical ineptitude. Lawrence had failed to use technique, he argued, "to discover the full meaning of his subject."[2] His well-known "impatience with technical resources," together with his use of fiction as personal therapy, had led to confusion rather than mastery of his themes. In this fictional exploration of his own early "sickness" as his mother's son and lover, he had become too personally involved with his material and had often contradicted his own intention to show "the crippling effects" of oedipal love.[3]

In this early application of New Critical formalism to fiction,

---

[1] D. H. Lawrence, *Sons and Lovers: A Facsimile of the Manuscript*, ed. Mark Schorer (Berkeley: University of California Press, 1977). Later in the essay I use the Viking Compass edition of the novel (1958) for comparative purposes.

[2] Mark Schorer, "Technique as Discovery," in *The World We Imagine* (New York: Farrar, Straus & Giroux, 1968), 3–23.

[3] Ibid., 11–12.

Schorer himself contradicts two formal principles: he prefers Lawrence's stated intentions in a letter to his editor, Edward Garnett, to his actual intentions as the novel itself reveals them; and he takes Jessie Chambers's complaints against the novel in her memoir, *D. H. Lawrence: A Personal Record* (1935), at face value:

> The handling of the girl, Miriam, if viewed closely, is pathetic in what it signifies for Lawrence, both as man and artist. For Miriam is made the mother's scapegoat, and in a different way from the way that she was in life. The central section of the novel is shot through with alternate statements as to the source of the difficulty: Paul is unable to love Miriam wholly, and Miriam can only love his spirit. These contradictions appear sometimes within single paragraphs, and the point of view is never adequately objectified and sustained to tell us which is true.[4]

Of course, both statements are true; they are coexisting conditions, and Lawrence even devotes specific chapters to their alternating predominance. In "The Defeat of Miriam" the mother's hold on Paul predominates and pulls him away from the girl; but in a subsequent chapter, "The Test on Miriam," where Paul finally breaks his mother's hold sufficiently to go to Miriam for passionate love, the girl defeats herself through her own deficiencies—on which her prototype, Jessie Chambers, might well be the last person to comment fairly.

Lawrence's intentions were far richer than Schorer realized, and in this early novel he had begun to discover the techniques needed to explore them. As Schorer rightly insists, "point of view" was not one of them, and without that Jamesian control Lawrence did sometimes yield to his prejudices. But he was more complex in his attitudes and in his own non-Jamesian techniques than Schorer at this point could allow. By 1951, however, Schorer had begun a radical shift in his own critical attitudes. In his introduction to the Harper's Modern Classics edition of *Sons and Lovers,* Schorer again traced the novel's many formal flaws to Lawrence's personal failure to confront his own split nature: but now he saw that self-betrayal as the first important sign of a lifelong "struggle for self-responsibility" and integrated being by which Lawrence would challenge the assumptions of his age and would become one of its "few truly affirmative writers." Within the space of three years, then, the "personal weakness" that so damaged the novel had become the source of Lawrence's future "literary strength"! It was a strength defined, moreover, by life-affirming

[4]Ibid., 13–14.

motives, not by technical control; and within that context some of the novel's merits now began to surface—its "superb characterizations," the "intense purity" of its natural descriptions, the "shimmer" of "inside reality" even in its human lives and loves. What had caused so great a change of mind and heart? Apparently, for Schorer as for most of Lawrence's recent admirers, it was *Women in Love*. In 1953, writing on *Women in Love* and death, he came out strongly for the prophetic value of a novel that, however nauseating it seemed on first reading, was "so tremendous" in its intentions, "so central to our lives," that readers must for their own sakes "make an effort to tolerate it."[5]

In this brilliant essay the newly tolerant Schorer succeeds in isolating "the realm of psychic drama" as Lawrence's peculiar forte. Such drama poses problems for a genre defined by social context, he argues, which Lawrence does not altogether solve; but Schorer applauds his attempt to go beyond generic limits, and though still concerned with them himself, he seems profoundly moved by the novel's extraordinary power in exploring psychosocial conflicts through fluid, dancelike movements and visionary scenes. "No novelist speaks more directly to us than Lawrence, and if we can't hear him, we are, I quite believe, lost," he says eloquently toward the end. Then he commends to our unregenerate hearing "the real Russian bang" in the last fifty pages—"the death of Gerald in the snow, and Birkin's grievous pathos without him."[6]

Three years later, in his introduction to Harry T. Moore's *Poste Restante: A Lawrence Travel Calendar* (1956), Schorer suspends his formal reservations and celebrates unquestioningly the Lawrencian impulse to move beyond corrupting social contexts into healing landscapes.[7] In that essay too, as he defines the polar opposition of mines and fields, an unmixed view of *Sons and Lovers* emerges. Lawrence's ability to convey "the unique quality of physical experience," "the physical essences of things outside the personality," now accounts for "his power of communicating the spirit of places" in this novel and becomes the basis too for his developing "sense of individual integrity and human relationships." Soon Lawrence would show how "deeply interdependent" men and places are, how "the corruptions of place and the corruptions of men are a single process," and how—to escape that deadly process—men must look for wilder landscapes, uncor-

[5]Schorer, "*Women in Love* and Death," in *World*, 107–21.
[6]Ibid., 120–21.
[7]Schorer, "Poste Restante: Lawrence as Traveler," in *World*, 147–61.

rupted places where the "vital connections with life outside themselves" can still be kept intact.[8]

Schorer's newfound sympathy for Lawrencian quests was shown in other ways. In another essay of 1953, on the Florentine villas of Sinclair Lewis and Lawrence, he records how Lawrence had schooled himself in loneliness in the Florentine woods and had written *Lady Chatterley's Lover* there, backing "almost entirely out of society in order to give us this measure of it";[9] and in his essay of 1957 on *Lady Chatterley,* which became the introduction to the unexpurgated Grove Press edition in 1959, he connects that Florentine setting with *Sons and Lovers* country—the Haggs Farm and its environs, which Lawrence still called "the country of my heart"—and shows how the polarities of place in *Chatterley* derive from that abandoned but still beloved farm, where life values were first affirmed for Lawrence and the encroaching mechanizations of human nature first resisted.[10]

Thus Lawrence, slowly dying, beginning to build his ship of death, had come full circle in this novel—as would Schorer himself, some twenty years later, in his own return to the world of *Sons and Lovers.* It seems fair to say that his facsimile edition makes ample amends for early critical misdemeanors—though in fact he never quite forgoes them. He is still partial, for instance, to Jessie Chambers's account of Lawrence's self-betrayal as a man and artist. He presents it now, however, without comment as that stage in the manuscript's progress when Jessie, having moved Lawrence to retell the story of his early life "as it really happened" (p. 2), had been disappointed by the courting chapters, where he gives his mother the supremacy that Jessie thought was hers. In a similar vein, Schorer still has hidden qualms about Lawrence's early artistry; but he transposes them now to Duckworth's "brilliant editor," Edward Garnett, whose "drastic trimming" of ten to fifteen thousand words from the final manuscript implies that Lawrence—if not artistically confused—did in fact need heroic help in getting his novel into formal shape (pp. 4, 8–9). Schorer is so impressed by Garnett that—perhaps with Maxwell Perkins and Thomas Wolfe in mind—he concludes his introduction with twenty-four lines

[8]Ibid., 152–53.

[9]Schorer, "Two Houses, Two Ways: The Florentine Villas of Lewis and Lawrence," in *World,* 195–218; see especially p. 217.

[10]Schorer, "Lady Chatterley's Lover," in *World,* 122–46; see especially pp. 123, 125, 130. It seems worth noting here that *Lady Chatterley* is Schorer's favorite in the Lawrence canon, the only novel that satisfies his formal and generic requirements while still appealing to his acquired taste for prophetic psychodrama. He believes that the novel concludes a history of Lawrencian forms (p. 132) and that it successfully combines social and psychic reality through its own richly symbolic form.

of praise for his editing to nine for Lawrence's manuscript revisions, the analysis of which he leaves, "reluctantly . . . yet happily," to younger scholars (pp. 8–9). Meanwhile he spends four of his nine pages tracing the manuscript's peregrinations from its completion in 1913 to its California purchase in 1963. His account of that purchase recalls the legend of his own lost book on Lawrence—in a steamer trunk that somehow disappeared—for which *this* retrieval may have seemed like partial compensation. Certainly he has retrieved for us this lost documentation of emerging stylistic power and its editorial redemption— now happily available for unreluctant study.

What the redeemed document reveals, however, is that Garnett was as much attuned to Lawrence's gifts as to his deficiencies. Heinemann, to whom Lawrence had first submitted the novel, had turned it down in July 1912 on the grounds that it lacked unity, that it was likely to be banned for want of reticence, and that none of its characters—not even Paul—commanded the reader's sympathy. Even Walter de la Mare, a friendly adviser, had felt that the novel needed pulling together and was "not of a piece," its real theme delayed "till half way through."[11] So Lawrence had again revised the manuscript—his fifth version!—and by November 1912 had sent it on to Garnett, who saw that it still needed the "drastic trimming" Schorer rightly praises, but who also saw its essential unity and commanding power and, as we shall see, was not much troubled by its "want of reticence." Thus Garnett at once accepted the novel for Duckworth and, as Schorer acknowledges, confined his trimmings to irrelevant or repetitious passages, tonal lapses, and minor matters of taste and consistency. If Lawrence was deficient in these formal amenities and still impatient with them, the essentially unified thrust of his novel was now quite evident. Unlike Perkins with Wolfe, Garnett did not create unity out of chaos; he removed whatever impeded it.

Lawrence himself was grateful for that sharp-eyed service. Though he had initially defended the manuscript for its patiently wrought form and its lifelike (or "slow like growth") development, when the proofs came in he praised Garnett for the jolly pruning, felt himself deep in his debt, and even dedicated the novel to him. Indeed, he hoped Garnett would "live a long long time" so as "to barber up" all his novels for him before they were published.[12] But such barbering became less and less necessary over the next few years. From the

---

[11]*The Letters of D. H. Lawrence*, vol. 1, ed. James T. Boulton (Cambridge: Cambridge University Press, 1979), 421–24.
[12]Ibid., 476–77, 496, 501, 517.

[33]

struggle with *Sons and Lovers* Lawrence had learned how to keep his own slow growth going without falling into irrelevancies; he became surer of his aims, more confident of the tone and manner needed to convey them; and as he moved further into the realm of psychic drama his creative intelligence burgeoned: he became his own best editor. The *Sons and Lovers* manuscript is likely to be studied less on its own merits, then, than as the initial phase of that development, when Lawrence first discovered the possibilities of slow organic growth and learned to proceed through successive versions of the same essential story. Unlike Joyce, whose static laminations Schorer so admired in 1948, Lawrence was a developer of kinetic forms; he moved through changing versions of his stories as he moved through changing landscapes.

The fact that he could "trim and garnish" when he had to do so may be incidental to that larger process. Schorer's interpretation of it, in his brief remarks, is accordingly worth challenging:

> As for Lawrence's manuscript revisions, they provide us with a most astonishing laboratory for stylistic studies. Anyone interested in the operations of the literary intelligence at a high level can only exclaim with delight as he examines these changes. It is more than merely exciting to observe how Lawrence activates prose, his own, that was at first rather inert, makes specific the more abstract, censures his own youthful impulse to write purple prose and to overwrite in general, changes passive authorial descriptions into dramatic character participations, sharpens throughout and deepens his character delineation. These are only some of the kinds of changes that his manuscript reveals. His alterations require and will certainly have much closer examination than this and infinitely more detailed analysis. [P. 9]

Perhaps they do and will. But Schorer's five stylistic observations, while readily documented, do not take us very far into the operations of high literary intelligence; they merely show Lawrence in the process of overcoming fairly obvious literary deficiencies. Here is an example of inert, relatively unspecific prose and shallow characterization from chapter 2:

> Then he went upstairs to his wife.
> "How are ter feelin' lass?" he said.
> "I'm all right," she replied. "Why do you bother?"
> "Dunna thee ma'e th' beds, I'll do it."
> "All right—There's apples simmering in the middle drawer. Did you sniff them out?"

"I didna," he said heartily, pleased.
"It's a wonder, for you're like a mouse after cheese."
"Ay, an' I s'll be glad on 'em," he said, with awkward thanks. [P. 42]

And here is the revised passage, written over the above crossed-out lines:

Then he went upstairs to his wife, with a cup of tea because she was ill, and because it occurred to him.
"I've brought thee a cup o' tea, lass," he said.
"Well you needn't, for you know I don't like it," she replied.
"Drink it up, it'll pop thee off to sleep again."
She accepted the tea. He loved to see her take it and sip it.
"I'll back my life there's no sugar in," she said.
"Yi'—there's one big un," he replied, injured.
"It's a wonder," she said, sipping again.
She had a winsome face when her hair was loose. He loved her to grumble at him like this, teasing.

Lawrence was unsure of the last word, "teasing," which in his revision replaces "warmly and friendly." In the proofs he would replace the final phrase, "like this, teasing," with the noncommittal "in this manner" (Compass, p. 28). But for me the word "teasing" captures more precisely the mildly peevish concession at stake in this exchange. In the first version, when Morel tries to please his wife, she does him one better; her shift from peevishness to playfulness, his slightly fatuous gratitude, is merely flavorful reporting of familiar traits. In the second version we learn that she is ill, and Morel's verbal concern is deepened into a thoughtful action that catches and disarms her guarded hostility, converts it into friendly grumbling with a hostile edge. If she injures him now, he has also won for the moment her grudging and winsome acceptance of his gift. Our sympathies at this point are with him, and since he has just shut her out in the garden in the previous chapter, in his drunken anger, we glimpse an unexpectedly tender side of his makeup and of their relationship. A rather lifeless passage has been vitalized and made to serve the novel's deeper purposes. But aside from those marvelously terse adverbial observations—"injured," "teasing"—which speak so directly to feelings and relations, we gain little stylistic knowledge from our close examination.

It seems to me more crucial that the improved passage comes after several paragraphs devoted to Morel's solitary pleasure in preparing his own breakfast. Lawrence's detailed delineation of his morning habits is part of the novel's documentary function—what Doris Lessing would later deprecate as journalistic reportage on "the existence of an area of society, a type of person, not yet admitted to the general literate consciousness."[13] Here Lawrence exploits his inside knowledge of life in a mining community and in a miner's family. He describes, for instance, how Morel prefers to eat his bread and bacon with a clasp-knife rather than that "modern introduction," a fork, "which has still scarcely reached common people"; he tells us too that the pit-singlet Morel puts on is "a vest of thick flannel cut low round the neck, and with short sleeves like a chemise" (Compass, p. 27). But his effort to convey through such documentary details the typicality of a miner's morning is more than mere reportage. For the first time in his longer fiction Lawrence is creating the conditional quality of the emotional life he knew best. He is creating emotional rhythms, daily cycles, and the fact that he moves from those daily rhythms into an improved revelation of actual intimacies, dramatic instances of typical relations, seems to me instructive. Here we see the beginnings of those timeless effects that Roger Sale long ago analyzed in *The Rainbow:* those paragraphs of conditional and subjunctive activity—how Brangwen *would* behave and feel in certain typical circumstances—followed by a dramatic exchange that animates those feelings for us.[14] Lawrence's immersion in the details of his own family life, before and after his birth, his attempt to document its typicality, and the enforced revisions by which he learned to animate the feelings appropriate to that life, prepared him for his later movement into the realm of psychic drama that best engaged his talents.

That seems to me one lesson we may learn from this "astonishing laboratory for stylistic studies": how in *Sons and Lovers* Lawrence began to evolve those timeless moments that give what I elsewhere call a "religious dimension" to his fiction. His more conscious attempts to create such movements are evident in the floral scenes throughout the novel, on which Dorothy Van Ghent and I first commented in the 1950s.[15] Contrasting attitudes toward flowers in this novel—Paul's, Miriam's, Clara's, Mrs. Morel's—are for the first time in his fiction construed as relations *with* nature as well as with the self and others.

---

[13]Doris Lessing, *The Golden Notebook* (New York: Ballantine, 1962), 60–61.

[14]Roger Sale, "The Narrative Technique of *The Rainbow*," *Modern Fiction Studies* 5 (Spring 1959), 29–38.

[15]Dorothy Van Ghent, "On *Sons and Lovers*," in *The English Novel: Form and Function* (New York: Harper, 1961), 245–61 (see especially pp. 256–57); Mark Spilka, "How to Pick Flowers," in *The Love Ethic of D. H. Lawrence* (Bloomington: Indiana University Press, 1955), 39–59.

One of the passages deleted by Garnett confirms the deliberateness of this pattern. In chapter 10, shortly after Paul gets a job for Clara at Jordan's factory, he begins to bait her for her apparent aloofness from the other factory girls and from himself. In the excised passage he has avoided seeing her for several days after being impudent with her (see Compass, p. 266); then he goes down to discuss an order with her, his wrath hidden under a cheerful mask:

> "You are wearing a flower," he said. "I thought that was against your rule."
> "I have no *rule*," she said, raising the head of a rather bruised red rose.
> "No, of course, only a preference. But you don't as a rule, I believe, *choose* to wear the languishing heads of decapitated flowers, on your bosom."
> She let fall the rose with a sharp movement.
> "This," she said, "is a flower I found in the street."
> "Jetsam of lost ladies," he said. "I'd hold a conversation with it, if I were you—'The Rose and the Tomb'! Know that poem?" [Pp. 373–74]

When she says she does not, he begins to mock her, then loses his head, saying they must act the poem out: he will ventriloquize the rose, she the tomb, which she can do well enough since—as everyone feels—there is a skeleton in her vault.

Garnett cuts this passage because a similar argument falls hard upon it—one of many points where Lawrence gives more instances than he needs of the same emotional impasse. But this floral argument goes back to the scene in chapter 9 where Paul scatters flowers over Clara's head as she kneels in the grass, in response to her belief that flowers "want to be left" unpicked, that picked flowers are corpses. "I thought you wanted a funeral," says Paul after his strange response to her forlorn beauty (Compass, pp. 238–39). Clara's bruised red rose in chapter 10 is a sign, then, that she has moved emotionally closer to Paul, has begun to rue her unpicked state, and will eventually be ready for the smashing of the red carnations he gives her when they first make love in Clifton Woods. It is a relational sign, moreover, of a kind that Lawrence would develop with greater depth and power in later fiction. In this novel it confirms his conscious movement in that direction.

Still other deletions in this facsimile volume will have confirming value for Lawrence scholars. There is, for example, Schorer's prize specimen: the moment in chapter 12 when Paul, alone in his "pyjamas" in Clara's bedroom, waiting for her mother to fall asleep in a nearby room, pulls on a pair of Clara's stockings and decides that he

[37]

must have her, then sits on the bed with his feet doubled up beneath him, listening for his chance (p. 472). Given the woolly warmth of women's stockings in bygone days and the coldness of British bedrooms, Paul may have done the sensible thing. But more probably the incident tells us something about his sexual confusions, his "ambiguous state of mind about 'sex' and 'soul,'" as Schorer notes (p. 5). And in fact Paul does identify himself physically with Clara in the previous scene in the theater, when, desiring her, "he was Clara's white heavy arms, her throat, her moving bosom. That seemed to be himself. Then away somewhere the play went on, and he was identified with that also. There was no himself" (p. 466; Compass, p. 331). Whatever the case, the stocking incident, which Garnett allowed to stand uncut in manuscript, was removed in proofs by a senior editor—possibly Duckworth himself—who seems to have censored several other scenes that Garnett allowed and that Lawrence himself toned down, involving nakedness and the kissing of cupped breasts (pp. 473–74, 491).

Obviously Lawrence's difficulties with censorship had begun even before the banning of *The Rainbow* in 1915. But the unusual point here is his early depiction of perverse behavior, comparable to the scene in the second version of *Lady Chatterley*, recently published as *John Thomas and Lady Jane*, where the embarrassed gamekeeper tells of being frightened as a boy of his future wife's pubic hair, which she had impudently exposed to him then, and of being unable to make love to her when they marry until she has him shave it off.[16] These odd sexual fetishes, now retrieved for public scrutiny, show that Lawrence felt closer to the Freudian outlook than he cared to admit. They are fair game, certainly, for Freudian and feminist critics, who have already made much of his homosexual and misogynistic leanings.

But Lawrence was so openly engaged in psychological self-exposures, and so willing to include Freudian insights within his larger and more creative purview, as to elude finally such reductive views. It seems more useful now to approach him through more inclusive problems, like the taboo on tenderness that he shares with many modern writers, which he was able to resolve, though only partially, in the late novel—*Lady Chatterley's Lover*—that he once wanted to call *Tenderness*. The *Paul Morel* fragments contain some interesting clues on the origin of that taboo in his early family life. Paul's father, for instance, is identified in several passages as being grossly sentimental in ways that offend his wife and children; whereas Paul's mother is

---

[16]Lawrence, *John Thomas and Lady Jane* (New York: Viking, 1972), 225–26.

characterized as unsentimental and straightforward. Morel's "sentimental play-acting" (p. 53) and "sentimental cravings" (p. 69) are
given full sway in Fragment 5 when his friend Jerry Purdy comes to
visit him while he convalesces, and he deliberately exaggerates his
illness, adopting "a strewn, pitiful attitude on the pillows," and putting on "a worn expression" (p. 72). The dialectic as he plays up to
Jerry's sympathy while his wife tries to cut through his feigning, and
as he accepts two swigs of smuggled whiskey when she leaves the
room, is that rare thing for Lawrence—an effective comic sequence;
and Mrs. Morel's amusement at the "fondling, lavish affection" between the two men helps to define its indulgent tone. The scene is
dropped from the final version, where Morel's self-pity and his wife's
bluffness are more flatly exposed, but it helps here to set off a crucial
difference between emotional honesty and emotional feigning from
which certain startling conclusions can be drawn. Miriam's cloying
spirituality and Clara's stifling possessiveness with Paul, for instance,
come closer to his father's ways than to his mother's; and Paul's
harshness with these women, and his inability to sustain his own affections, may stem as much from his father's poor example as from his
mother's binding love. The absence of any doctrine of male tenderness in this novel, like that in *Lady Chatterley,* may not be Morel's fault.
He tries often to be gentle with his son, and sometimes with his wife,
but since his gentleness often dissolves into maudlin feigning or gives
way to brutal rages, he sets a poor example to his son. For this reason,
perhaps, the sexual doctrine that does emerge in this novel, which
Paul openly derives from his father's early passion with his mother—
the "baptism of fire in passion" that "almost seems to fertilise your
soul and make it that you can go on and mature" (Compass, pp. 317–
18)—does not seem to work for Morel, any more than it works for
Clara Dawes, Paul's baptismal partner, who like Morel is sensually
vital but emotionally suspect. Only Paul and his mother, unsentimental and emotionally honest, seem to qualify for maturity—perhaps
because of their genuine affection for each other.

A fellow Lawrencian, Martin Green, once said to me that Paul
Morel does not really have an Oedipus complex. At the time the
statement seemed far-fetched, though I had myself emphasized the
essential health of Paul's relations with his mother before his brother's
death, *after* which he became her favored son and lover, and the
genuineness even then of their affections. But as I have since come to
see, Paul suffers from a still more important problem—male identity—that owes as much to his father's emotional default as to his mother's ultimately absorbing and possessive love. Immersion in the *Paul*

Morel fragments and in the *Sons and Lovers* deletions helps me at least to clarify that problem. I think now that Paul Morel might well be able to share and sustain his affections with a tough-minded woman like his mother, a woman strong enough to give him a rough time and plenty of leeway while he solves his male identity problem for himself—a woman, that is, like Frieda von Richthofen Weekley. For Paul too is tough-minded, like his mother, and sensually vital, like his father; but when he goes to other women, he is afraid of blundering through their "feminine sanctities," as his father did before him (Compass, p. 279), and has only his mother's bluffness and his father's feigning to guide him. He favors the former, at some expense to genuinely affectionate relations; but with a tough-minded sensualist like himself, he might eventually arrive at the creaturely tenderness he senses in his father—and perhaps in Baxter Dawes—and make that his emotional credo, as Lawrence did in *Lady Chatterley's Lover.*

It seems instructive, at any rate, that Oliver Mellors, Lawrence's gruff and occasionally surly gamekeeper, who shares with Walter Morel a number of obvious traits—his dialect speech, his work and bathing habits, his creaturely sureness—has been stripped free of Morel's "sentimental play-acting." The creaturely tenderness that emerges in its place, which derives from manly sureness, was an attribute that Lawrence came to value increasingly in his later years, as his enriched conception of types like the gamekeeper well attests. Like some of the unsettled heroes of Lawrence's middle period, Mellors tries at times to impose his masculine will upon his aristocratic mistress, Lady Chatterley; but chiefly he allows the love between them to flower spontaneously. He is gifted, moreover, with what Lady Chatterley calls "the courage of [his] own tenderness," a capacity for male nurture that he is able to exercise without falling into mawkishness, like the hapless Morel, and perhaps more important, without losing his masculine pride.

That the essence of maleness lies not in dominating phallic power but in nurturing tenderness, was not altogether a new idea for Lawrence. Much is made, for instance, of Paul Morel's regenerative touch in restoring sexual pride to Clara Dawes. Rather it was an old idea revivified, and for the first time prominently conceptualized, after the sexual and political wars of the middle period, the flirtation with leadership, and with male superiority and dominance, for which Lawrence has often been criticized. But the germ of the idea was there in *Sons and Lovers,* in the creaturely quickness, sureness, and tenderness that Paul implicitly shares with his sensual father. And perhaps it was there too, in potential, in the surly gruffness of the unsentimental bully Baxter Dawes, another older broken male to whom Paul is oddly attracted and whose marital dilemma he oddly tries to solve. As now seems abundantly clear, it would take a long, conflictual wandering life with the combative Frieda, and some patient schooling in his own creaturely separateness, before Lawrence could solve such problems for such recurring characters and could arrive at his own delayed version of male sureness.[17]

Immersion in this facsimile edition of *Sons and Lovers* may have similarly clarifying effects for other Lawrence scholars. Those interested in the religious Lawrence, for instance, may want to look at some of the "lost" precisions of the original manuscript, as when Lawrence compares Morel and his wife on religious grounds:

> He had no religion, she said bitterly to herself. What he felt just at the minute, that was all to him. He would sacrifice his own pleasure never, unless on an impulse, for he had plenty of impulsive charity. But of the deep charity, which will make a man sacrifice one of his appetites, not merely one of his transitory desires, he was quite unaware. He was strictly irreligious. There was nothing to live for, except to live pleasurably. She was deeply religious. She felt that God had sent her on an errand, that she must choose for God from her sense of right and wrong. So she kept undaunted, her sense of duty and responsibility bearing her onward. [Pp. 20–21]

Lawrence crosses out most of this passage in the manuscript and revises it as follows: "He had no grit, she said bitterly to herself. What he felt just at the minute, that was all to him. He could not abide by anything. There was nothing at the back of all his show" (Compass, p. 14).[18]

Lawrence's reasons for making this revision become clearer in the next crossed-out passage in the manuscript, where Mrs. Morel is depicted as the sheepdog in charge of Morel's soul, who must bark in front of him and turn his own "petty meannesses back into himself," to keep him from straying, but who drives him mad instead with "moral suffering." The unhappy sheepdog image, the abstract comparison before it, and the desire to do better by Morel—to balance the terms of conflict—must have moved Lawrence to focus on essentials

---

[17]For further discussion of the male identity problem, see my essays "Lawrence's Quarrel with Tenderness," *Critical Quarterly* 9 (Winter 1967), 363–77, and "On Lawrence's Hostility to Willful Women: The Chatterley Solution," in *Lawrence and Women*, ed. Anne Smith (London: Vision, 1978), 189–211.

[18]Within these crossed-out lines, the phrase "to live pleasurably" has also been crossed out and has been replaced by "the pleasant sensation of living" (p. 21).

in both passages. Thus "religion" becomes "grit" and, in the next passage, shiftless impulse is more fairly and deeply founded in sensuality: "His nature was purely sensuous, and she strove to make him moral, religious. . . . He could not endure it" (Compass, p. 14). But as the sacrifice of moral ideas to emotional dynamics implies, Lawrence was shifting religious grounds as he revised his way deeper into parental conflict. Ultimately he would choose Morel's impulsive ways while on his own errand for God—the God of Isness rather than Oughtness—thus fusing something of his mother's religious "grit" with his father's sensuous spontaneity.

Still other signs of his religious heritage may be found in these pages. In the *Paul Morel* fragments we learn, surprisingly, that Mrs. Morel not only befriends a clergyman, here called Mr. Revell, but also composes his sermons for him. Clumsy in his speech, scoffed at by the miners and tradespeople, he turns to her for translations of his ideas into terms and circumstances that will appeal to his congregation (Fragment 3, pp. 47–52). In the completed version, moreover, we get a sample of one such sermon, deleted by Garnett, on the Wedding at Cana. The minister, here called Mr. Heaton, has just interpreted the changing of water into wine as a symbol of the transformation into spirit of "the ordinary life, even the blood, of the married husband and wife, which had before been uninspired, . . . because when love enters, the whole spiritual constitution of a man changes, is filled with the Holy Ghost" (Compass, p. 33). Mrs. Morel, who thinks to herself that the poor man, his young wife dead, has made his love into the Holy Ghost, then says aloud:

"No, . . . don't make things into symbols. Say: "it was a wedding, and the wine ran out. Then the father-in-law was put about, because there was nothing to offer the guests, except water—there was no tea, no coffee, in those days, only wine. And how would he like to see all the people sitting with glasses of water in front of them. The host and his wife were ashamed, the bride was miserable, and the bridegroom was disagreeable. And Jesus saw them whispering together, and looking worried. And He knew they were poor. They were only, perhaps, farm-labouring people. So He thought to himself 'What a shame! All the wedding spoiled.' And so He made wine, as quickly as he could. You can say, wine isn't beer, not so intoxicating—and people in the East never get drunk. It's getting drunk makes beer so bad."

The poor man looked at her. He wanted badly to say how human love is the presence of the Holy Ghost, making the lovers divine and immortal. Mrs. Morel insisted on his making the bible real to the people, and on his having only bits of his own stuff in between. They were both very excited, and very happy. [P. 54]

At this point her son William enters and Mrs. Morel, beginning to make tea, hopes that her husband will not intrude upon her happiness. Garnett cut the passage, apparently, because it fails to advance that intrusion. But it adds a dimension to Mrs. Morel's life and character as a gifted woman who can reach others only by "bullying her clergyman over his sermons" (p. 54); and beyond the novel itself, it gives us an example of how Lawrence's mother must have influenced his own later penchant for literary sermons. In *The Man Who Died* (1928), Lawrence would himself attempt to make a Bible story more real to people of his own post-Christian persuasion; and in earlier works, such as *The Rainbow* (1915) and *Women in Love* (1920), he would restore the Holy Ghost to his own earthy version of mystic marriage, whereby blood (rather than love) enters the spiritual constitution of his characters and brings the Holy Ghost to life. He was like his spirited mother, then, in trying to bring "quaint and fantastic" religious ideas "judiciously to earth" (Compass, p. 33); and like his mother's minister in his spirited view of sensual relations.

In a later passage deleted by Garnett, Paul discusses a Good Friday sermon with the Leivers family. They listen avidly as he tries—"earnest and wrathful"—to show them how the minister spoiled the Bible chapter chosen as his text. "It was thus Miriam loved him," writes Lawrence, and he then indicates that it was the Disciple in Paul, the presence of the Messiah, that Miriam loved, and not the man (pp. 314–15). Though the passage repeats things we already know about Paul and Miriam, it also helps to explain why his mother's religious grit appeals more to Paul than Miriam's religious adoration; and if we extend our view to Ursula's earthy scorn, in *Women in Love,* which appeals more to Birkin than the love of spiritual brides like Hermione, we begin to understand why Lawrence himself preferred Frieda's combative love to that of adoring disciples like Dorothy Brett, who also confused the preacher in him, or even the poet, with the man who contained them. It took grit, scorn, and battle, apparently, to rouse that inclusive but elusive fellow into godly being, and he liked ladies who would do that for him.

It may have been in recognition of such distinctions that Mark Schorer concludes his remarks in the supplement on textual variants with a fitting coincidence: "I am delivering the editorial apparatus for this publication to the people at the University of California Press on, as only I now see, the anniversary of Lawrence's birth, September 11, 1885. Can one imagine him alive today, in *this* world, at ninety-one? Where? In Taos? A shaky Dorothy Brett, still there, supporting his shaky frame? Impossible!" (p. 610).

[43]

Of course, Brett is dead now; so too is Schorer; and if I compliment him on coming closer to the rousable Lawrence in his supplement than in his introduction, it is not from any lack of gratitude for his labors. I agree, for the most part, with his heroic view of Garnett's editing. Nonetheless, as I have been laboring to show myself, it is that emerging hero Lawrence, with the gallant Frieda at his back, who provides us all with rich fare for literary redemption.

I have not touched on all that resurrected fare: the library scene in which Paul eagerly awaits for Miriam; the alley scene in which the weird religious cries of the "Barm-O" man stand in counterpoint to an irate neighbor's attack on William's conduct; the several passages in which Paul's attitudes toward the new feminism seem more sympathetic than the printed novel suggests; the nice psychological touches, such as William's sibling rivalry with Paul and the common hatred of Paul and Baxter Dawes for Clara; the magnificent death scenes and others like them where the pen seldom falters; the improvements on the *Paul Morel* fragments in the final version; and still other scenes and possibilities that will bemuse Lawrence scholars for some time to come. My intent instead has been to show—as Schorer never does— that many deletions reveal ideas and preoccupations that helped Lawrence to become the man whose prophetic art-speech still commands our hearing; that some of those deletions might have been retained; and—to complete my own Lawrencian circle—that Schorer's inordinate satisfaction with them betrays his original misgivings about this novel, which, though now subdued, are still substantially intact.[19] But finally Schorer comes to his task as a dying man who, like Lawrence before him, wants to build his ship of death out of vital literary strivings, and whose own vital effort is to deliver the recorded traces of those strivings trimly and efficiently into living hands. He performs this dying task, I think, with admirable success; but in *this* world, where all too many shaky disciples support our shaky frames, I think also that he would prefer a combative reception of his views, if not his labors, to an adoring one. To my departed namesake, then—much combative love, much thorny thanks for your last Lawrencian errand, much heartfelt praise for your own brave and godly going. *Poste Restante.*

---

[19]Schorer's view of Garnett's infallibility should be cited here: "Every deletion that Garnett made seems to me to have been to the novel's advantage. Nothing important is lost, ineptitudes disappear, and the novel emerges as tighter and more smoothly paced than it would otherwise have been" (p. 9).

[3]

"Logic of the Soul": Prothalamic Pattern in *The Rainbow*

PETER BALBERT

I

Lawrence's letters during a confident stage in his composition of *The Rainbow* and *The Lost Girl,* in which he claims that his work is "not a bit visualized" and "really a stratum deeper" than the fiction of other novelists, suggest the importance of focusing on the internal emotional life of his characters.[1] In his many comments on the fiction of this period, no evidence exists of an attempt to duplicate the pictorial documentations of England such as those in *Sons and Lovers.* Critics generally recognize the focus on emotional life in *The Rainbow* and properly relate it to that novel's concern with habits of love and courtship through three generations. Yet relatively little attention has been drawn to the significance of such repetitive domestic struggles. Similarly, there has been insufficient discussion of the seminal theme of marriage in *The Rainbow,* a theme that Lawrence uses as a form of visionary ligature to integrate the pattern of repetition and to provide the doctrinal insistence so important to him.[2] As he relentlessly travels

[1]*The Letters of D. H. Lawrence,* vol. 1, ed. James T. Boulton (Cambridge: Cambridge University Press, 1979), 526.
[2]There has been much discussion of the "special" qualities of each generation in *The Rainbow,* and several essays deal with the recurrent motifs and images that unify the Brangwen saga; but critics rarely stress in an integrated fashion both Lawrence's vision of marriage and the compulsions in his characters that inform the doctrine and structural repetitions. F. R. Leavis was among the first to note that "the effort of realization and discovery starts again in each generation. . . , and it is an essential part of the undertaking of *The Rainbow* to deal with three generations" (*D. H. Lawrence: Novelist* [New York: Simon & Schuster, 1969], 101). But Leavis isolates this pattern primarily to make his argument about class, English culture, and the tradition of the novel, while the correlative themes of marriage and instinctive need receive little attention from

in exile, works through disagreements with Frieda over her commit-
ment to her Weekley family, and struggles with what would become a
companion novel to *The Rainbow*, Lawrence conveys a preoccupation
of both his impassioned life and his recent fiction when he tells his
friend McLeod: "I think *the* one thing to do, is for men to have the
courage to draw nearer to women, expose themselves to them. . . .
Because the source of all life and knowledge is in man and woman,
and the source of all living is in the interchange and the meeting and
mingling of these two."[3] Lawrence thus insists (implicitly in his acceptance of the ostracism caused by his then "illicit" connection to Frieda)
that marriage amounts to an organic necessity; it remains the only
institution that can sanction, legally and socially, the rigors of the
mandate contained in his remarks to McLeod.

We must marvel at Lawrence's characteristic ability here to put his
courage where his doctrine is: he permits his own instinctive sense of
what is right to triumph over the natural temptation, which had to be
strong in his beleaguered period early in the war, to renounce marriage altogether. Who could begrudge him resentment toward an
institution so central to the bourgeois society that was attacking Lawrence for his alleged draft evasion, pornography, and libertinism?

---

him. Leavis makes partial amends for such omission in his later essay when he examines
the rainbow symbol to demonstrate Lawrence's concern with the interrelationship of
marriage and individual growth; Leavis shows "how the distinctive offer of *The Rainbow*
is to render development concretely—the complex change from generation to generation and the interweaving of the generations" (*Thoughts, Words and Creativity* [New
York: Oxford University Press, 1976], 125). Julian Moynahan emphasizes that "the
crucial relation in *The Rainbow* is between a man and a woman in marital and sexual
experience"; Moynahan sees marriage "as the major recurring event in *The Rainbow*,"
and he stresses a doctrine of "individuation" within the context of Lawrence's depiction
of marital struggle (*The Deed of Life* [Princeton: Princeton University Press, 1963], 43–
44). Yet Moynahan's analysis of the passionate scenes between the Brangwens under-
estimates the extent to which Lawrence documents an intrinsic, instinctive momentum
in marriage toward reconciliation and compromise; Moynahan seems more concerned
with Lawrence's mystical ideas on salvation and transfiguration than with the tensions
in the marital discord. H. M. Daleski integrates the marriage theme with both Lawrence's doctrine and the structure of the novel. He maintains that *The Rainbow* is more
"than a psychological study of marriage," and he shows how it functions as the "first
stage in an attempt to discover the necessary conditions for a meaningful life." Although Daleski illustrates how "Lawrence deals with three generations in order to
discover what is consistent in the lives of men and women," he does not sufficiently
explain the seminal relation of Lawrence's use of the "unknown" to the sense of primitive urgency that operates in many of the scenes Daleski discusses. See Daleski, *The
Forked Flame: A Study of D. H. Lawrence* (Evanston: Northwestern University Press,
1965), 75.

[3]Reported by Harry T. Moore, in *The Priest of Love: A Life of D. H. Lawrence*, rev. ed.
(New York: Farrar, Straus & Giroux, 1974), 197.

But he provocatively creates, in the midst of destroying one marriage in favor of the promise of his own, a virtual hymn in *The Rainbow* to the spirit of marriage; the creation becomes, in effect, a prothalamic embodiment of the kind of union he wishes to achieve with Frieda, which Frieda lacks in the marriage she abandons. He writes a novel that describes the continual "exposure" and "interchange" he regards as "the source of life." Lawrence never seriously considers, throughout these years of turmoil, any compromise in his stress on *legal* status; his letters show a resolute discomfort with the idea of a private romance with Frieda that would lack the contractual obligations of official marriage.[4]

The Rainbow is a testament to the conservative impulse in Lawrence that is at the heart of his most apocalyptic doctrines; it reflects a sensibility inclined toward traditional forms of worship, stability, and passion, even though he wishes to transmute and invigorate the forms. Indeed, his radical notions of the vital relations between men and women in *The Rainbow* are framed by an affirmation in each Brangwen generation of the legal state that sanctions a marriage. The words of another writer, whose self-proclaimed designation is "left-conservative," help illuminate significant aspects of Lawrence's beliefs. In a summary of the ethical imperatives that he believes underlie Lawrence's fictional representations of love and sex, Norman Mailer writes: "Lawrence's point . . . is that . . . people can win at love only when they are ready to lose everything they bring to it of ego, position, or identity—love is more stern than war—and men and women can survive only if they reach the depths of their own sex down within themselves. They have to deliver themselves 'over to the unknown.' No more existential statement of love exists, for it is a way of saying we do not know how the love will turn out."[5] Mailer's lines suggest the demands of the dual process of self-definition and transcendence that is central to the many communion scenes in Lawrence's fiction. Lawrence insists on a love that begins as an existential assertion of the sexual separateness of each lover—a drive toward a sexual singling out—identified by a character's unintimidated accep-

---

[4]Here are a few of the many relevant comments contained in *The Letters:* "Remember, you are to be my wife" (I, 393). "*Is* the divorce coming off? . . . Have you settled anything definite with Ernst? . . . My next coming to you is solemn, intrinsically—I am solemn over it—not sad, oh no—but it is my marriage, after all, and a great thing—not a thing to be snatched and clumsily handled" (p. 401). "Dear God, I am marrying you, now, don't you see. It's a far greater thing than ever I knew" (p. 403).

[5]Norman Mailer, *The Prisoner of Sex* (New York: New American Library, 1971), 107. Mailer first refers to himself as "left-conservative" in *The Armies of the Night* (New York: New American Library, 1968), 185.

tance of the "otherness" of his partner.[6] Through this balanced (or "polarized") forging of male and female energies, each lover—in separate and often uneasy ways—is then able to recognize the spirit of the overarching "unknown" that is the animating force in Lawrence's universe. In Lawrence's necessarily circular dialectic, just as self-definition relies on a person's initial faith in the beyond, so a person must desire this unknown to legitimize the process of singling out. The circularity becomes a fail-safe testament to the organic nature of Lawrence's vision, which never envisages a felt connection to the transcendent without a perception of the pristine, sexual self.

In *The Rainbow*, men have the greater difficulty in accepting this pure unknown in their mates; thus they exhibit, in moments of extreme stress, a fear and uncertainty about the cosmos (that is, fear of the sky, wind, stars, moon, and so forth)—the looming "beyond" that is both animator and confirming principle of the sexual otherness they struggle to accept in each other. The quest for the unknown is no less intense in the men than in the women, but often inhibitions and egocentric worry hamper the male. Tom, Will, and Skrebensky wish to feel the impulse to the transcendent even as they draw back from that naked exposure to their wives or lovers; Lawrence believes that such restraint compromises the courage he mentioned to McLeod for "*the* one thing to do." The consistent depiction in *The Rainbow* of the willingness in women to embrace the unknown, and the strength imputed to them because of such courage, is Lawrence's fictional version of a doctrine of female speciality that has ample precedent in religious, mythic, and psychological structures of belief. In his essay "The Crown," which Lawrence writes while revising *The Rainbow*, he expresses a faith in the innate power of women that sounds like a shorthand fusion of the clinical concepts of anatomic destiny promulgated by Freud and Erikson, the mystical awe of Mary urged by the Catholic Church, and the poetic adoration directed at Dante's Beatrice and Eliot's *Lady of Silences*. Put simply, Lawrence envisages women as a step closer to the unknown than men, since "the womb is full of darkness and also flooded with the strange white light of eternity."[7] Although the lack of a uterus puts the male at an unbridgeable dis-

---

[6]See my related discussions of this process in "The Loving of Lady Chatterley: D. H. Lawrence and the Phallic Imagination," in *D. H. Lawrence: The Man Who Lived,* ed. Robert B. Partlow and Harry T. Moore (Carbondale: Southern Illinois University Press, 1980), 143–58, and in "Forging and Feminism: *Sons and Lovers* and the Phallic Imagination," *D. H. Lawrence Review* 11 (1978), 93–113.

[7]Lawrence, "The Crown," in *Phoenix II: Uncollected, Unpublished, and Other Prose Work by D. H. Lawrence* (New York: Viking, 1970), 367.

tance behind the female in proximity to the transcendent, his need to perceive that unknown is as urgent as the female's. Yet in the discriminatory nature of Lawrence's vision, the stabilizing biology of a womb, that ingrown potential for linking with eternity, makes a woman's search for the beyond less fraught with self-consciousness and fear of failure. Her body's structure thus gives confident direction to her quest.

Lawrence portrays the men in *The Rainbow* as always looking to the institution of marriage as the social instrument for delivery to the unknown. That portrayal is consistent with his views in another work simultaneous with *The Rainbow*, the "Study of Thomas Hardy," in which he claims that man "dare not leap into the unknown save from the sure stability of the unyielding female."[8] The women in *The Rainbow* try to show the men that as males they instinctually desire a link to eternity through their wives. But their civilized male egos, which have been conditioned to settle for the wages of a protective day's work on the farm, urge them to avoid risking their souls in enterprises that depend on acts of faith. The novel becomes a three-generation battle between female persuasion, which can become vindictive, and male inhibition, which can become self-destructive. In a letter to Sir Thomas Dunlop in July 1914, Lawrence writes prescriptive lines that could serve as an introduction to the preoccupations he dramatizes in *The Rainbow*:

> One must learn to love, and go through a good deal of suffering to get to
> it, like any knight of the Grail, and the journey is always *towards* the other

[8]Lawrence, "Study of Thomas Hardy," in *Phoenix: The Posthumous Papers of D. H. Lawrence*, ed. Edward D. McDonald (New York: Viking, 1972), 446–47. Mark Kinkead-Weekes provides significant criticism on the relation of Lawrence's doctrine in "Study of Thomas Hardy" to both the theme of marriage in *The Rainbow* and the function of the novel's tripartite structure. Kinkead-Weekes's essay is based on the development of Lawrence's thoughts about marriage and selfhood from the manuscript of *The Wedding Ring* to the completion of *The Rainbow*. His essay focuses on how Lawrence's basic ideas on "male" and "female" principles in the "Study of Thomas Hardy" provide insights into the complexities of characterization in *The Rainbow*. My major objection to that essay is the degree to which it relies on the dialectic in the Hardy study to corroborate (or initiate) the conclusions Kinkead-Weekes reaches about the revisions in Lawrence's composition of the novel. Although Kinkead-Weekes maintained that the "Study of Thomas Hardy" "is not a skeleton key" for *The Rainbow* "and must not be misused as one," he does not clearly observe his own warning ("The Marble and the Statue: The Exploratory Imagination of D. H. Lawrence," in *Imagined Worlds: Essays in Honor of John Butt*, ed. Ian Gregor and Maynard Mack [London: Methuen, 1968], partly reprinted in *Twentieth-Century Interpretations of "The Rainbow*," ed. Mark Kinkead-Weekes [Englewood Cliffs: Prentice-Hall, 1971], 110). Except for his interpretation of the Lincoln Cathedral scene, he does not subject his conclusions about marriage to a close scrutiny of relevant scenes in the novel.

soul, not away from it. . . . It is damnably difficult and painful, but it is the only thing which endures. You mustn't think that your desire or your fundamental need is to make a good career, or to fill your life with activity, or even to provide for your family materially. It isn't. Your most vital necessity in this life is that you shall love your wife completely and implicitly and in entire nakedness of body and spirit.[9]

II

The opening page of *The Rainbow* introduces a theme that reverberates through more than fifty years of Brangwens: "There was a look in the eyes of the Brangwens as if they were expecting something unknown, about which they were eager."[10] A "look" is all Lawrence provides about this eagerness, as if only a glance can catch the inarticulate quality of the Brangwen desire. The men are in the grip of a need as powerful as the lust for sex or the drive for success in their farming occupation. It is the instinctive urge to find a reason for existence, to feel a sense of affirmation beyond the duties of work, to connect with something "foreign" and beyond familial responsibility. But they are farming men, aware that the requirements behind their look must somehow be accommodated to their working presence at Marsh Farm. For the men this look stays in living suspension in their blood and circulates only when the men feel ready both to embrace a woman "in entire nakedness of body and spirit" and to affirm the presumed permanence of that embrace in matrimony.

The inexorable drift toward that "vital necessity in life" is first chronicled in Tom Brangwen. Although a robust and capable young man, he matures slowly; his experiences with a prostitute and a flirtatious young woman do little to confirm his sense of manhood. Yet his immaturity does not delay his need to deliver himself to that unknown embodied in Lydia Lensky. He feels ready for her, motivated by what Lawrence soon calls "a logic of the soul" (p. 36). All Tom requires is the slightest glance at this inscrutable woman: " 'That's her,' he said involuntarily" (p. 24)—an involuntary mutter from his instinct, his soul, and not from his knowledge or experience. That Lydia is also literally "foreign" accelerates Tom's sense of polarized attraction to her when they first meet. Later this foreign element

[9]*The Letters of D. H. Lawrence*, vol. 2, ed. George J. Zytaruk and James T. Boulton (Cambridge: Cambridge University Press, 1981), 191.

[10]Lawrence, *The Rainbow* (New York: Viking, 1961), 1. Page numbers in my text refer to this edition.

will demand the full measure of Tom's adjustment when he undertakes marriage with a wife whose history and manner are so unusual in his community. The early scenes between Tom and Lydia convey a sense of anticipatory tension beneath the apparent nonchalance of the encounters; they show the heightened readiness in Tom that results from months of eager waiting for "something to get hold of. . . . Steadfastly he looked at the young women, to find a one he could marry" (p. 20). The slightest gesture becomes filled with meaning, as it moves like a luminous movie, run strangely slow motion through an imagination in Tom that is vibrantly alive with his desire:

> And he also stooped for the button. But she had got it, and she stood back with it pressed against her little coat, her black eyes flaring at him, as if to forbid him to notice her. Then, having silenced him, she turned with a swift "Mother—," and was gone down the path.
> The mother had stood watching impassive, looking not at the child, but at Brangwen. He became aware of the woman looking at him, standing there isolated yet for him dominant in her foreign existence. [P. 28]

The perspective here is multiple and resonant, for as Tom makes his discovery, the widow carefully measures him as her potential man, and even the daughter is vaguely aware—"Mother" sounds the frightened declaration of *her* allegiance—that stakes of family destiny silently are enacted at this encounter. Several pages later Tom's decision to propose is captured in a poignant scene with his wise servant:

> All these things were only words to him, the fact of her superior birth, the fact that her husband had been a brilliant doctor, the fact that he himself was her inferior in almost every way of distinction. There was an inner reality, a logic of the soul, which connected her with him. . . . Tilly brought down one of the linen shirts he had inherited from his father, putting it before him to air at the fire. She loved him with a dumb, aching love, as he sat leaning with his arms on his knees, still and absorbed, unaware of her. . . . "It's got to be done," he said as he stooped to take the shirt out of the fender, "it's got to be done, so why balk it?" [P. 36]

For years Tilly has lovingly ministered to the Brangwen family's needs, and as she recognizes why there is ritual in Tom's preparations, so must she prepare him for a man's most crucial calling even as she loses the part of him that was her own. Although Tom senses the momentousness inherent in his marital decision, he seems uncertain about where all this ceremonial fuss might lead.

Mailer's comment about the existential uncertainty in Lawrence's work of how the love will turn out seems particularly appropriate to that lingering image of Tom walking to Lydia as a man who has exposed himself to forces larger than he can manage: "He went up the hill and on towards the vicarage, the wind roaring through the hedges, whilst he tried to shelter his bunch of daffodils by his side. He did not think of anything, only knew that the wind was blowing" (p. 37). Tom walks as if under the spell of a private god; he is motivated by "an inner reality" and "he did not think of anything"—he moves toward his woman with that combination of mystical mandate and deductive conviction conveyed by the oxymoronic phrase "logic of the soul." When Tom reaches Lydia's house to make the actual proposal, Lawrence establishes the risk involved with Tom's faith in his soul's logic. Tom peers in at a world separated by barrier and prohibition:

> There was a light streaming on to the bushes at the back from the kitchen window. He began to hesitate. How could he do this? Looking through the window, he saw her seated in the rocking-chair with the child, already in its nightdress, sitting on her knee. The fair head with its wild, fierce hair was drooping towards the fire-warmth, which reflected on the bright cheeks and clear skin of the child, who seemed to be musing, almost like a grown-up person. The mother's face was dark and still, and he saw, with a pang, that she was away back in the life that had been. The child's hair gleamed like spun glass, her face was illuminated till it seemed like wax lit up from the inside. The wind boomed strongly. Mother and child sat motionless, silent, the child staring with vacant dark eyes into the fire, the mother looking into space. The little girl was almost asleep. It was her will which kept her eyes so wide. . . .
> Then he heard the low, monotonous murmur of a song in a foreign language. [Pp. 37–38]

The warmth of maternal blood connection, the magic of shared history, the sensuous allure of flesh and soft hair, and the tacit link between the hidden past and the transcendence of nature—Lawrence is rarely better and never more composite. Tom is as cut off from the world beyond the glass as Heathcliff is when he looks through the window at the foreign domain of the Lintons. But Tom Brangwen wants to join the tableau spread before him. He understandably hesitates before the bond of history and blood between mother and daughter that he can never share. The sounds of foreign words and a "life that had been" with a husband he can never know intimidate him. Their contented contact with each other and their indecipherable murmurs keep him imprisoned outside. He perceives the scene through a window that is as admonishing as it is transparent; are they priceless artifacts, wax museum pieces he dare not touch, much less propose to protect?

As the window passage concludes, Lawrence characteristically moves, in the second of several analogous movements in the novel, from the issue of a Brangwen's struggle to experience the unknown, to a complementary depiction of the overarching cosmos that is source and overseer of the primal force Tom struggles to comprehend: "Then a great burst of wind, the mother seemed to have drifted away, the child's eyes were black and dilated. Brangwen looked up at the clouds which packed in a great, alarming haste across the dark sky" (p. 38). The impulsive feel of the wind and the hasty, alarming clouds reflect both the immediate proximity of Tom's quest—just *beyond* the glass, as it were—and his fear of the confrontation itself. Although Tom enters the house and Lydia accepts his proposal, the frozen moment of his observation at the window, filled with his sense of desire and fear, anticipates the rhythm of his relation to her during their engagement and marriage. The foreign element in Lydia that spurs his attraction is also a wedge that complicates his emergence from the strait jacket of ego and consequently hampers delivery to the unknown demanded by her: "When he approached her, he came to such a terrible painful unknown. . . . What was it then that she was, to which he must also deliver himself up, and which at the same time he must embrace, contain" (p. 53)? At the end of the proposal scene Tom still has not won the struggle to abide by the logic of his soul. Although he knows "it's got to be done" he cannot give himself up to her. As he leaves his betrothed, Lawrence again turns to a view of the firmament that insists, as a choral reminder throughout the novel, that his struggle take place: "He went out into the wind. Big holes were blown into the sky. . . . And all the sky was teeming and tearing along, a vast disorder of flying shapes . . . . then the terror of the moon running liquid-brilliant into the open for a moment, hurting the eyes before she plunged under cover of cloud again" (p. 44). The enveloping cosmos presents no merely symbolic correspondence to Tom's unpredictable relations with Lydia and not any pantheistic celebration of inscrutable natural energy. It becomes a felt and *participatory* reflection of what Tom has achieved with his fiancée; in effect, his vitalistic perception of the unknown in her will lead him to his fundamental appreciation of the energy beyond her. What Tom perceives in Lydia is as actual as the wind and moon that take part in the prescient feeling with which he leaves. "Hurting the eyes before she plunged under cover of cloud again"—a celestial body becomes

[53]

Lawrence's counterpoint, in a universe that itself ebbs and flows, to Tom's strained willingness, just a page earlier, to meet Lydia in a kiss "till he could bear no more" and must retreat, as "he drew away, white, unbreathing" (p. 43).

It is not surprising that Tom's greatest difficulty in accommodating himself to his wife's "unknown" occurs when she is pregnant, when she is most adamantly "other." During this period Lydia remains isolated and confident, her body brimming with the confirmation (which Lawrence describes in "The Crown") of her direct connection to the forces of creation. Tom returns home with a mixture of trepidation and excitement to the bedside of a womb-aloof wife who is about to give birth:

> There was the sound of the owls—the moaning of the woman. What an uncanny sound! It was not human—at least to a man.
>
> He went down to her room, entering softly. She was lying still, with eyes shut, pale, tired. His heart leapt, fearing she was dead. Yet he knew perfectly well she was not. He saw the way her hair went loose over her temples, her mouth was shut with suffering in a sort of grin. She was beautiful to him—but it was not human. He had a dread of her as she lay there. What had she to do with him? She was other than himself.
>
> Something made him go and touch her fingers that were still grasped on the sheet. Her brown-grey eyes opened and looked at him. She did not know him as himself. But she knew him as the man. She looked at him as a woman in childbirth looks at the man who begot the child in her: an impersonal look, in the extreme hour, female to male. Her eyes closed again. A great, scalding peace went over him, burning his heart and his entrails, passing off into the infinite.
>
> When her pains began afresh, tearing her, he turned aside, and could not look. But his heart in torture was at peace, his bowels were glad. [P. 76]

The scene is alive with the paradox of the "logic of the soul" that motivates Tom. He is roused to anticipation of death by the portentous darkness, owls, and silence while he waits with tentative pleasure for the first life he created. Here is a man who cannot comprehend the "suffering grin" of his woman, for hers is the painful joy that belongs to an anatomy unlike his own. Here is a husband in love with his pregnant wife; yet here also is a man so bewitched by the transformations of parturition that he feels his woman's humanity as something "not human." Lawrence dramatizes the developing breach in her body as establishing a necessary breach with him—an archetypal singling out of the pure polarity of pregnant mother and expectant father. Tom fears this separation from Lydia, and he remains more perplexed than respectful that she is "other than himself." Although Tom cannot fully appreciate its primeval simplicity, her look at him is the regard of ultimate recognition. The scene works not only as a faithful and poetic rendering of the most essential aspects of Lawrencian doctrine but also as an appropriate depiction of the truths about childbirth a century ago.

Once again Mailer supplies direction, this time with a clue to the reason for the relative absence of such a haunting vignette in the technologized world often reflected in contemporary fiction:

> Sometimes the Prisoner thought women had begun to withdraw respect from men about the time pregnancy lost its danger. For once Semmelweiss uncovered the cause of puerperal fever, and the doctor could take over from the midwife, once anesthesia, antiseptics, obstetrics, and delivery by fluorescent light were able to replace boiling water, the lamp by the bed, and the long drum roll of labor, then women began to be insulated from the dramatic possibility of a fatal end. If that had once been a possibility real enough for them to look at their mate with eyes of love or eyes of hate but know their man might yet be the agent of their death, conceive then of the lost gravity of the act, and the diminishment of man from a creature equally mysterious to woman (since he could introduce a creation to her which could yet be her doom) down to the fellow who took lessons on how to satisfy his wife from Masters and Johnson.[11]

Such *is* the gravity of this scene in *The Rainbow* as Tom and Lydia are reduced to "creatures"; they are shorn of the habits of civilized discourse by the silence and metamorphosis that accompany the fate that Lydia risks. Finally Tom leaves the room while "his heart in torture was at peace," which suggests that he begins to comprehend the measuring look by Lydia, who sees him as "her man." Tom's functioning instinct, which is summarized in the beats of his pacified heart and the message of his "entrails," is the pulse of the transcendent as he begins to accept the otherness of Lydia. So Lawrence, for the fourth time in thirty pages, moves from Tom's organic struggles to the climate of the infinite, but this time—caught in his first acceptance of the proper sense of awe—Tom has moved from fear to the larger truth that overwhelms: "He went downstairs, and to the door, outside, lifted his face to the rain, and felt the darkness striking unseen and steadily upon him. The swift, unseen threshing of the night upon him si-

[11]Mailer, *The Prisoner of Sex*, 93.

lenced him and he was overcome. He turned away indoors, humbly. There was the infinite world, eternal, unchanging, as well as the world of life" (p. 76). Tom seems properly initiated to the visionary sensations he has begun to accept. Years later when he is present at the wedding of Anna, his stepdaughter, he tries to defend marriage to his unconvinced elder brother, Alfred: "There's very little else, on earth, but marriage. You can talk about making money, or saving souls. You can save your own soul seven times over, and you may have a mint of money, but your soul goes gnawin', gnawin', gnawin', and it says there's something it must have. In heaven there is no marriage. But on earth there *is* marriage, else heaven drops out, and there's no bottom to it" (p. 134). Tom's remarks conveniently allude to both the matrimonial urge felt as the logic of the soul and the connection to transcendent truth provided on earth through marriage. The young man who once timidly peered through a window at his future family now speaks for a vision he has grown to understand.

III

The intention of this analysis is not to detail Lawrence's painstaking portrait, "really a stratum deeper," of the emotional history of Will's and Anna's marriage, but it needs to be stressed that the primary struggle between Tom and Lydia is recapitulated in the second generation in more elaborate terms. Although the assignment of "blame" for specific periods of their discord varies according to the prominence of Anna's self-involvement or Will's inhibitions, Lawrence presents their problem with a language that holds the husband primarily at fault: "Always, her husband was to her the unknown to which she was delivered up . . . . he seemed to expect her to be part of himself, the extension of his will" (p. 166).[12] Like his father-in-law, Will experiences an immobilizing insecurity when he confronts his wife in her pregnancy. When she reveals to him that she is pregnant, the turbulent wind again charts a comment on his fear: "And he trembled as if a wind blew on to him in strong gusts, out of the unseen. He was afraid. He was afraid to know he was alone. For she seemed fulfilled and separate and sufficient in her half of the world" (p. 175). When

[12]See Charles L. Ross, "The Revisions of the Second Generation in *The Rainbow*," in *Review of English Studies* 27 (1976), 277–95, and *The Composition of "The Rainbow" and "Women in Love": A History* (Charlottesville: University Press of Virginia, 1979), who builds on several of Kinkead-Weekes's conclusions.

Anna understandably becomes alienated by Will's obvious resentment of this "fulfillment" in her, she punishes him by means of her naked dance. This primitive pantomime of his emasculation and execution summarizes the concern with marriage and the unknown that constitutes the ethical core of this novel. It is an extraordinary scene, not only for its sexual intensity and unrestrained cruelty, but also for its reflection of the special dispensations of Lawrence's art: it stands as both symbolic and literal rendering of that final recourse that Will's abrogations have forced Anna to take. Although the logic of Will's soul urges his marriage to Anna, he still resists delivery to the unknown, the essence of marital communion. Anna's pregnancy provides her with the natural temptation—doubly attractive because of her bitterness over Will's failure—to reach for the transcendent without her husband. So a pregnant Anna mobilizes within herself. She enacts a blasphemous version of Lawrence's prothalamic vision. She takes a cruel, logical, and heretical shortcut to the "beyond" that is the ultimate direction of the logic of the soul. In essence, she capitalizes on her self-contained link with the infinite, bypasses her defaulting husband, and communes with the unknown by herself: "She would dance his nullification, she would dance to her unseen Lord. . . . And she lifted her hands and danced again, to annul him" (p. 180). The legalistic ring of "nullification" and "annul" registers a contractual failure by her husband. Will has not adhered to the marriage sacrament, so Anna sidesteps her man to engage her "Lord" directly. Will senses that her preemptive dance signifies his ritual murder, and the pain he feels is more organic than analogical, as was the wind "out of the unseen" that had just made him tremble. These fires burn through the real flesh of people who default on sacramental responsibility: "Her face was rapt and beautiful, she danced exulting before her Lord, and knew no man. It hurt him as he watched as if he were at the stake" (p. 181).

The revivifying potential of sex in a Lawrencian marriage is evident when Will and Anna reestablish their vital connection to each other. In his "Study of Thomas Hardy" Lawrence proposes a doctrinal explanation for the logic in a husband that urges him to conceive children despite his fear of the profound "separateness" in his wife occasioned by her pregnancy and maternal commitments. Lawrence writes of a man who, "taking the superb and supreme risk, deposits a security of life in the womb," but he immediately clarifies the reasons for undertaking such a risk with a terminology that infiltrates *The Rainbow*: "It is so arranged that the very act which carries us out into the unknown shall probably deposit seed for security to be left behind."[13] Thus Will undergoes the penalty implicit in the risk when he observes his wife's annihilating dance, as an angry Anna presides over his emasculation in that confident period of her life that Lawrence describes as the "fecund of storm life," when "she felt like the earth, the maker of everything" (p. 205). Only when Will rouses her to a sensual duel of discovery—as if to call her back after her frenzied years of pregnancy—do they demonstrate how they remain each other's crucial link to the beyond. The inviolable primacy of sexual intercourse, apart from procreation, Lawrence stresses in his "Study of Thomas Hardy": "But the act, called the sexual act, is not for the depositing of the seed. It is for leaping off into the unknown."[14]

Lawrence concludes the Will and Anna section with an interlude that links the fate of young Ursula with the prothalamic theme that frames the novel. Ursula listens intently to Lydia's nostalgic and contemplative description of her two marriages. Lydia shows that she loves both men, and she emphasizes the importance of her granddaughter's understanding that her grandmother's loving and varied life was given baptismal form and meaning through the institution of marriage. Lydia's advice to Ursula was prompted by the child's curiosity about the wedding rings on her fingers. The next mention in *The Rainbow* of a wedding ring (aside from its use as the early title of *The Rainbow*) occurs several years later and is so strategically casual that it recalls the contrasting context of Lydia's warm and serious remarks about the significance of her rings. It happens in the midst of Ursula's courtship with Skrebensky immediately after Ursula remarks, "I don't think I want to marry you" (p. 453). There is nothing unexpected about this renunciation of Skrebensky's proposal of marriage, an offer that he makes with a characteristic pretense of aplomb: "I suppose we ought to get married" (p. 452). Ursula's refusal reflects her developing sense of his inadequacy for her, even as the phrasing also suggests her inability to break off sexual dependency on him, for she does not offer to end the affair. Yet a few lines later, as if she had not just declined his offer, she happily joins him in a conventional play act of young lovers by purchasing "a wedding-ring for a shilling, from a shop in a poor quarter" (p. 453). Her participation in this charade of betrothal contrasts with her earnest attention to her grandmother's benedictive consideration of marriage. Ursula's adolescent behavior with a wedding ring functions as a denial of her

---

[13]Lawrence, "Study of Thomas Hardy," 441.
[14]Ibid.

awareness of Skrebensky's inadequacy, and it anticipates her perverse proposal of marriage that she writes to him late in the novel.

The history of Ursula's long affair with Skrebensky, which concludes with the antiprothalamic trappings of a miscarriage, an emasculated male, and a sick female, stands as Lawrence's warning of the pathology in a love that does not produce a joint singling out. Through her early sexual experiences with Skrebensky, Ursula realizes that she can never reach the unknown with him because "as a distinct male he had no core" (p. 321); however, Ursula later realizes she at least can attain self-definition at his expense.[15] Mailer's earlier comments about the modern tendency to adulterate the apocalyptic possibility in sex provide a pertinent index to the pattern of Skrebensky's decline; his gradual physical and emotional deterioration, urged on by that "terrible knowledge" Ursula gains of him under the moon, recalls Mailer's fears about "the lost gravity" of the sexual act and "the diminishment of man from a creature equally mysterious to woman." Yet it would be wrong to castigate Ursula's exploitation of their sexual relationship. Her compulsion to follow the logic of her soul into an affair with him is not merely the manifestation of either physical desire or ego. Her sexual triumphs over Skrebensky are apprentice efforts at her own singling out. So she indulges in a form of competitive sex with him that is both necessarily at his expense and necessary for her own growth into the woman who marries Rupert Birkin, a man who will demand that otherness be achieved through polarity or "star-equilibrium."

In *Psychoanalysis and the Unconscious*, which explores certain "pollyanalytical" principles dramatized in his fiction, Lawrence provides a doctrinal explanation for the relentless impulse behind Ursula's treatment of Skrebensky: "It is perhaps difficult for us to realize the strong, blind power of the unconscious on its first plane of activity. It is something quite different from what we call *egoism*—which is really mentally derived—for the ego is merely the sum total of what we conceive ourselves to be. The powerful pristine subjectivity of the unconscious on its first plane is, on the other hand, the root of all our consciousness and being, darkly tenacious."[16] In a complementary

---

[15]My explanation in this paragraph of Ursula's sense of self is a reformulation of my original discussion in *D. H. Lawrence and the Psychology of Rhythm* (The Hague: Mouton, 1974), a book that discusses in greater detail the relation of *The Rainbow* to the principles Lawrence enunciates in his major psychological essays.

[16]Lawrence, *Psychoanalysis and the Unconscious* (New York: Viking, Compass Books, 1960), 28.

letter to his friend Edward Garnett, Lawrence in effect discourages criticism of Ursula's manipulative but instinctive brand of sex. He also provides an explanation for the abrupt sequence of changes in Ursula's mood and health in the novel's last pages: "You mustn't look in my novel for the old stable ego of the character. There is another ego, according to whose action the individual is unrecognizable, and passes through, as it were, allotropic states which it needs a deeper sense than any we've been used to exercise."[17] This passage through allotropic states, which seems to demand obedience of a person's instinctive passion, is dramatized when Ursula and Skrebensky make love: "It was begun now, this passion, and must go on, the passion of Ursula to know her own maximum self, limited and so defined against him. She could limit and define herself against him, the male, she could be her maximum self, female, oh female, triumphant for one moment in exquisite assertion against the male, in supreme contradistinction to the male" (p. 301). Such language, with its repetitive emphasis on isolated male and female movements toward self-definition, is revealing for what it suggests about both the prerogatives of Ursula's singling out and the instrumentality of Skrebensky's role in that process. Once the allotropic process begins, once Ursula begins to exert her primal female self, "her own maximum self," the forging to elementals develops a momentum of its own; the porous Skrebensky, who cannot single out, is easy prey for the slaughter. Why should Ursula enjoy such predatory behavior, and why should Lawrence devote so many scenes to the chronicling of this victory over Skrebensky? Lawrence's response in *Fantasia of the Unconscious*, with its distinct echo of phrasing from *The Rainbow*, goes to the crux of Ursula's instinctive achievement; he summarizes why the stakes implicit in her intercourse with Skrebensky under the moon seem heightened beyond the needs of orgasm or ego: "And only at his maximum does an individual surpass all his derivative elements and become purely himself."[18] Ursula's quest for her maximum self is most graphically described in the act of love, where the potential for singling out is greatest, and where Lawrence can employ the moon and stars as participatory representatives, respectively, of Ursula's quest for self-definition and for transcendence.[19]

---

[17]Lawrence, *Letters*, ii, 183.

[18]Lawrence, *Fantasia of the Unconscious* (New York: Viking, Compass Books, 1960), 71.

[19]Mark Spilka first stressed the significance of the moon scenes in his pioneering work on Lawrence more than a quarter of a century ago. He explains that Ursula resembles both Diana, the moon goddess who protects women, and the daughter of Aphrodite, whom "Lawrence calls the goddess of dissolution and death." *The Love Ethic*

The act of intercourse is not the only context used by Lawrence in the Ursula section to dramatize aspects of his prothalamic theme. In the barge scene, for instance, he reestablishes the novel's emphasis on the values of stability and vitality in marriage that Lydia had enunciated years earlier in her talk with Ursula. The husband and wife whom Ursula meets on their boat exist in that state of lively and delicate balance that Lawrence would describe in *Women in Love*. The man exhibits a competent independence without resorting to the chauvinistic slogans that Skrebensky had just praised in a previous conversation with Ursula. Although the husband loves his wife, speaking of her "with just pride" (p. 311), he also demonstrates an appreciation of Ursula's charm; he has a respectful flirtation with Ursula that moves beyond Skrebensky's games of ego and conquest. Similarly, Ursula's abandonment of Uncle Tom's necklace during her visit on the barge anticipates her coming awareness, for she soon identifies Uncle Tom with a cynical view of love and marriage. It is not surprising that, after she breaks off with Winifred, because she senses the mechanization and organic dislocation that underlie Winifred's flaunted independence, she realizes the appropriateness of Winifred's union with Tom. Ursula has come a long way. As an impressionable innocent she had listened passively to her mistress's pontifications that held her "by a kind of spell": "Miss Inger was telling Ursula of a friend, how she had died in child-birth, and what she had suffered; then she told of a prostitute, and of some of her experiences with men" (p. 338). Ursula does not yet realize that Winifred's preoccupations with suffering, dirty sex, and death in childbirth tell more about Winifred's relation to love and sexuality than about normative realities of passion and nurturing affections. When she begins to sense the truth about Winifred, she is content to lose her to the equally manipulative Uncle Tom. Lawrence's deadpan description of the motivations and hopes for such a marriage reads as a litany of the values he despises:

---

of D. H. Lawrence (Bloomington: Indiana University Press, 1953), 112. Thus as Ursula seeks rhythmic communion with the moon, she asserts her triumphant female self as a woman whose psychology calls upon her to destroy the oppressive weight on her (e.g., "Skrebensky, like a load-stone weighed on her," p. 317) and as a mythical goddess (beyond psychology, as it were) whose very triumph is ensured by her name and the moon environment. When Ursula makes love to him late in the novel, she brings to a climax his need to bypass his enclosed self—"not on any side did he lead into the unknown" (p. 473)—and she has her intercourse with the stars. It is a version of the legitimate sexual bypass of a lover that Lawrence depicted in Anna's dance in front of Will.

Brangwen and Winifred Inger continued engaged for another term. Then they married. Brangwen had reached the age when he wanted children. He wanted children. Neither marriage nor the domestic establishment meant anything to him. . . . He had the instinct of a growing inertia. . . . He would let the machinery carry him. . . . As for Winifred, she was an educated woman, and of the same sort as himself. She would make a good companion. She was his mate. [P. 351]

It is instructive to contrast Uncle Tom's needs with the instinctive "look in the eyes" of the Brangwens on the first page of the novel. He has no real interest in either marriage or the unknown, for he only "wanted children" to propagate his mechanical view of existence. He is spurred in this desire by no vital logic of his soul but only by "the instinct of growing inertia," which recognizes a kinship with the deadness at the core of Winifred. The flat repetition of "he wanted children," with its suggestion of apathy and pragmatism, makes Uncle Tom appear as an early version of Clifford Chatterley. Like the paralyzed magnate, who literally "let the machinery carry him," Uncle Tom speaks without respect for institutions and metaphors such as marriage, fatherhood, and the infinite—all of which exist beyond the easy control of a machine or marketable idea. As for Winifred, Lawrence mocks her fashionable pretense with his use of "an educated woman," "a good companion," and a "mate"; those vapid and trendy terms indicate her lack of connection to the flesh and blood realities of passionate marriage.

IV

But, it may be argued, does not the apocalyptic conclusion of the novel contradict the bedrock celebration of marriage that Lawrence develops throughout *The Rainbow*? Are not the final pages—as much feminist criticism insists—a declaration of the birth of an eminently single and "modern" woman, an ending that shows conclusively the influence on Lawrence of his recent exposure to the radical ideas of Cambridge?[20] In the independence and stoic optimism that Ursula's

[20]Carolyn Heilbrun, for instance, speaks of Ursula as a "new woman" at the end who "is entirely alone"; she remarks, "Hindsight suggests that there was no one less likely than Lawrence to have created her," but she never subjects the purported isolation to an analysis that would reveal the unlikeliness of her own interpretation. Heilbrun sees Ursula's only future option as "ordinary marriage for the sake of social recognition," when, in fact, the final page posits something quite apart from the "ordinary." *Toward a Recognition of Androgyny* (New York: Harper & Row, 1974), 109–10. Kate Millett dis-

vision of the rainbow seems to suggest, does she not reject the prothalamic doctrines of this work?

The ending of *The Rainbow* reflects neither a rejection of Ursula's
need and desire for marriage nor Lawrence's deemphasis of the critical importance of marriage in shaping the instinctive life of men and
women. Indeed, it is not really an ending at all but an announcement
of Ursula's realization of the kind of marriage she needs—a declaration, in effect, of her intention to prepare for that "discovery" of the
proper husband in *Women in Love*. Lawrence's companion novel begins with a discussion between Ursula and Gudrun Brangwen on the
subject of marriage; although Ursula confesses that she has rejected
several offers, it is the inadequacy of the men in her life rather than
an abiding antagonism to the institution that has kept her single. One
of the offers of marriage was from Anthony Schofield, a generous
and competent young man from *The Rainbow*, whom Ursula turns
down because the life he offers her is unstimulating and unsuitable.
Before she rejects him Lawrence scarcely hides the continued importance Ursula places on a husband when he writes with odd coyness:
"But having more freedom she only became more profoundly aware
of the big want . . . . she wanted to know big, free people; and there
remained always the want she could put no name to" (p. 406).

Several reasons exist for the unfortunate consensus in Lawrencian
criticism that finds Ursula more determinedly isolated and self-contained at the conclusion of *The Rainbow* than she really is. A willingness to see the Ursula on the last page as complete and emblematic
tends to serve the fashionable interests of sexual politics. Ignorance of
some relevant facts about the composition of *The Rainbow* deflects
needed attention from the suspiciously preemptory nature of the
novel's concluding incidents; a tendency not to be wary of an interpretation of the ending that contradicts Lawrencian belief permits
a reading that strangely asserts Lawrence's celebration of Ursula's

---

torts the compulsions that operate in Ursula's treatment of Skrebensky, as she argues
that "Anton must be sacrificed as an object lesson in how monstrous the new woman
can be." *Sexual Politics* (Garden City: Doubleday, 1970), 262. This peculiar reading
results from such an overriding desire in Millett to charge Lawrence with sexism that
she ironically misses the justifications of Ursula's attack on the man. More recently,
Lydia Blanchard mars an otherwise balanced appraisal of familial structures in *The
Rainbow* with her stress on Adrienne Rich's delimiting theories of motherhood and
power relationships. Blanchard is one of the few critics to realize that "the ending of the
novel is not a resolution," but she steers clear of any crucial admission that Ursula's
quest for self-definition requires the opposite sex. "Mothers and Daughters in D. H.
Lawrence: *The Rainbow* and Selected Shorter Works," in *Lawrence and Women*, ed. Anne
Smith (New York: Barnes & Noble, 1978), 75–100.

glorious chances for spinsterhood. These interpretations distort the significance of an aspect of Ursula's rainbow vision by not considering the concluding lines in a context broad enough to integrate notions in Ursula's dramatized past, her "realized" present, and her likely future.

No doubt the subservient letter that she writes to Skrebensky persuades many readers that Ursula's fortuitous escape from marriage to him suggests her intention to pursue life without a man.[21] But Ursula's ultimate realization about her pathetic letter and the threat posed by Skrebensky have taught her to be wary of flawed men and inadequate marriages. It is important not to give Ursula's fawning letter to Skrebensky any weight on the subject of normative marriage. Its tone of maudlin imploring—" 'It was given to me to love you' " (p. 484)—describes a nearly hysterical Ursula not seen before; the self-abnegating sentiments she expresses about marriage and her wifely role stand in contradiction to the portrait throughout the novel of Ursula's reliable instinct and developing insight. In short, the letter must be construed as a reflection of her understandable panic and illness when she discovers she is alone and pregnant and not as a program for recommended wedlock. Even her analysis of her parents' marriage is glib and reductive, failing to catch the complexity of the adjustments between Will and Anna: "Was it not enough for her, as it had been enough for her mother? She would marry and love her husband and fill her place simply" (p. 484). There is nothing "simple" about either Lydia's or Anna's definition of "place."

College-educated and emancipated Ursula is an adamantly different woman than her mother and grandmother, and she entertains ideas about her destiny that do not rest comfortably with Lydia's and Anna's emphasis on maternity. Lawrence accommodates his understanding of Ursula's special power and requirements in the implications of the novel's final lines. Lawrence forecasts without any self-consciousness a kind of "royal" marriage for Ursula that he memorializes in *Women in Love;* he has created the only woman who might be an appropriate wife for Birkin: "Who was she to have a man according to her own desire? It was not for her to create, but to recognize a man created by God. The man should come from the Infinite and she should hail him" (p. 493).

---

[21]The letter is less significant for ideological criticism, which rejects Ursula altogether—whether she is single, engaged, or pleading for marriage. Millett, for instance, derides the single Ursula as Lawrence's attempt "to make the lot of the independent woman repellent," and she despises the engaged Ursula as a subtle reflection of Lawrence's reactionary and "half derogatory, half vaporous" relation to feminism (*Sexual Politics*, 260–61).

This inflated style, with its sense of grandiose expectation, is not mere metaphor; it suggests that Ursula readies herself for neither the submissive marriage to Skrebensky nor the traditional marriage of the previous two generations of Brangwens but for that advocate of star-equilibrium whom she will meet in the novel originally conceived as *The Sisters*, before Lawrence split it into *The Rainbow* and *Women in Love*.[22] Only a Lawrence would dare suggest the coming of Birkin-Lawrence in terms so hyperbolic, but he never was modest about his talent or mission. When Birkin does "arrive" for Ursula in *Women in Love*, his significance for her recalls the tone and imagery suggested by Ursula's concluding mandate in *The Rainbow* "to recognize a man created by God": "It was here she discovered him one of the sons of God such as were in the beginning of the world, not a man, something other, something more."[23]

There is a more crucial reason for anticipating the next novel. The history of the composition of *The Rainbow* and *Women in Love* supports the view that the end of *The Rainbow* is really the beginning of Ursula's search for the right husband. In a concise discussion of the final revisions of *The Rainbow*, Harry T. Moore writes: "Apparently Ursula's experiences toward the end of *The Rainbow* had occurred near the beginning of *The Sisters;* the surviving manuscript of *The Rainbow* indicates, with its alterations of page numbers and in order of chapters, that these experiences had been moved back, a process which evidently pushed Birkin (the school inspector) into the second book."[24] Such information helps explain the "addendum" tone of *The Rainbow*'s final lines that makes many readers feel the end amounts to a beginning. Ursula's final experiences were originally part of a longer work that would more decisively chronicle her straight-line movement from Skrebensky to a suitable mate. Lawrence's final revisions and his decision to write two novels make the ending of *The Rainbow* more declarative than dramatized; the assertion of the conclusion tends to disguise the original function of the final episodes as a mediating stage in Lawrence's prothalamic vision.

Just a few months before Lawrence began work on what would

[22]Since Lawrence writes that his novel is about "woman becoming individual, self-responsible, taking her own initiative," it is important to regard the new and exclusive grounds of Ursula's search for a husband within the context of Lawrence's stress on such virtues. Lawrence, *Letters,* II, 165. The marriage she contemplates in her future does not involve escape, easy dependency, or empty conventionality.

[23]Lawrence, *Women in Love* (New York: Viking, 1960), 305.

[24]Moore, *The Priest of Love,* 224. Moore's discussion is a summary of the initial findings of Kinkead-Weekes and a preview of the more detailed corroborations of Ross, both cited above.

become *The Rainbow* and *Women in Love,* he wrote a letter to Frieda that not only reveals something about himself but also summarizes a pattern of concern in his fiction: "Can't you feel how certainly I love you and how certainly we shall be married. . . . Do you know, like the old knights, I seem to want a certain time to prepare myself—a sort of vigil with myself. Because it is a great thing for me to marry you, not a quick, passionate coming together. I know in my heart 'here's my marriage.' "[25]

[25]Lawrence, *Letters,* i, 403.

[4]

Women in Love:
D. H. Lawrence's Judgment Book

MARIA DiBATTISTA

I

It was Frieda Lawrence who wanted the sequel to *The Rainbow* entitled *Dies Irae*, the Days of Wrath, the Final Days.[1] Lawrence preferred the less apocalyptically charged *Women in Love*. Frieda's suggestion preserved for Lawrence's proposed "double" novel the grace of symmetry: Genesis and Apocalypse, the total history of Creation recapitulated and reinterpreted in modern times. *The Rainbow* was a novel chronicling the creation of the first woman in "the Essential Days";[2] *Women in Love* actually concerns the destiny of the last men in the final days: the death of Gerald Crich, the Nietzschean captain of industry; and the eclipse, whether temporary or terminal, of Rupert Birkin, the artist as social prophet and sage.

As a novelist and polemicist of the final days, Lawrence always insists, as he does in *Fantasia of the Unconscious*, that he is merely "trying to stammer out the first terms of a forgotten knowledge." For him, the first terms are always the primary principles of a metaphysic that is both comprehended and lived: "Men live and see according to some gradually developing and gradually withering vision. This vision exists also as a dynamic idea or metaphysics—exists first as such.

---

[1] *The Letters of D. H. Lawrence*, vol. 2, ed. George J. Zytaruk and James T. Boulton (Cambridge: Cambridge University Press, 1981), 669; hereafter cited as *L*. Lawrence would later write to Catherine Carswell: "Shall keep the title *Women in Love*. The book frightens me: it is so end-of-the-world. But it is, it must be, the beginning of a new world too." See *The Collected Letters of D. H. Lawrence*, ed. Harry T. Moore, 2 vols. (New York: Viking, 1962), 1, 482.

[2] Lawrence, *The Rainbow* (New York: Viking, 1961), 274. Hereafter cited as *R*.

Then it is unfolded into life and art. Our vision, our belief, our metaphysic is wearing woefully thin, and the art is wearing absolutely threadbare. We have no future; neither for our hopes nor our aims nor our art."[3] In Lawrence's view, the dependency of art on a metaphysic, its secondariness before the larger forms of an authentic cosmology, is compensated by art's transparency as the expressive medium for an unknown time, what Lawrence calls the "next future," an odd and apparently redundant locution that testifies to the Lawrencian belief that the future is what succeeds the present yet remains unconditioned by it. The present always contains the possibility of a "renewed chaos" from which emerges "the strangeness and rainbow-change of ever-renewed creative civilisations."[4] As a symbolic object, the rainbow recommends itself as a model of historical development because it possesses both the aura of natural phenomena—hence its familiar and reassuring presence in the world's landscapes—and the strangeness of a numinous object invested with the prestige and power of the sacred, a promissory sign of the eternal word keeping faith with the world of time.

However, the "earth's new architecture" announced in *The Rainbow*'s final transformative vision of "a world built up in a living fabric of Truth, fitting to the over-arching heaven" (*R*, 495) is only experienced through the visionary ecstasies of the redeemed female. The New Eve always precedes the newly awakened Adam into a paradise of fulfilled desire; the Old Adam, that typological and typical Lawrencian hero, dies belatedly, if at all. Men in *The Rainbow*, as in *Women in Love*, are the preservers of the past; they are the lovers of the Gothic "which always asserted the broken desire of mankind," abjuring the spectacle of "Absolute Beauty" (*R*, 234). Most of Lawrence's men are the artists of the elegiac for whom "a temple is never perfectly a temple, till it was ruined" (*R*, 203). For such men, the sublime is ineluctably connected with the sites of the ruined past.

The Rainbow thus adumbrates the sexual dialectic that informs the struggle for imaginative mastery in its successor fiction. But unlike Lawrence's generational novel, *Women in Love* places its human subjects against a backdrop largely absent from *The Rainbow*, the "great retrogression" of mankind into a "process of active corruption."[5] Lawrence insists on distinguishing between the degenerate meta-

[3]Lawrence, *"Psychoanalysis and the Unconscious" and "Fantasia of the Unconscious"* (New York: Viking, 1960), 57.

[4]Lawrence, *Psychoanalysis*, 57.

[5]Lawrence, *Women in Love* (New York: Viking, 1982), 475. This edition is cited as *WL*. It reproduces Thomas Seltzer's 1920 edition, the least "corrupt" version of the text.

physic that precipitates the historical decline of the West and his own resurgent sexual symbolism that issues from this renewed chaos born of decay. From the opening chapter of *The Rainbow* through the last major polemic of his career, *Apocalypse*, Lawrence argues, both as a predicate of his metaphysic and as a structure of his fiction that, "when there is a touch of true symbolism, it is not of the nature of a ruin or a remains embedded in the present structure, it is rather an archaic reminiscence."[6] Finally, it is Lawrence's generic memory that determines the forgotten knowledge his novels seek to revive and communicate. And it is his controversial genius that traces all inherited symbolic codes to their origin in sexual difference.

II

The first terms of a forgotten knowledge are summarily recalled in the Foreword to *Women in Love*, where Lawrence announces the absolute equality of desire and destiny as coefficients in the balanced equation of creation. The business of the novelist is to express this true fate: "The creative, spontaneous soul sends forth its promptings of desire and aspiration in us. These promptings are our true fate, which is our business to fulfil. A fate dictated from outside, from theory or from circumstance, is a false fate."[7] In his "Study of Thomas Hardy," Lawrence had complained that the novels of the great metaphysical realists Hardy and Tolstoy projected a false rather than a true image of fate by confusing the individual's war against society with the individual's struggle with God. The novels of classical realism are predicated on a false judgment and a fatal imagining of necessity "where transgression against the social code is made to bring destruction, as though the social code worked our irrevocable fate."[8] Exhaustive criticism of Hardy's characters, Lawrence maintained, "would fill the Judgment book,"[9] a final accounting of life novelistically rendered. Unable to liberate themselves from "the greater

[6]Lawrence, *Apocalypse* (New York: Penguin, 1980), 33.

[7]Lawrence, *Women in Love* (New York: Penguin, 1983), vii.

[8]Lawrence, "Study of Thomas Hardy," in *Phoenix: The Posthumous Papers of D. H. Lawrence*, ed. Edward D. McDonald (New York: Viking, 1972), 420. For a descriptive summary of Lawrence's interpretation of Thomas Hardy's fiction, see Richard Swigg's *Lawrence, Hardy, and American Literature* (London: Oxford University Press, 1972), especially 3–31, 58–80. Paul Delany's work is also helpful in defining the biographical and historical context of Lawrence's views on Hardy. See his *D. H. Lawrence's Nightmare: The Writer and His Circle in the Years of the Great War* (New York: Basic, 1978), 30–36.

[9]Lawrence, "Study of Hardy," 410.

idea of self-preservation, which is formulated in the State, in the whole modelling of the community," Hardy's heroes and heroines are doomed to perish in the wilderness: "This is the tragedy of Hardy, always the same: the tragedy of those who, more or less pioneers, have died in the wilderness, whither they had escaped for free action, after having left the walled security, and the comparative imprisonment, of the established convention."[10]

Hardy's walled city is the novelistic space defined by the false fate dictated by theory (religious or biological determinism), or by circumstance (society in its practical and moral forms). The wilderness is the precarious open that designates the creative prodigalities of the eternal origin whose spontaneous activities always impress us as "the waste enormity of Nature."[11] But waste, Blakean excess, is the principle that rules in nature and authorizes what Lawrence insists is the "greater morality" of unfathomed Nature. In the true Judgment Book, *Women in Love*, unfathomed Nature becomes the backdrop of the lesser morality play enacted in that walled city, the novel of manners (with its central plot—the double love stories of Birkin and Ursula, Gerald and Gudrun). It would take, as Lawrence well knew, a radical revisioning of novelistic convention to release his characters from the established representations of life. But to reform generic conventions is, of course, to subject novelistic characters to yet another set of conventions (however "natural" their unfolding) and therefore, potentially, to a false fate.

Lawrence ignores the paradox at the novel's beginning, but it reappears to exact its full metaphysical payment at the novel's ending. The opening chapter, "Sisters,"[12] echoes, with characteristic Lawrencian self-overcoming, *The Rainbow*'s familial and generational interest in a female destiny. Yet this apparent continuity disguises a real disjunction between the initial and final segments of the double novel. In *Women in Love*'s original opening, the canceled prologue, the state of the male soul, the sexual torments of Rupert Birkin, was symptomatic of modernist dis-ease. Birkin's obsession was with the male body,

---

[10]Ibid., 411.

[11]Ibid., 419.

[12]The chapter headings were not added until the 1921 edition by Martin Secker. But I have interpreted them, and I believe Lawrence intended them, as a kind of shorthand denoting the generic and thematic codes of the realist novel. "Sisters" was, of course, also the original working title of the narrative that grew into Lawrence's double novel; *The Letters of D. H. Lawrence*, vol. 1, ed. James T. Boulton (Cambridge: Cambridge University Press, 1979), 550; *L*, 256. Judith Wilt has an extremely suggestive discussion of Lawrence's transvaluing evocation of the Gothic in her *Ghosts of the Gothic* (Princeton: Princeton University Press, 1980), 231–92.

"whilst he studied the women as *sisters,* knowing their meaning and intents" (emphasis added): "It was the men's physique which held the passion and mystery to him. The women he seemed to be kin to, he looked for the soul in them."[13] Birkin's erotic longings merely duplicate, under the sign of sexual difference, the very soul/body dualism that his sexual ideal would abolish: "to love completely, in one and the same act: both body and soul at once."[14] Women will appear in *Women in Love* as sisters, but they are no longer represented as Birkin's spiritual kin. If writers shed sicknesses in books, as Lawrence claimed (*L,* 90), it is Lawrence's own soulfulness that *Women in Love* exorcises. The novel consciously disavows the knowledge of the female soul acquired in the writing of *The Rainbow.* It restores to women their mystery and freedom as novelistic subjects whose meaning and intents cannot, as the prologue mistakenly implied, be foreknown.

The passional mystery of female desire is renewed in the opening discussion between Gudrun and Ursula about their marriage "prospects." To marry or not to marry—that is the question that conventionally defines the choices open to novelistic heroines. But never has the dilemma been formulated in such pained alternatives: Gudrun ironically insisting that marriage, whatever the desire or the fitness of the individuals, is "bound to be an experience of some sort," and Ursula, in her first display of apocalyptic thinking, suggesting that marriage is "more likely the end of experience" (*WL,* 53).

The marriage question is not just linked to the modernist crisis of disassociation and anomie but precipitates it. Nietzsche asserts in that gnomic book, *Twilight of the Idols,* that "modern" marriage and its supporting mythology of Romantic love bear witness to the decadence in the modern's "valuating instinct," a spiritual decline so pronounced that the modern *"instinctively prefer[s]* that which leads to dissolution, that which hastens the end." The objection to modern marriage lies not in marriage but in modernity, which has lost the beneficial instincts out "of which institutions grow, out of which the *future* grows": "The rationale of marriage lay in its indissolubility in principle: it thereby acquired an accent which could *make itself heard* against the accidents of feeling, passion, and the moment."[15] For Lawrence, who like Nietzsche desires a permanent marriage not susceptible to the

[13]Lawrence, "Prologue to *Women in Love," Phoenix II: Uncollected, Unpublished, and Other Prose Works by D. H. Lawrence,* ed. Warren Roberts and Harry T. Moore (New York: Viking, 1968), 104.
[14]Ibid., 103.
[15]Friedrich Nietzsche, *Twilight of the Idols and the Anti-Christ,* trans. R. J. Hollingdale (New York: Penguin, 1968), 94.

vagaries of passion, feeling, or the moment, marriage is also the final test of the instinct for life, the modern riddle whose solution would unveil the mystery of being. Marriage, he claimed, is the great puzzle of modern times, its sphinx riddle. "Solve it or be torn to pieces" is the decree.

Failure to solve the riddle of marriage entails the ritual penalty known as *sparagmos*, the dismemberment of the sacred body, without the ritualistic consolations and controls of ancient Dionysian rites. Modern attitudes toward marriage inevitably fragment the unitary fullness of being into subjective particles, novelistic (Jamesian) "points of view" instead of comprehensive cosmologies. It is at this point that Ursula and Gudrun begin taking "last stands" before they need to do so, a symptom of their fall into the fragmented world of modernity. " 'When it comes to the point, one isn't even tempted—oh, if I were tempted, I'd marry like a shot.—I'm only tempted *not* to.' The faces of both sisters suddenly lit up with amusement. 'Isn't it an amazing thing,' cried Gudrun, 'how strong the temptation is, not to!' They both laughed, looking at each other. In their hearts they were frightened" (*WL,* 54).

The exchange of secret looks, "whilst each sister vaguely considered her fate," communicates more than the malaise of diminished desire; it introduces into the novel's emergent sexual dialectic a primary female negativity before any external forces of prohibition or interdiction are called into play. This negativity, registered in the sisters' denial of their own possible future, is essentially temporal; it signals a collapse of the time needed for the self's unfolding into the compacted and airless space of irony (Gudrun) or anomie (Ursula). Both responses measure the distance separating female desire from the established familial system of filiation and alliance. This distance between desire and the concrete forms of marriage Lawrence's novel must either traverse or abolish entirely.

"Sisters" centers on the radical isolation of the modern woman, alienated from marriage and its central affirmations: the principle of existential security—the promise of indissolubility—and the principle of temporal security, the insured destiny of future generations. The next chapter of *Women in Love,* "Shortlands" (the manor of the Crich dynasty), considers the same problem, but from the perspective of the male will. Lawrence dramatizes in the career of Gerald Crich the peculiarly modern tragedy of the anarchic Dionysian spirit trying to express itself in the Apollonian (degraded) forms of industrial production. Gerald reminds Ursula "of Dionysus, because his hair was really yellow, his figure so full and laughing" (*WL,* 159); this reminder

[72]

anticipates the male fate he must reenact: the modern god dying in the Nordic rite of ice annihilation. At issue in Gerald's destiny is the very meaning of "purpose" in the modern world, an issue addressed in the Lawrencian critique of work, the activity by which man, directed by the spontaneous aspirations of his creative soul, both reclaims his past and organizes his future.

Man works, writes Lawrence in his "Study of Thomas Hardy," because the source of his life is overfull and thus "presses for utterance."[16] "Weltschmerz and other unlocalized pains" signify the pressures within man to "produce" himself. Work therefore constitutes both an inherent passion, a craving "to produce, to create, to be as God," and a faulty mimesis, for in craving to be as God, man can only repeat and reproduce "the movement life made in its initial passage, the movement life still makes, and will continue to make, as a habit, the movement already made so unthinkably often that rather than a movement it has become a state, a condition of all life; it has become matter, or the force of gravity, or cohesion, or heat, or light. These old, old habits of life man rejoices to rediscover in all their detail."[17]

Work entails a conscious reminiscence of those generative movements that have congealed into immemorial "habits" that constitute the given, known conditions of nature: matter, gravity, cohesion, heat, light. The purpose of work is thus present in its basic form as *repetition,* "the repetition of some one of those rediscovered movements, the enacting of some part imitated from life, the attaining of a similar result as life attained." The motive of labor should be consonant with the meaning of work: "to bring all life into the human consciousness."[18]

The mystic harmony between knowledge and life that obtains in the truly creative work is never realized in *Women in Love.* Lawrence's philosophy of work, derived from his reading of Hardy, finds expression only in its demonic opposite: the mechanical philosophy justifying the "life-work" of Gerald Crich. Lawrence, in a rare moment of conventional psychologizing, exposes the grounds of Gerald's savage materialism, tracing it to an early repression of his authentic desire for the epic existence of Homeric days: "During his childhood and his boyhood he had wanted a sort of savagedom. The days of Homer were his ideal, when a man was chief of an army of heroes, or spent his years in wonderful Odyssey" (*WL,* 294). Gerald's drive to

---

[16]Lawrence, "Study of Thomas Hardy," 422.
[17]Ibid., 429.
[18]Ibid., 430–31.

impose his will on the material universe is analyzed as a corrupt form of quixotic idealism. His idealizing compulsion, unlike Quixote's inventive madness, seeks to subjugate the world with "the sword of mechanical necessity" (*WL*, 298) rather than with the broadsword of romance. But like all mad constructionists, Gerald elaborates a system of life that is internally consistent but weakly founded, predicated as it is on two faulty acts of translation—Gerald's mistaking the mystic word "harmony" for the practical word "organization" and his grotesque mistranslation of the godhead into pure mechanism: "He found his eternal and his infinite in the pure machine-principle of perfect coordination into one pure, complex infinitely repeated motion, like the spinning of a wheel: but a productive spinning, as the revolving of the universe may be called a productive spinning, a productive repetition through eternity, to infinity. And this is the God-motion, this productive repetition ad infinitum. And Gerald was the God of the machine, Deus ex Machina" (*WL*, 301).

Not just the echo of Blake's Satanic Mills but the entire antirationalist tradition empowers Lawrence's parody of the materialist analytics that makes the godhead immanent in the world's material motions. Lawrence appropriates Blake's critique in his own polemical diagnosis of the "pure orders" valorized by rationalist metaphysics, the ideology whose historical products—the Krupp Mills, German militarism, and "the sick Man of Europe"—are fabled in the family chronicle of the Crich dynasty, from its sick and dying patriarch, Thomas Crich, to its Bismarckian savior, Gerald Crich. In fact, this historical dimension of the novel is so obvious that, like the Great War, its informing presence can, as Lawrence said, merely be taken for granted.[19]

III

I began my treatment of *Women in Love* with mention of its initial chapters, "Sisters" and "Shortlands," because these early installments recapitulate the old novelistic themes that the unfolding narrative will seek to work through until they are either transmuted into something "new" or are dispersed by the energy of Lawrence's own apocalyptic

[19]Lawrence relates in his Foreword to *Women in Love* that his novel "took its final shape in the midst of the period of war, though it does not concern the war itself." Then he adds: "I should wish the time to remain unfixed, so that the bitterness of the war may be taken for granted in the characters" (*WL*, vii).

imaginings. I have perhaps reductively identified these old themes as marriage and work, the private and public destinies apportioned to novelistic character. The novel's visionary plot to inaugurate a genuinely free, unpredictable course of narrative development actually commences with the third chapter, "Class-Room." "Class-Room" initiates the novel's real effort at a new beginning, a radical departure from the moribund traditions of realist fiction.

The formal attempt to purge the novel of its sentimental and sickly conventions is thematized in the personal drama enacted in "Class-Room": Birkin's attempt to dissassociate himself from Hermione, both as a lover and as a demonic double who mimics his ideas on spontaneous animal joy. Hermione is a Cassandra,[20] but unlike the ancient prophetess whose knowledge is authentic and whose words are discredited, the modern Cassandra is a spectral presence whose agonies result not from the ironic reception of her predictions but from the ironic distance between her speech and the knowledge she would communicate. Her ecstatic language is derided as the "worst and last form of intellectualism," her transports as the convulsions of a will that can only experience the "animalistic" nature of the body as a mental abstraction. Hermione is not only a Cassandra but the Lady of Shalott, another cursed female visionary whose will-bound imagination condemns her to a mirror world of shadows that will never materialize: "You've got that mirror, your own fixed will, your immortal understanding, your own tight conscious world, and there is nothing beyond it" (*WL*, 91).

Birkin's struggle with Hermione, whose rhetoric shadows Birkin's in the vampirish form of unconscious parody and conscious mockery, and who reflects his fear of self-mirroring, is thus part of the larger struggle the novel seeks to portray: the "struggle for verbal consciousness," as Lawrence identifies it in his Foreword. Only the verbalizing "instinct" possesses the eruptive force needed to reclaim the past and to project a future in one totalizing movement. The ceaseless promptings of desire *must* find their way into language where they can be materialized into living forms, or else they will languish in the mind. Lawrence's famous manifesto on novelistic character insists on replacing "the old forms and sentimentalities" of novelistic discourse with this new *materializing* language:

[20]Lawrence wrote Lady Ottoline Morrell, the model for Hermione, that she belonged to a "special race of women: like Cassandra in Greece, and some of the great women saints. They were the great *media* of truth, of the deepest truth: through them, as through Cassandra, the truth came as through a fissure from the depths and the burning darkness that lies out of the depth of time." See *L*, 297.

You mustn't look in my novel for the old stable ego of the character. There is another ego according to whose action the individual is unrecognizable, and passes through, as it were, allotropic states which it needs a deeper sense than any we've been used to exercise, to discover are states of the same single radically-unchanged element. (Like as diamond and coal are the same pure single element of carbon. The ordinary novel would trace the history of the diamond—but I say "diamond, what! This is carbon." And my diamond might be coal or soot, and my theme is carbon.) [L, 183]

To chronicle this allotropic development, in which the elemental ego passes through the successive stages of its potentiality, Lawrence appropriates an archaic language that posited the existence of multiple states, the language of totemism. Totemism is the atavistic language by which the constituent elements that collectively compose the given themes of any culture find their living expression. Totemism provides a serviceable nomenclature for an otherwise "unrecognizable" and therefore potentially *unrepresentable* Lawrencian ego because, as Birkin implies in the chapter entitled "Totem," totemic objects convey the complete truth of a "state" without vitiating or compromising it under the morally static signs of analytic language (WL, 72).[21]

Lawrence, of course, read widely in the burgeoning anthropological literature (Frazer, Weston, Tylor, Harrison) that helped inspire the pancultural myths of modernist works such as *Ulysses* and *The Waste Land* or *Totem and Taboo* (1913). His particular interest in totemism may have derived from totemism's privileged position in the anthropological descriptions of primitive cultures. According to Frazer's *Totemism and Exogamy*, religion itself emerged out of the disruption and decay of totemism; and totemism survives as an elemental remainder and reminder of older social forms in the "later phase of religious evolution."[22] Totemism's capacity to survive as an "archaic reminiscence" of the collective mind thus accounts for its pancultural *and* panhistorical vitality. As Frazer observes, "There is nothing in the institution itself incompatible with the pastoral, agricultural, even the commercial and industrial modes of life, since in point of fact it remains to this day in vogue among hunters, fishers, farmers, traders, weavers, leather-makers, and stone-masons, not to

[21]Lawrence's language has been the focus of many recent studies. Among the most notable are Michael Ragussis, *The Subterfuge of Art* (Baltimore: Johns Hopkins University Press, 1978), especially 178–225, and Garrett Stewart, "Lawrence, 'Being' and the Allotropic Style," *Novel* 9 (1976), 217–42.

[22]J. G. Frazer, *Totemism and Exogamy* (London: Macmillan, 1910), IV, 6.

mention the less reputable professions of quackery, fortune-telling, and robbery."[23]

The real appeal of totemism for Lawrence, whatever its diversionary interest as a patron institution for quacks and fortune tellers, is that it constitutes a system of relationships—animalistic, spiritual, and social—that honors the law of difference,[24] primarily through the stabilizing institution of exogamy. Lawrence's criticism of the modern democratic "isms" (Fabianism, liberalism, socialism, and communism) is that each system advocates a social state based on the utopian goal of material and spiritual equality. Speaking through the bitter declamations of Birkin, Lawrence maintains that social life must reflect and foster the original and originating purpose of life: differentiation. "We are all abstractly or mathematically equal, if you like. Every man has hunger and thirst, two eyes, one nose and two legs. We're all the same in point of number. But spiritually, there is pure difference and neither equality nor inequality counts. It is upon these two bits of knowledge that you must found a state. . . . One man isn't any better than another, not because they are equal, but because they are intrinsically *other*, that there is no term of comparison" (*WL,* 161). Equality is a theoretical construct abstracted out of the data of material necessity; hence Birkin banishes it to the realm of number, wherein its truth and utility, if any, are to be found. In the essay "Democracy," Lawrence converts the primal fact of Otherness into the first term of his "metaphysics of presence." "Our life, our being depends upon the incalculable issue from the central Mystery into indefinable *presence*. This sounds in itself an abstraction. But not so. It is rather the perfect absence of abstraction. The central Mystery is no generalized abstraction. It is each man's primal original soul or self, within him."[25]

The metaphysics of presence demands a language purified of any false "term of comparison" if it is to preserve the inviolability of its "central Mystery." Yet how is the absolute law of otherness to be fulfilled (or even monitored) in the verbal and social contacts of individuals and to retain its ontological status as "the undefinable"? This problem Birkin himself encounters in a rather playful dialectical conversation with Ursula about the "nature" of daisies.

"They are nice flowers," he said, her emotional tones putting a constraint on him.

[23]Ibid., 18.
[24]Ibid., 13.
[25]Lawrence, "Democracy," in *Phoenix,* 714.

"You know that a daisy is a company of florets, a concourse, become individual. Don't the botanists put it highest in the line of development? I believe they do."

"The compositae, yes, I think so," said Ursula, who was never very sure of anything. Things she knew perfectly well, at one moment, seemed to become doubtful the next.

"Explain it so, then," he said. "The daisy is a perfect little democracy, so it's the highest of flowers, hence its charm."

"No," she cried, "no—never. It isn't democratic."

"No," he admitted. "It's the golden mob of the proletariat, surrounded by a showy white fence of the idle rich."

"How hateful—your hateful social orders!" she cried.

"Quite! It's a daisy—we'll leave it alone." [WL, 192]

The ease with which Birkin can postulate the terms of comparison between democracy and the composite structure of the daisy, the facility with which he can transform the daisy into an emblem of the class divisions segregating the proletariat from the idle rich testify to the seductiveness of analogical language. Resisting the temptations of false resemblance is part of the struggle for verbal consciousness that the novel recounts. Birkin must forebear seeking explanations in the concave mirror of false analogy; therein lies the significance of his deferential act in the presence of the daisy: "It's a daisy—we'll leave it alone." The verbal gesture is slight, even comic, but Birkin honors the uniqueness of the daisy as the absolute *other*.

Lawrence's rhetoric of difference found inspiration in the naturalistic language of totemism. Totemism establishes a classificatory system of relationships predicated on the imaginary brotherhood of resemblances in difference.[26] Totemic language externalizes the "primal, original soul within"; it signifies the living realities issuing from the depths of the central mystery and posits their organic relationships. The authority of this totemic identity justifies Lawrence's banishment of the old "stable ego" hypostasized in the novelistic cult of "personality" and the "great Mind" from which it descends.

You can't have life two ways. Either everything is created from the mind, downwards; or else everything preceeds from the creative quick, outwards into exfoliation and blossom. Either a great Mind floats in space:

[26]Claude Lévi-Strauss, who dismisses the "totemic illusion" as a false category of cultural description, attempts to "get to the bottom of the alleged problem of totemism" through the structure of "so called totemic representations." In totemic representations, "it is not the resemblances, but the differences, which resemble each other." See Claude Lévi-Strauss, *Totemism,* trans. Rodney Needham (Boston: Beacon, 1963), 77.

God, the Anima Mundi, the Oversoul, drawing with a pair of compasses and making everything to scale, even emotions and self-conscious effusions; or else creation proceeds from the forever inscrutable quicks of living beings, men, women, animals, plants. The actual living quick itself is alone the creative reality.[27]

The struggle for verbal consciousness is waged in the unspoken battle raging between Birkin, the metaphysician of presence, who celebrates the inscrutable quick of living beings, and Gudrun, that formidable apostle of Mind for whom the world is a spectacle of descending creations, life defined (and degenerating) downward, abstracted, "preconcluded." Committed to the notion of personality, she regards the human being "as a complete figure, like a character in a book, or a subject in a picture, or a marionette in a theatre, a finished creation." When she sees Gerald for the first time, the novel, adopting her mode of perception, lapses into the language typical of "old" narrative habits of representation. Gerald is described in terms of externals, "a fair, sun-tanned type, rather above middle height, well-made, and almost exaggeratedly well-dressed": "But about him also was the strange, guarded look, the unconscious glisten, as if he did not belong to the same creation as the people about him" (*WL*, 61).

Gudrun can only express the unconscious glisten that identifies Gerald as *another*, not the *same* creation as the fixed and finished characters about him, by invoking his totemic reality: "'His totem is the wolf,' she repeated to herself. 'His mother is an old, unbroken wolf.' And then she experienced a keen paroxysm, a transport, as if she had made some incredible discovery, known to nobody else on earth" (*WL*, 61). Gudrun's "powerful apprehension" of Gerald's essence is not the result of conscious metaphor making, that is, metaphor making as an exercise of the will intent on connecting the known with the unknown. "His totem is the wolf" is rather a kind of double metaphor, the first part, totem, assimilating even as it traverses the second part, wolf. Totemistically, Gerald is that doubly unknown and undefinable reality, wolf manifest. Wolf is the ancestral and universal reality struggling to express itself through him. The totemic depths of Gerald's individuality are brought to the narrative surface through a process of charged language that does not bother to discriminate between generative forces and their individual manifestations. Lawrence's language here is designed to radicalize metaphor and all other "terms of comparison" by eliminating the mediating middle term in

[27]Lawrence, "Democracy," 712.

the vital transfer of meaning from the depths to the surfaces. He wants his language to destroy or incapacitate that part of the verbal consciousness, best represented in the "mind" of Gudrun, which habitually employs language to encircle, complete, and define (fix) the real.

Thus language determines novelistic destiny in *Women in Love*. The novel's climactic moment of reckoning may be seen in the great chapter "Gudrun in the Pompadour," which stages the secular spectacle of the Logos "harrowing hell," Birkin's excoriation of the decadent Halliday crowd with his prophetic "letter" proclaiming the unalterable law that will prevail in *Dies Irae:* "the Flux of corruption . . . , the reducing back of the created body of life" (*WL,* 375). The episode's dramatic power issues from the charged interplay between the novel's two competing "artists," the absent Birkin (present by virtue of his jeremiad on modernism) and Gudrun, the fashioner of miniatures, the respecter of the old virtues and corrupt privileges of the dead letter "I," and Birkin's only real rival in *Women in Love.*

Gudrun incarnates "a desire for the reduction process in oneself" that Birkin identifies as the sign of modern decadence. Her art represents "the process of active corruption" that results in Baudelairian "fleurs du mal," those (literary) flowers of evil that hauntingly contrast with Birkin's pristine daisies. When Gudrun overhears the Halliday party ridiculing Birkin's "genuine letter," she goes over to their table, retrieves the letter, and walks out of the Pompadour "in her measured fashion" (*WL,* 476). In the ethos of a traditional novel, Gudrun's act is praiseworthy, a dignified defense of a friend's right to privacy, the decorous rescue of a private letter from mocking public scrutiny. But Gudrun is defending values that Lawrence cannot and will not endorse: the value of privacy and family loyalty, the affiliative ties that defined the obligations and prescribed the roles of an "older," stable ego. Her act is justly recorded in the language of the narrative commentary as a misdeed.[28] Gudrun rescues the letter at the expense of its spirit, and the novel, after her dramatic act of retrieval and repossession, reverts to the literalism of "realistic" description in narrating her triumphant exit:

> From Halliday's table came half articulate cries, then somebody booed, then all the far end of the place began booing after Gudrun's retreating

---

[28]Delany details the origins of this episode in the notorious "Café Royal" incident in which Katherine Mansfield, one of Lawrence's models for Gudrun, retrieved a book of Lawrence's poems from the mocking coterie of "Café Society" intellectuals. See *D. H. Lawrence's Nightmare,* 247–48.

form. She was fashionably dressed in blackish-green and silver, her hat was brilliant green, like the sheen on an insect, but the brim was soft dark green, a falling edge with fine silver, her coat was dark green, brillantly glossy, with a high collar of grey fur, and great fur cuffs, the edge of her dress showed silver and black velvet, her stockings and shoes were silver grey. She moved with slow, fashionable indifference to the door. [*WL*, 476]

Gudrun's movements are tracked in this pure description of surfaces, a narrative gesture on Lawrence's part that is at best supererogatory and at worst damning. Gudrun moves within the colorful modalities of self-display, while the real existential issue for Birkin is nakedness. Birkin argues with Gerald and Ursula about the dispensability of clothes; he wrestles naked with Gerald in "Gladiatorial"; and he and Ursula ritually disrobe in "Excurse" to experience the "unrevealed nudity" of the mystic body of reality (*WL*, 403). Gudrun in the Pompadour acts out the old ethics—and psychology—of self-presentation; Birkin yearns for a kind of psychic nakedness in the reality of human encounters. Gudrun defines and defends the rhetoric of finality, the aesthetic of the finished and polished creation. Birkin attempts to stammer out the words of a new rhetoric of futurity in the last facts of nakedness. The novel as it nears its conclusion represents a battle between these two rhetorics, a struggle between Gudrun and Birkin, not just for mastery over the novelistic spaces they occupy, but over the soul of the last modern hero—Gerald Crich. Their competition generates a system of warring metaphysics (neither fully articulated nor fully sufficient), and the aesthetics appropriate to each: Birkin, the voyager into the unknown, the Hardyean "pioneer" who journeys into the fruitful wastes seeking his destiny in what he calls "mystic marriage"; Gudrun, the "Glucksritter," riding the unstable currents of fashion, the Eternal Feminine pursuing her own degradation as the whore of Fortune, whose vehicle is the wheel of mechanical transformation.

IV

Birkin's salvationist reimagining of the creative life is nowhere as dramatically figured as in "Moony," Lawrence's most controlled and condensed narrative meditation on modern love purged of its Meredithian "sickly cant." "Moony" describes Birkin's obsessive disfigurement of the image of the moon reflected in the surfaces of a pond.

This lunar reflection is not for him a natural icon for the order of mutability but a demonized image of Cybele, the "accursed Syria Dea" (*WL*, 323) of Asiatic mother cults. In an effort to discharge the powers of darkness gathering force within him, Birkin throws stone after stone into the motionless pond, turning it into "a battlefield of broken lights and shadows," a field of "white fragments" that mirrors his own obsession with those disintegrative processes that may portend, for all their negativity, a positive struggle to emerge from the womb of creation. Yet the moon's image remains unviolated—Nature sees to it that the "scattered fragments" course their way back to the still center: "He saw the moon regathering itself insidiously, saw the heart of the rose intertwining vigorously and blindly, calling back the scattered fragments, winning home the fragments, in a pulse and in effort of return" (*WL*, 324). Sparagmos to *nostos:* the winning home of fragments—that, of course, is the desired homecoming at the thematic and mythic heart of modern narratives from Joyce's *Ulysses* to Beckett's grimly ironic, vagrant fictions of disintegration. Winning home is the telos of modern art—to repair, no matter how tempting the urge to fall "back in panic," the "ragged rose," Dante's rose of the World. Winning home is what Birkin sees as "the remaining way" open to those weary of contemplating the modern mysteries of dissolution: "There was another way, the way of freedom. There was the paradisal entry into pure, single being, the individual soul taking precedence over love and desire for union, stronger than any pangs of emotion, a lovely state of free proud-singleness, which accepted the obligation of the permanent connection with others, and with the others, submits to the yoke and leash of love, but never forfeits its own proud individual singleness, even while it loves and yields" (*WL*, 331–32). Birkin, however, remains unsure whether his vision of free proud singleness is "only an idea, or . . . the interpretation of a profound yearning" (*WL*, 329). Love must be experienced as a "travelling together," a mobile nostos, an exploratory way, never a final destination. Lawrence's novel never abandons its desire to see the elemental ego find its own way into the unknown, its true fate.

The "love" story of Birkin and Ursula embedded in and illuminating the dark heart of *Women in Love* represents Lawrence's attempt to render the great, perhaps the last, epic adventure of modernity—the exploration of the as yet unknown. This love story generically attains its consummatory moment of winning home, its paradisal entry into a new world, in the chapter peripatetically entitled "Excurse," in which Birkin proposes to Ursula the terms of his star marriage, terms she will come to accept as the liberating fatality of love. The chapter opens with Birkin's decision to renounce the tutelage of Luck as a vulgar minister of destiny (*WL*, 385); he refuses to accept that life is "a series of accidents—like a picaresque novel" (*WL*, 383). "Excurse" thus becomes one of Lawrence's most successful fictional representations of a "generic" self-overcoming. The picaresque, the narrative of human destiny imaged forth as a series of accidents originating in the contingencies of history, social caste, and economic conditions, is invoked only to be revoked as a fictional legacy that validates a "false fate." In "Excurse" the promise of *The Rainbow* is realized: Ursula's "new knowledge of eternity in the flux of time" is fulfilled in her *internally* apprehended knowledge of "the inevitability and beauty of fate, fate which one asks for, which one accepts in full" (*WL*, 400) and in "this star-equilibrium which alone is freedom" (*WL*, 402).

Yet despite her revelatory vision of a self-generated fate, the true "fate which one asks for," not the untoward destiny one struggles against, like a picaresque heroine, Ursula does not always accede to the conditions of her newfound freedom in star-equilibrium. The reason is partly that Lawrence prefers to leave his characters in uncertainty and partly that Ursula remains for Lawrence totemically bound to her essence as Magna Mater, the Great Mother who insists on pressing for a reactionary and limited kind of love, love as ecstatic fusion. Like all of Lawrence's early heroines, from Mrs. Morel to Anna "Victrix" Brangwen, Ursula has a predilection for a consuming romance whose central episode is the idyll of a sexual paradise regained. Generically, romance is the narrative form that seeks to cancel out the differences separating love and its objects. For Lawrence, it is *the* female form of imaginative desire, born out of the female will to absorb the "Other" in the all-comprehending womb. The Great Mother would reclaim all individualized life into the undifferentiated Source, drawing all articulated meanings and distinctions into herself. For Ursula, who might be won over by love's (and Birkin's) excursionary nature, intercourse is still initially and perhaps finally the act of homecoming, the winning home of the errant male.

Birkin's suspicions that the Magna Mater's lust for "unspeakable intimacies" (*WL*, 343) lurks behind every female's urge to "mate" leave him dissatisfied with mystic marriage as the controlling metaphor for his transvaluing vision of life. Because marriage is disposed, by the sheer force of institutional inertia and by the reactionary demands of the "feminine" will to enforce a unity where none should exist, Birkin advocates the complementary, revolutionary relation of

Blutbrüderschaft.[29] The truly subversive content of *Women in Love,* its well-conceived threat to the conventional attitudes toward human relationships propagated by the "bourgeois" novel, is in expanding the idea of spiritual mating to encompass a male-to-male relation, a broader and less interested relation than the "égoïsme à deux" or "hunting in couples" (*WL,* 439) that characterizes modern marriages.

Birkin's rite of "bloodbrotherhood" is authorized both by his personal desire for a male relationship and by the more utilitarian need to populate the "new world" of his visions with as yet undefined human constellations in supposed star-equilibrium. But beneath Birkin's ideological justification for such a male rite as a "new utterance" issuing out of life's creative mysteries, there abides the epic striving condensed and displaced in the obsessions of Birkin's *Salvator Mundi* complex: his classical yearning for the "Gladiatorial" *virtus* embodied in the Homeric figure of Gerald Crich. Of course Gerald has ostensibly betrayed his heroic nature by dedicating himself to the "established world" and its decadent, moribund orders "in which he did not livingly believe." Conventional marriage would prove "the seal of his condemnation": it would condemn him to the underworld "like a soul damned but living forever in damnation." Birkin's offer of Blutbrüderschaft is the redemptive alliance that Gerald considers in the chapter "Marriage or Not": "If he pledged himself with the man he would later be able to pledge himself with the woman: not merely in legal marriage, but in absolute, mystic marriage" (*WL,* 440). But Gerald declines Rupert's offer, whether because of "unborn, absent volition or of atrophy" (*WL,* 440) Birkin declines to speculate and Lawrence refuses to say.

Of course Birkin's revolutionary offer to rescue Gerald from his impending doom is exposed as an illusory choice in the novel's depiction of the Final Days. For Gerald has already made his choice in the previous chapter, prophetically entitled "Death and Love." The death of his father brings Gerald to a crisis state in which, poised on the edge of the grave, the image of the perilous void, he "must take direction." Crisis, as Frank Kermode reminds us, citing the pun of St. John, comprises a moment both of judgment and of separation.[30] For

[29]Emile Delavenay's *D. H. Lawrence and Edward Carpenter: A Study in Edwardian Transition* (New York: Taplinger, 1971), 190–235, assesses the influential presence of Carpenter's ideas on sexuality and society in Lawrence's concept of Blutbrüderschaft. See also Samuel Hynes's "Science, Seers, and Sex," in *The Edwardian Turn of Mind* (Princeton: Princeton University Press, 1968), 132–71, for a more comprehensive account of the new attitude toward sexuality fostered by the work of Carpenter and Havelock Ellis.

[30]Frank Kermode, *The Sense of an Ending: Studies in the Theory of Fiction* (London: Oxford University Press, 1967), 25.

Gerald the moment of crisis resolves itself in a decision to separate himself from the "one center" authorized and inhabited by his father—"the unseen, raw grave": "No, he had nothing to stay here for." He then forms his "dangerous resolve"—to go to Gudrun, "persistently, like a wind, straight forwards, as if to his fate" (*WL*, 424). But this resolution issues in a false "separation" of love and death. Even as Gerald enters Gudrun's bedroom seeking comfort in love's restorative rites, he tracks in the cold clay of the grave. Death and love become dialectically wedded, composing the signs that dictate Gerald's true fate. Whatever Birkin might do to oppose it, Gerald is set on an irreversible course of self-destruction. In a letter to John Middleton Murry, Lawrence describes the limits of his own revolutionary vision of the millennium when the world will be repopulated with the new men and women of his imaginings: "I think that one day—before so very long—we shall come together again, this time on a living earth, not in the world of destructive going apart. I believe we shall do things together, and be happy. But we can't dictate the terms, nor the times. It has to come to pass in us. Yet one has the hope, that is the reality" (*L*, 662).

The *Götterdämmerung* finale of the novel confirms Lawrence's intuition that neither the terms nor the times ordained for the world's "destructive going apart" can be dictated by the human will—either the regenerate will of the prophet, or the corrupt will of the insane "ecstatics," like Gudrun and Loerke, who herald the dawn of "the obscene beyond." Birkin's vision thus acquires an ambiguous status in the novel's already tortuous eschatology—it expresses the hope for, not the imminence of, a new creative order. This hope diminishes as the novel relentlessly moves toward its last days, whose end terms are dominated not by Birkin's visionary excursions but by the sick "love story" of Gudrun and Gerald.

The destinies of Gerald and Gudrun constitute, as Lawrence once wrote of Dostoevsky's novels, "great parables . . . but false art" (*L*, 544). Their love story represents, that is, the dead life and the moribund forms of older (tragic) narratives whose formal integrity conformed to a deterministic notion of historical causality. This formalism appears in an early exchange between Gudrun and Gerald: "You have struck the first blow," Gerald reminds Gudrun, to which she responds with "confident assurance," "And I shall strike the last." That Gudrun's threat sounds like a prediction is a sign of her (and the reader's) confidence in the symmetry intrinsic to the resolutions of the classical novel. Lawrence's own analysis of Dostoevsky's "parables" helps illuminate his unwilling incorporation of this "false" yet inevitable formalism into the last stages of *Women in Love*. Writing again to Murry, who was working on a study of Dostoevsky, Lawrence observes: "The Christian ecstasy leads to imbecility (the Idiot). The sensual ecstasy leads to universal murder: for mind, the acme of sensual ecstasy lies in *devouring* the other, even in the pleasures of love, it is a devouring, like a tiger drinking blood (Rogozhin). But the full sensual ecstasy is never reached except by Rogozhin in murdering Nastasya. It is nipped in the last stages by the *will*, the social will" (*L*, 544).

This Dostoevskian insight shadows Lawrence's representation of Thomas Crich's sentimental Christianity and Gudrun's demonic sensuality. Christian ecstasy, which Thomas Crich seeks through his self-abnegating charities and his sentimental, "democratic" politics, leads to his final imbecility and the slow stupor of lingering death. Sensual ecstasy is the special lust of Gudrun, whose face betrays the insane will of the "demoniacal ecstatic" (*WL*, 69) and whose love affair with Gerald, like her nostalgic fascination with the underworld of his mines, grows out of her desire to experience the "perfect voluptuous finality" (*WL*, 560). Her affair with Gerald must end with her triumph in "the last stages" and, as the Dostoevskian parable instructs, in sensually gratifying murder.

Lawrence's unwilling but not inadvertent accommodation of Dostoevsky's spiritual determinism *as the only possible* resolution to his visionary narrative is also reflected in the larger structural configurations of the novel. *Women in Love* begins with an unstable triangle— Hermione, Ursula, and Birkin—that Birkin attempts to replace with the transforming relationships comprehended in mystic marriage. But as the novel moves toward the Continent and into its Götterdämmerung phase, the generic imperative to observe certain novelistic symmetries begins to reassert itself. The novel's initial sexual triangle reappears in the parodic and demonic trinity of Loerke, Gudrun, and Gerald. Moreover, the novel also regresses to a formalist rigidity in echoing Birkin's vision of male love in Loerke's relation to Leitner, an alliance that demystifies Birkin's mystic sense of Blutbrüderschaft in the perversions of "ecstatic" and exploitive homosexuality.

To discredit the determinism that is overwhelming his narrative, Lawrence has Gudrun mock the conventional explanation that the violence called forth in the final stages of her battle with Gerald is due to the tensions and jealousies traditionally associated with the "eternal" love triangle: " 'A pretty little sample of the eternal triangle!' And she turned ironically away, because she knew that the fight had been between Gerald and herself and that the presence of the third party was a mere contingency—an inevitable contingency perhaps, but a contingency none the less. But let them have it as an example of the eternal triangle, the trinity of hate. It would be simpler for them" (*WL*, 578). Gudrun's scathing dismissal of the idea that her triangular entanglements with Gerald and Loerke compose a trinity of hate, a demonic variation on the eternal triangle, is based on a quibble about the meaning and importance of "contingencies." But what does she, or even Lawrence, mean by the self-contradictory assertion that Loerke's presence operates as an "inevitable" contingency? How can a contingency be both accidental and forseeable, dependent on chance yet necessary as both a primary and secondary cause? What is important to Gudrun's self-interpretation is not her claim that her battle with Gerald represents a singular death struggle between two insane wills; rather, what emerges as significant and triumphant is Gudrun's power of dismissive irony, her tonal mastery over the reality of the last facts, the violent ends of *Dies Irae*.

In *Women in Love*, Gudrun's vision, the ironical vision of love and death, overwhelms the imaginations of the artist of life, Rupert Birkin. Birkin tries to inaugurate a reign of freedom, the new time of the transcendent individual who lives in close contact with the inexhaustible life source. Gudrun, with Loerke, her demonic consort, inaugurates the totalitarian regime of terror, the nightmare of history and historicism, the coming era of real social hatred. Gudrun's is a peculiarly "modern" madness, not the classical and even pathos-ridden madness of Hermione, who is partially redeemed by her mythic affinity with Cassandra. In her prophetic but unredeeming imagination, Gudrun confronts and then *becomes* the specter that haunts the modern mind, the specter of mechanical causation.

> Perhaps she was healthy. Perhaps it was only her unabatable health that left her so exposed to the truth. If she were sickly she would have her illusions, imaginations. As it was, there was no escape. She must always see and know and never escape. She could never escape. There she was, placed before the clock-face of life. . . . She was watching the fingers twitch across the eternal, mechanical, monotonous clock-face of time. She never really lived, she only watched. Indeed, she was like a little, twelve-hour clock, vis-à-vis with the enormous clock of eternity—there she was, like Dignity and Impudence, or Impudence and Dignity. (*WL*, 565)

Gudrun identifies with the eternal repetition of the clock face as the internal principle of her existence, thus alienating herself from the nurturing and restorative cycles of natural time: hence "her unripening nights, her unfruitful slumbers" (*WL*, 566). She is the mad prophetess who presides over the apocalyptic Terrors that proclaim the end of the world as a ceaseless duration. *Dies Irae* for Gudrun take the form of a perpetual *chronos*, to paraphrase Kermode's formulation of the modernist's "intemporal agony,"[31] chronos without kairos, without a transforming, all-reversing and all-renewing eruption of creative mystery into the remorseless chronicity of linear, clock-face time. Gudrun can neither envision nor hope for deliverance. She can only persist in fashioning the totalitarian, apocalyptic fantasies she plays out with Loerke, the "final craftsman" of "the last series of subtleties," who "did not deceive himself in the last issue":

> As for the future, that they never mentioned except one laughed out some mocking dream of the destruction of the world by a ridiculous catastrophe of man's invention: a man invented such a perfect explosive that it blew the earth in two, and the two halves set off in different directions through space, to the dismay of the inhabitants: or else the people of the world divided into two halves, and each half decided *it* was the perfect and right, the other half was wrong and must be destroyed; so another end of the world. [*WL*, 551]

Gudrun and Loerke translate the central rite of modernity—sparagmos—into global and genocidal terms: the earth torn in two, mankind's destructive dream of exterminating the ideologically corrupt other. As the final form in their last series of subtleties, Loerke and Gudrun construct this mad parody that inverts Plato's myth of the origin of sexual love in Zeus' punitive division of the original hermaphroditic body into halves, who thereafter seek to reunite through love. Time becomes a clock face onto which they project their false "Dignity" and their true "Impudence" as artists of the obscene whose ecstatic vision of the End finds its consummation in universal murder.

Gudrun's myth of finality is registered in the cold, life-betraying voice of irony: "Everything turned to irony with her: the last flavour of everything was ironical" (*WL*, 511). Kierkegaard claimed that irony was "in the strictest sense a mastered moment" and saw in the birth of ironic consciousness "the absolute beginning of the personal life."[32] For Kierkegaard, irony is the baptism of human beginning; for Lawrence irony is the last rites of the living-dead. That the creative moment could in any way be limited to and defined by the needs and desires, the dignities—and impudence—of the personal life is repug-

---

[31]Ibid., 63.

[32]See Sören Kierkegaard, *The Concept of Irony*, trans. Lee M. Capel (Bloomington: Indiana University Press, 1968), 337.

nant to his metaphysical and rhetorical doctrines of impersonality. For Lawrence language should adhere and inhere in the reality it denominates, in the new utterances it struggles to deliver over to verbal consciousness. Irony, the conscious displacement of meaning from its vehicles of expression, irony as the deliberate estrangement of essence and phenomena, is the last betrayal of the creative Source.

Gerald's death vindicates Gudrun's status as the ironical artist who has mastered the creative moments immanent in the "time" of Nature. It is Gudrun who regards Gerald's death as an inevitable contingency attending the Final Days, a necessary but "barren tragedy" without meaning or significance, but hers is the view of cold irony. It is at this point that Birkin returns to the novel that he has abandoned (and that has abandoned him) to contest Gudrun's ironical reading of Gerald's death. He mourns the fallen hero and retreats, not behind the frigid dignities of irony, but into the enclosed and emotionally charges spaces of elegy: "I didn't want it to be like this" (*WL*, 581). Ursula, to her horror, hears the accent of nostalgia in Birkin's valedictory lament and cannot help thinking of the Kaiser's "Ich habe es nicht gewollt." In exposing the historical retreat implicit in Birkin's elegiac meditations, Ursula argues for the "realities" honored in the resolutions of the classical novel and in so doing interprets Birkin's grief as a perversion, a refusal to accept the fate decreed by those impersonal forces that constitute the Real.

> "You can't have two kinds of love. Why should you!"
> "It seems as if I can't," he said. "Yet I wanted it."
> "You can't have it, because it's wrong, impossible," she said.
> "I don't believe that," he answered. [*WL*, 583]

Women in Love thus represents and advances the modernist crisis of separation and judgment. Its Götterdämmerung finale envisions the last symmetries in the form of an impasse and an argument. Birkin's perverse insistence that his desire to "save" Gerald was not a false, nor even a barren, hope, but a living expression of his heart's desire, his true fate, is contrasted with Gudrun's grim, ironical view of necessity. His quarrel with Gudrun over the meaning of history is perhaps less threatening to his metaphysic than his argument with Ursula over the visionary possibility of Blutbrüderschaft, men wedded in purpose and in love. Both the historical impasse and the emotional argument remain unresolved, their outcome temporarily suspended by a narrative moratorium dictated by Birkin's grief and Lawrence's own need to reimagine the presence of the creative mystery that will "carry on the embodiment of creation" even if mankind is exterminated—or annihilates itself. The novel opens itself up to the future only by insisting on a kind of blank space in time, empty yet still capable of being filled with new utterances, "miraculous unborn species" (*WL*, 580).

In an essay on modern painting, Lawrence pictured Cézanne's struggle with the visual clichés that composed the tainted inheritance, the corrupted legacy of pictorial form. His analysis illuminates and corresponds to Lawrence's own transvaluing critique of novelistic conventions. "In other pictures he seems to be saying: Landscape is not like this and not like this and not like this and not . . . etc.—and every *not* is a little blank space in the canvas, defined by the remains of an assertion. Sometimes Cézanne builds up a landscape essentially out of omissions. He puts fringes on the complicated vacuum of the cliché, so to speak, and offers us that. It is interesting in a repudiative fashion but it is not the new thing."[33] *Women in Love*, despite its efforts to imagine and realize a "new thing," comes to rest on the fringe of the complicated vacuum of novelistic cliché. Birkin's belief that life need "not," is "not," like this and this—contains the remains of an assertion, but it is hard to determine whether his refusal to submit to Ursula's pragmatic and historical view of the limits of human desire is anything more than mental repudiation. *Women in Love* begins but cannot conclude Lawrence's own struggle with the memory of classical narrative, which trusted, not naively, but livingly, in a final day of historical reckoning. *Women in Love* is the Judgment Book that publishes the decrees of a Providence that Lawrence could neither ignore nor accept.

[33]Lawrence, "Introduction to These Paintings," in *Phoenix*, 581. Ragussis first commented on the importance of this passage to the novel's "open-ended" ending; see *The Subterfuge of Art*, 224.

[5]

Accident and Purpose: "Bad Form" in Lawrence's Fiction

ROBERT KIELY

Though D. H. Lawrence is accepted as one of the major English writers of the twentieth century, he is still regarded, except by his most loyal defenders, as an author for whom we must make apologies. There is wisdom and profound insight, but there are also ideas that are naive and illiberal. There are deft economies of detail and powerfully realized characterizations, but there are also tedious pages of repetitious exposition. Most of Lawrence's admirers have learned to excuse the unattractive ideas and language as lapses in the work of an unruly genius. Some of his detractors have argued that the faults are not incidental but rather symptoms of an essentially crude mentality.

Lawrence probably would have preferred the latter judgment to the former, since he was not one for half measures or polite evasions. Though he was not always a consistent thinker, he admired integrity. He wanted "wholeness," and though he did not readily accept conventional explanations, he believed in a universal coherence of things and thought that it was the business of human beings to discover the connections within themselves and with others. Despite his well-known dislike of Freud, he too thought that "slips of the tongue" and sporadic departures from ordinary behavior were meaningful expressions of the whole personality.

Certainly, Lawrence without the lapses would not be Lawrence. His sins against "good form" and "straight thinking," however we may explain them, are, unless we reedit his books, part of his literary legacy. In exploring his own fictional characters, he himself hardly overlooks or deemphasizes the rough spots. On the contrary, much of what we admire in him is his ability to reveal precisely those thoughts, actions, and traits often discounted by other writers as significant indicators of character.

My question is not "How can we forgive this gifted eccentric?" but rather "How was what he did a necessary part of what he was trying to do?" Lawrence warns his readers to trust the tale, not the teller. But in exercising discretion with regard to the intentional fallacy, critics have not always been fair to Lawrence. What is self-conscious in Joyce and Eliot, for example, is usually treated as the ultimate in sophisticated modernism. These are writers who knew what they wanted to do and did it. The image of Lawrence as spontaneous to the point of carelessness has too often overshadowed his own typically modern tendency to reflect on the nature of his art.

Of course, Lawrence's manner of writing criticism no less than his manner of writing fiction has created this image. Lawrence has not simply been the victim of obtuse critics. To a large extent, he is the author of his own reputation. Joyce never fails to remind us of the discipline—classical and Ignatian—of his vocation as an artist. Lawrence, on the contrary, pictures himself as a sloppy, loud-mouthed intruder, not a literary man himself, certainly not restrained or careful about what he says, one who enjoys smashing things and shocking people.

Sometimes in his critical writing, Lawrence sounds as though he were opposed to all received forms of art and literature. "The moment man became aware of himself he made a picture of himself, and began to live from the picture. . . . If we could once get into our heads . . . that we are *not* the picture, and the picture is not what we are, then we might lay a new hold on life. For the picture is really the death, and certainly the neurosis, of us all."[1] Elsewhere he refers to art as a "tomb" inside which mankind is trapped like a corpse.[2] The great need is to "break the present great picture."[3] Such talk conjures up images of hammers smashing pianos, of a new breed of "artists" able to express themselves only through their hatred of the inherited picture.

But Lawrence was not that kind of artist. Despite his anger and rebelliousness, his books represent much less of an assault on the tradition than those of contemporaries such as Stein, Pound, or Joyce. Furthermore, he was not really that kind of critic either. As one reads on in his essays, the source of his irritation becomes more clearly and

[1]*Phoenix: The Posthumous Papers of D. H. Lawrence*, ed. Edward D. McDonald (New York: Viking, 1972), 380.
[2]Ibid., 569.
[3]Ibid., 382.

narrowly defined. In a suggestive essay on Thomas Mann, Lawrence makes it plain that he mistrusts not art but a certain conception of form.

Form, as he finds it in Mann, is "like logic," impersonal, abstract, definite, and externally imposed. In recalling *Death in Venice*, Lawrence considers the morbidity of the theme in perfect keeping with the too carefully schematized narrative, the neatly placed symbols, the unswerving logic of the protagonist's motivation. These strict patternings have a death hold on art, according to Lawrence, not simply because they impose severe limits on its range but because they represent a spiritual malaise. "This craving for form is the outcome, not of artistic conscience, but of a certain attitude to life."[4] He compares Mann with Pope and Flaubert, resorting to aesthetic absolutes because of their distaste for physical life, seeking invented perfections as alternatives to a life that fills them with loathing.

The picture that Lawrence wishes to smash is not only one of Victorian prudery and sentimentality but the more modern and to him even more deadly one of world-weary despair and self-hatred. He was never so naive as to believe that an artist could proceed without design, but he thought that when design became an end in itself, inflexible and absolute, it undermined the highest purpose of art and cast a shadow over life. In his discussion of the principles of Law and Love in the essay on Thomas Hardy, he expresses his belief that art, like morality, must continually seek a balance between stability and motion, order and change. He singles out Shelley's "To a Skylark" as a successful representation of "conflict contained within a reconciliation," in which the poet creates a vital tension between the bird as creature and pure spirit.[5]

There is no doubt that Lawrence's views of organic form and the fluidity of symbolic language owe much to the ideas and practices of the English Romantic poets. But he was much more than a Romantic willing to deal more frankly with "up-to-date" subject matter. His versions of the "conflict" between order and change have an intensity, an urgency touched by Shelley and Blake but stressed and sustained in a fashion unique to him and his century. For Lawrence, as for many of his contemporaries, life seemed peculiarly threatened by the attitudes and events of the early twentieth century. His use of terms such as "adventurer" or "explorer" to describe the modern artist sound overblown, but he did believe that the situation was desperate

[4]Ibid., 308.
[5]Ibid., 478.

enough to require risks. Moving into unknown territories seemed infinitely better than staying where you were.

Despite the vigor with which he stated his critical opinions, Lawrence, like Eliot and Joyce, believed that the work of art must exist and must be considered separately from the personality and prejudices of the artist. He reserves some of his highest critical praise for Cézanne and, in doing so, moves beyond the Romantics and locates himself in the modern world: "Cézanne's apples are a real attempt to let the apple exist in its own separate entity, without transfusing it with personal emotion. Cézanne's great effort was, as it were, to shove the apple away from him, and let it live of itself."[6]

Lawrence's characterization of Cézanne's artistic effort sounds so much like noninterference that it raises questions about the motivation of the artist or writer. Why paint or write at all if the best that can be done is to let things "live of themselves?" The simplest way to do that, it would seem, is to leave the apples to their own devices, to let nature alone. But though Lawrence admired Cézanne's attempt to withhold "personal emotion" from the objects of his art, he did not equate this attitude with a relinquishing of contact. The best art for Lawrence and what he seemed to want to attain in his own writing was a relationship with the natural world that was unpossessive, balancing intimacy with the familiar and reverence for that which is unalterably separate.

Like many of his modernist contemporaries, Lawrence frequently reveals his preoccupation with art in his creative work. But unlike James, Eliot, Woolf, Pound, and Joyce, he rarely seems at his best when doing so. For the more he seems bent on naturalizing art, on eliminating personal emotion and setting nature free, the more he seems to intrude and destroy the balance. Few readers can fail to notice the disparity between Lawrence's "natural" artistry and his fevered attempts to persuade us that he can remove all artifice from art and batter it back into the earth. His successful books rarely resemble the notions about art or works of art described in them. Paul Morel's comments about his painting ("as if I'd painted the shimmering protoplasm in the leaves . . . and not the stiffness of the shape")[7] may be "pure" Lawrence, but they are not especially accurate reflections of the structure or quality of *Sons and Lovers*, which Virginia Woolf, among many others, praised for its craftsmanship and clarity of form.

---

[6]Ibid., 567.
[7]Lawrence, *Sons and Lovers* (New York: Viking, 1958), 152.

In two fascinating but highly flawed novels—*The Lost Girl* and *Aaron's Rod*—promising narratives go disastrously out of control when Lawrence allows his preoccupation with the naturalization of art to become an obsession. *The Lost Girl* begins as an imitation of Arnold Bennett, a brilliant imitation full of an energy unique to Lawrence. The stifling atmosphere of a Midlands town and the frustrations of the young heroine are vividly realized until various troupes of visiting performers appear on the stage of the local theater and provide Lawrence with the opportunity to assail his heroine and reader with the hypnotic attractions of art and sexuality all rolled up into one confusing "whole." One of the heroine's first awakenings comes when she sees a tatooed Japanese appear on stage: "She wished she could jump across the distance. Particularly with the Jap, who was almost quite naked, but clothed with the most exquisite tatooing. Never would she forget the eagle that flew with terrible spread wings between his shoulders, or the strange mazy pattern that netted the roundness of his buttocks."[8]

As an isolated instance of inhibition thawed by the exposure to flesh "clothed" by a design, this is pardonable. But the tattooed "Jap" is only a preamble. Another troupe appears from the continent ready to dress up as American Indians and dance about the stage. When the heroine falls in love with a handsome Italian, the entire course of her life and the novel changes. Significantly, it is when she first sees him in costume, his face "wonderfully and terribly painted," that she is deeply and irreversibly moved. Along with his obvious relish in the encounter between a kind of bohemian primitivism and the stuffy inhabitants of the Midlands English town, Lawrence has a more complicated interest in the situation he has created. He is intrigued by the notion of the imprinted skin, the flesh as canvas or page. The foreignness of the imprinted figures betrays a touch of Edwardian decadence, but it also suggests the possibility of a nonverbal language, of powerful systems of communication not dependent on a common vocabulary.

The difficulty we have in taking Lawrence's tattooed man and masquerade Indians seriously stems not, as is often assumed, from their inherent "vulgarity." Shakespeare and Dickens made powerful use of amateur theatricals; circuses and clowns have often been employed as effective symbols of art and artists. However, in *The Lost Girl*, it is not only the heroine but the author who seems to wish to "jump across the

[8]Lawrence, *The Lost Girl*, ed. John Worthen (Cambridge: Cambridge University Press, 1981), 119.

distance" between art and nature. It is partly because the players in *Hamlet* make so little claim to credibility that they astonish us and the king with the "truth" of their performance. As Lawrence's perspective converges more and more completely with that of his heroine and she becomes more and more submerged in the attractions of the imprinted male body, the narrative swerves out of control. By trying to force a union of design and flesh, Lawrence succeeds in reminding us of their disparity. We resist the equation and can only watch with morbid curiosity as author and heroine pursue the decorated physique in search of a code but instead become lost in a muddle.

Aaron's Rod provides another illustration of Lawrence's impulse to naturalize art. It too is an odd combination of promising starts and unresolved muddles. The piccolo of the musician hero is so often likened to a flower or branch of a tree that the reader is prevented from inventing associations that a freer, less insistent use of metaphor invites. The phallic identification is even more dominant. When Aaron plays his flute for a woman with whom he has an affair, the music is described as a "pure male voice";[9] when the affair comes to an end, his flute is broken, his sense of purpose gone. Lawrence chooses not to make clear whether Aaron's failure is musical or sexual because he seems to want the reader to see them as the same, or at least as so closely meshed as to be inseparable. Once again, we rebel at the forced connection. The narrative collapses under the weight of abstract theories, which Lawrence always said were the death of art.

It is tempting merely to ridicule or apologize for these and similar "lapses" in Lawrence's fiction. But it is worth remembering that the failures in these books are not deviations from some main Lawrencian current; they are parts of that current. In both *The Lost Girl* and *Aaron's Rod,* Lawrence is trying to rescue art from the moral and formal confines of the middle class. The seamy theatrics of the one and the pagan pipe of the other, whether or not convincing, are consistent with Lawrence's refusal to see art as polite and mildly uplifting entertainment. He always believed, as writers of his generation had good reason to believe, that respectability and creativity were inimical. But Lawrence's social fervor was never distinct from his urgent sense of individual need. Above all else, he wanted an art that could reestablish contact between human beings, their own nature, and that of the living world.

Even in his most successful fiction, Lawrence never gave up the desire to "jump across the distance" between the self, isolated by

---

[9]Lawrence, *Aaron's Rod* (London: Penguin, 1975), 296.

experience, intelligence, and conscience, and the completeness of un-reflective nature. The most memorable chapters in *Women in Love*, for example, bring powerful intensity to individual efforts to conquer isolation through natural contact: Gerald breaking the horse; Her-mione attacking Birkin with a paperweight; Gudrun dancing before the bullocks; Ursula and Birkin coming together in the fields; Gerald and Birkin wrestling; Birkin dashing stones at the moon's reflection. Though there are survivors, the drowning of the newlyweds and Gerald's death in the snow seem inevitable consequences of rela-tionships with nature that are unrelentingly aggressive and com-petitive. The wish for harmony appears to be confused with the will to dominate. That, of course, is a major theme of the novel, as it is of all of Lawrence's work. But, as has often been noted, this is not only Lawrence's main theme but also one of his problems as a writer. He too often "jumps across the distance" and wrestles his subject to the death.

Yet there is another crucially important side to Lawrence, as much a hallmark of his genius as his notorious and passionate intensity. There is a Lawrence that lets the gaps between man and nature be, an ironical, humorous, relaxed though never resigned Lawrence, who *does not insist on anything.* Nowhere is this side more effectively in evidence than in *Women in Love.* For among the vividly memorable chapters are others, quieter, less graphic, a bit rambling, without which the novel could not stand and which the reader cannot afford to forget.

Three such chapters—"Shortlands," "Sketch-Book," and "A Chair"—contain structural and thematic elements in common, which at the same time link them to the other chapters of the novel and set them apart from them. Most significantly in this book of large prob-lems and strong wills, each of these chapters dramatizes a small "mis-take," a trivial accident surrounded by implications of psychological intention. Equally surprising, given the potent and rather solemn symbolism of the "strong" chapters, is the fact that each of these chapters introduces an ordinary object—a hat, a sketch, a chair—momentarily made meaningful by the characters and then abruptly released from imposed significance. Each chapter also introduces a familiar activity—a wedding reception, sketching, buying furniture—the conventional course of which is interrupted, challenged, de-familiarized. In each there is a character or several characters who seem out of place but who nonetheless have a magnetic attraction for one of the main characters. The dialogue, even more than is usual in Lawrence, tends to the philosophical and beyond, to a kind of parody of philosophical inquiry in which all questions seem to be asked as if for the first time. None of these chapters concludes with an air of finality. On the contrary, the situations and dialogues they introduce invariably drift into irresolution.

In chapter 2, "Shortlands," the wedding reception of a conventionally happy and well-matched young couple serves as the context for unpremeditated and socially uncategorizable "pairings." Birkin, the outsider, feels unaccountably attracted by old Mrs. Crich, a stranger in her own house, and by her stolid son, Gerald:

> Suddenly Mrs. Crich came noiselessly into the room, peering about with her strong, clear face. She was still wearing her hat. . . .
>
> "What is it, mother?" said Gerald.
>
> "Nothing, nothing!" she answered vaguely. And she went straight towards Birkin. . . .
>
> "How do you do, Mr. Birkin," she said in her low voice, that seemed to take no count of her guests. . . . "I don't know half the people here."
>
> "And you don't like strangers?" laughed Birkin. "I myself can never see why one should take account of people, just because they happen to be in the room . . . : why *should* I know they are there?"
>
> "Why indeed, why indeed!" said Mrs. Crich, in her low tense voice. "Except that they *are* there. I don't know people whom I find in the house. The children introduce them to me. . . . I am no further. What has Mr. So-and-so to do with his own name?—and what have I to do with either him or his name?"
>
> She looked up at Birkin. She startled him. He was flattered. . . . He noticed . . . how her hair looped in slack, slovenly strands over her rather beautiful ears, which were not quite clean. Neither was her neck perfectly clean. Even in that he seemed to belong to her, rather than to the rest of the company, though . . . he was always well washed . . . . he and the elderly, estranged woman were conferring together like traitors.[10]

When Birkin suggests that most other people do not exist, Mrs. Crich punctures his airy assertion:

> "But we don't imagine them," she said sharply.
>
> "There's nothing to imagine, that's why they don't exist."
>
> "Well," she said, "I would hardly go as far as that. There they are, whether they exist or no. It doesn't rest with me to decide on their existence. I only know that I can't be expected to take count of them all." [P. 19]

[10]Lawrence, *Women in Love* (New York: Viking, 1960), 18. Page numbers in text below refer to this edition.

On the way to the dining room, one of the Crich daughters suggests, with some embarrassment, that her mother, as hostess in her own house, should remove her hat. Whether the guests have noticed the social impropriety is not mentioned, but within a few moments Lawrence introduces an exchange in which the word "hat" accumulates and sheds meaning. Gerald begins in earnest:

> "If I go and take a man's hat from off his head, that hat becomes a symbol of that man's liberty. . . ."
> Hermione was nonplussed. . . . "But that way of arguing by imaginary instances is not supposed to be genuine, is it? A man does *not* come and take my hat from off my head, does he?"
> "Only because the law prevents him," said Gerald.
> "Not only," said Birkin. "Ninety-nine men out of a hundred don't want my hat."
> "That's a matter of opinion," said Gerald.
> "Or the hat," laughed the bridegroom. [P. 23]

When pressed about what she would do if someone did try to take her hat, Hermione shifts the mood abruptly. "Probably I should kill him." Trying to return to a lighter, more bantering tone, Birkin calls Gerald's nationalism "old hat" and the conversation is broken off by the call for toasts:

> Birkin, thinking about race or national death, watched his glass being filled with champagne. . . . Feeling a sudden thirst at the sight of the fresh wine, Birkin drank up his glass. A queer little tension in the room roused him. He felt a sharp constraint.
> "Did I do it by accident, or on purpose?" he asked himself. And he decided that, according to the vulgar phrase, he had done it "accidentally on purpose." [Pp. 24–25]

The chapter concludes with an "inconsequential" dialogue between Birkin and Gerald. As with Birkin and Mrs. Crich, there is an undercurrent of attraction that neither understands. And there is an unmistakable irony in the fact that, for the world that celebrates weddings and worries about when to put on and take off hats, such attractions have no significance. Indeed, they might as well not exist.

The entire chapter, a bit slack and meandering on first reading, seems to resemble those chapters in long Victorian novels that accomplish certain necessary business but are not otherwise interesting or important. Particular characters and situations are brought to the reader's attention, background information is provided, and a credible time lapse is provided between the more dramatic moments. On closer reading, however, the chapter is not at all loose in construction, nor does it function largely as filler for the plot. Indeed, the main narrative line of the novel could survive very well without it. Nor is this chapter merely a relief from some of the intensities of the novel as a whole. Rather it is an alternative to them and a comment on them. The best-laid human plans—whether for weddings or novels—are subjected to odd quirks of chance; encounters with no future, debates without bearings, words adrift between high symbolism and commonplace literality. The chapter itself seems to be the author's purposeful "accident," the exposure of his own masterly design to contradictory elements.

What the characters discuss and enact refers as much to the creative process as it does to the various human relationships that are the subject of the novel. The debates about true existence—whether of the people in the room or of British rights—mean, for the artist, as for Mrs. Crich, whether or not one "takes account" of them. The writer brings into existence what he notices, and he notices, according to the logic of this chapter, not always what makes a "good story" or satisfying moral but what attracts him. The social or ethical justification for the attraction may or may not be clear, but for Lawrence, to ignore it is to let the work of art die. Yet in "taking account" of certain things, it is inevitable that the artist will risk making "too much" of them, like the characters who force too much weight on the poor old hat until it collapses and reasserts its *insignificance*. The author who would be honest and produce a vital work of art must move with a particular kind of alertness. He must exercise his judgment and will in conceiving a plan and, at the same time, must remain sufficiently passive to be open to the unexpected interventions that seem to threaten the plan but in fact keep it alive.

Chapter 10, "Sketch-Book," opens with a sensual description of the unmistakably phallic waterplants being painted by Gudrun. There is at first no indication of irony in these descriptions, no indication that Lawrence is up to anything other than his characteristic form of sexual symbolism. Suddenly a rowboat with two figures in it appears on the lake. It is Gerald and Hermione, who are composing another kind of picture; he in white, she with a Japanese parasol look, at a distance, like the figures in a Romantic idyll. But as the gap between Gudrun and the boat narrows, the hazy illusion is pierced by the emotions of each character reacting with unexpected violence to a seemingly trivial meeting. At first, Hermione insists on approaching Gudrun because it seems daring to show an interest in someone of her class.

Gerald has no interest in her, and Gudrun is annoyed by the interruption, "for she always hated to have her unfinished work exposed."

However, when Hermione insists, Gudrun hands her sketch over to be inspected. The real "event" that occurs during this forced encounter between the two women is a wordless but powerful current of attraction between Gudrun and Gerald. Gudrun's phallic imagination is transferred from the water plants to Gerald. When the boat begins to drift, "he lifted the oar to bring it back. And the exquisite pleasure of slowly arresting the boat, in the heavy-soft water, was complete as a swoon." The paragraph in which this attraction occurs begins with Gudrun's point of view ("Gudrun was aware of his body"), but "the exquisite pleasure" is a mutual one. It forms a link of communication in which Hermione has no part. Her awareness of exclusion infuriates her and when Gerald asks to see the sketch, there is an "accident":

> A little shock, a storm of revulsion against him, shook Hermione unconsciously. She released the book when he had not properly got it, and it tumbled against the side of the boat and bounced into the water.
> "There!" sang Hermione, with a strange ring of malevolent victory. "I'm so sorry, so awfully sorry. Can't you get it, Gerald?" [P. 113]

As Gerald reaches into the water to retrieve the book, he realizes that "his position is ridiculous." Indeed, the entire episode hovers between heavy sensuality and ludicrous slapstick. It is important to say that the wavering mood is not the result of narrative ineptitude but appears to be very much part of the pattern of the purposeful accident by which the solemnity and coherence of the primary narrative design are temporarily broken. As in the wedding reception, the social niceties appear particularly thin in comparison with the strong undertones of feeling. As Hermione continues to repeat her apologies, words seem less and less capable of reflecting the truth of the situation. Yet even this assumption is broken when Gudrun speaks out: "'I assure you,' said Gudrun, with cutting distinctness, 'the drawings are quite as good as ever they were, for my purpose. I want them only for reference.'" (p. 114).

Hermione, who exerts her will in trying to convert art as well as sexual emotion into social categories, is defeated by Gudrun's notion of her art as personal and "referential." Hermione's purposeful "accident," her little joke at the expense of Gudrun, plays right to an aesthetic attitude that she cannot understand. The unfinished sketch "spoiled" by water is also an emblem of art immersed in nature (concrete reality untransformed by the ordering imagination) and not, according to some views, the worse for it. If the drifts and currents of nature are not permitted now and then to "spoil" the perfect plan of the artist, the result will be neat but, in Lawrence's terminology, "decadent," without life. As Gerald rows away absentmindedly, watching Gudrun with her wet sketchbook, the boat drifts off course and Hermione is more furious than ever.

As with the hat in the discussion at the wedding reception, Lawrence uses the sketchbook for a variety of purposes, including as an occasion to reflect on the process of symbol making. Whereas the debate in "Shortlands" is a satire on inflated political rhetoric, Gudrun's view of her sketchbook comes close to Lawrence's theories of art. He does not undermine these theories with mockery but illustrates aspects of them and gives them life. In order to function effectively in a symbolic pattern, objects must be allowed their own reality. This seems Lawrence's meaning when he says that Cézanne "shoves the apple away from him." For Lawrence, the artist does not "convert" reality to his own purposes without recognizing the tenuousness of that process in the face of the intractability and waywardness of things. Symbols may fly as long as matter is not deprived of gravity.

As in chapter 10, "Sketch-Book," an object with symbolic possibilities is the central figure of chapter 26, "A Chair." Ursula and Birkin are browsing in an open market when they come upon a patched-up antique chair of elegant proportions. The classically harmonious design, associated with Jane Austen's England, pleases the couple, and there is no indication from the narrative that Lawrence does not share their admiration for its "fine delicacy." Impulsively, the couple buys the chair, and almost immediately it becomes in their eyes something more than the well-designed "arm-chair of simple wood" that had first attracted their attention.

The chair becomes a representative object, a sign of the past, of materialism, of the accumulation of ideas and things that point to a "settling down" that Birkin particularly wishes to resist. They decide that they have made a "mistake" in buying the chair. But like the earlier "accidents," this one has its purpose. As Birkin tries to explain his desire to leave certain aspects of his life unsettled, he resorts to an artistic analogy: "You have to be like Rodin, Michelangelo, and leave a piece of raw rock unfinished to your figure. You must leave your surroundings sketchy, unfinished, so that you are never contained, never confined, never dominated from the outside" (p. 349).

The analogy brings the reader back to the chair, whose perfect finish is "spoiled" by a poor attempt to repair a break: "'It was once,' said Birkin, 'gilded—and it had a cane seat. Somebody has nailed this wooden seat in. . . . It is the fine unity of the lines that is so attractive. . . . But of course the wooden seat is wrong. . . . I like it though'" (p. 347).

In the context of Birkin's philosophy and his reference to Rodin and Michelangelo, the chair assumes another kind of significance. Its attraction resides partly in its broken symmetry, since its perfect lines appear to have an effect similar to the careful plans of a neatly arranged life. Both have their attractions, but completeness, their most apparent virtue, is a trap. The claim to perfect harmony is confining to the spirit and is, for Lawrence, a false representation of reality. The greatest artistic masterpieces pay homage to nature by acknowledging their own defects. Of course, as Lawrence realized, the "defect" itself can quickly be imitated until it too is absorbed into conventional notions of harmony. Nothing is more mannered than poor copies of Rodin, Michelangelo and, for that matter, Lawrence. The artist's "purposeful accident" is as much a part of his peculiar genius as his most graceful and self-contained designs.

Though the impulsive act itself cannot be undone, Lawrence manages to keep its significance alive without attaching it neatly to a linear chain of events in his plot. One of his major objections to Hardy was his habit of stringing fatal consequences onto chance events. Such carefully determined pessimism, he felt, was as untrue to life as its sentimental opposite. In the introduction to *Women in Love*, he wrote: "Fate dictated from outside, from theory or circumstance, is a false fate" (p. viii). Lawrence believed that individuals could change the direction of their lives, that accidents could be meaningful without being fatal.

It is interesting that a writer who studied Hardy with such care and obviously learned much from him does not often choose to introduce nature into his fiction by means of the external "acts of God." There are mining accidents in *Sons and Lovers* and floods in *The Rainbow*, but when lightning strikes a Lawrence character, it is much more likely to strike from within. Obsessive, violent, or ecstatic passions well up inside his characters, causing unexpected behavior. When external nature seems to duplicate their internal state, the effect is not really that of the pathetic fallacy, a cosmic echo, but rather a blurring of the boundaries between the individual and the world.

Every internal tremor does not signal an earthquake, however. The impulsive actions of Lawrence's characters *may* be bursting with serious consequences; then again, they may not. An even greater departure from Hardy is represented by those moments in Lawrence when a chance encounter or "fatal" mistake is raised to high symbolic potential and is then abruptly deflated.

Ursula and Birkin decide to give the chair to a young couple whom they do not know but have observed browsing at the market. Their attitude toward the couple is at first a mixture of pity and condescension; they are lower class, and the woman, not yet a wife, is pregnant. Suddenly, to her surprise, Ursula finds herself attracted to the young man. He disarms her by stripping the chair of any special meaning and treating it as a chair, which Birkin cannot do: " 'Ave a sit in it, you'll wish you'd kept it,' said the young man. Ursula promptly sat down in the middle of the marketplace. 'Awfully comfortable,' she said. 'But rather hard. You try it' " (pp. 352–353).

The mild flirtation leads nowhere. Ursula does not run off with the young man, and Birkin hardly notices the undercurrent. But the chair has been returned to its unsymbolic state, and Ursula's character is shown to have its own built-in resistance to finality. The chapter concludes, foreshadowing the end of the novel, with a discussion between Ursula and Birkin about his seeming need for Gerald's love. On this subject, even Birkin has no answers. "His face was full of real perplexity. . . . 'It's the problem I can't solve.' " (p. 355).

The recurrence of certain patterns in these three chapters suggests a strong impulse in Lawrence's narrative imagination. While disrupting some structures, he is building and reinforcing others. He does not obliterate familiar forms. Each of these episodes, like most of those in his fiction, contains easily recognizable elements of social and literary convention. But he does open up familiar forms, exposes them to uncertainty, removes their "finish," and thereby brings them closer to reality as he conceives of it. For Lawrence, reality was not chaotic, but neither was it in any of its aspects completely knowable. Thus, the most honest artist had to allow room for the "unplanned" in his plan.

To try to overcome this contradiction by means of sheer rhetorical willpower is, as in the examples from *The Lost Girl* and *Aaron's Rod*, to destroy both the conventional coherences and the liberating effect of natural spontaneity. The problem with Lawrence's weaker fiction is not mere sloppiness but a forced, strident, insistent sloppiness. The "purposeful accident" becomes a long disaster, the justification for which too often takes on the duration and tone of a crusade. The "accidents" in *Women in Love*, by contrast, are beautifully poised between playfulness and high seriousness, as they are between literal objectivity and symbolism. The "quiet" chapters are unfinished in the sense that they end with inconclusive encounters or dialogues and because throughout they dramatize an endless dialectic on the definitions of art and reality.

Lawrence does not force a union between the two in *Women in Love* without at the same time showing his awareness of the irony or danger of doing so. The hat, the sketch-book, and the chair are never allowed to "take leave of themselves" once and for all, as Aaron's rod does. Though he does not acknowledge clear boundaries between art and reality, Lawrence does in *Women in Love* treat them as different from each other. The thing and the thing perceived (and named) are not the same. Yet he does not accept the kind of distinction that he attributes to Flaubert and Mann: that art is mostly will, and nature random chance. Lawrence believed that nature has design, whether or not mankind can understand it, and that, in allowing "accident" to enter in, the writer can create an art that imitates a design larger, deeper, than he himself or any of his characters can fully know.

There is no doubt that Lawrence could pursue spontaneity with a zeal so deliberate as to scare the quarry. But it is worth noting that he could also laugh at the chase, showing, despite Eliot, that he had a sense of humor and that he was not working in the dark. Lawrence's apparent alternation between loosening and tightening of control throughout *Women in Love,* the rhythm he establishes between the symbolic, sharply visual, emotionally intense chapters and those of a more meandering, discursive, humorous character, produces a symphonic variety of near discords working always toward unexpected resolutions.

The meeting with Loerke and Leitner in the Alps near the novel's end is not an accident in the sense that has been discussed thus far. But it is an odd, unexpected, seemingly gratuitous introduction of at least one important character so late in the narrative as to appear an afterthought. The malicious, implike Loerke seems an excuse for Lawrence to enter into a satiric diatribe against a conception of art particularly distasteful to him. In the midst of the agonizing relationship of Gerald and Gudrun and the forced gaiety of the Alpine holiday, Lawrence's timing and focus at first seem questionable. Why such long discussions of art with an obsessive German throughout a fatal idyll of lovers?

In the first place, the subject of art in both the "quiet" and the more dramatic chapters is never completely absent from the narrative. Furthermore, in one form or another, Lawrence never ceases trying to search out ways in which art and love intersect. That is one of the major subjects of the novel. His characters, like Birkin and Ursula, either find a way to balance between design and passion, purpose and accident, or, like Gudrun and Gerald, they find themselves engaged in a struggle to the death. In Loerke, small, dark, cerebral, and dogmatic, Lawrence creates a Wagnerian emanation of Gerald's will, the will to order, dominate, annihilate. In his fair, "well-built," handsome young companion, Leitner, who dances with Gudrun, he creates the sensuous, unformed, potentially lovable Gerald who had appealed from the first to Birkin.

Gerald's unintegrated self is shown in the Loerke-Leitner projection to be a menacing, absurd grotesque. Yet Gudrun had once characterized one side of Gerald in terms that bear a striking resemblance to certain classical definitions of the artist, especially the narrative artist: "He had the faculty of making order out of confusion. Only let him grip hold of a situation, and he would bring to pass an inevitable conclusion" (p. 407). In Loerke, Lawrence shows a perverse and dehumanized version of this mentality stripped of class and sexual glamor. What Gerald comes to represent in social, political, and sexual terms, Loerke defends in art.

When Ursula is repelled by the "stiffness" of his sculpture of a horse, Loerke lashes out in a summary of everything that Lawrence hated about the theories of certain of his contemporaries:

It is a work of art, it is a picture of nothing, of absolutely nothing. It has nothing to do with anything but itself, it has no relation with the everyday world of this and other, there is no connection between them, absolutely none, they are two different and distinct planes of existence, and to translate one into the other is worse than foolish, it is a darkening of all counsel, a making confusion everywhere. [P. 421]

It is the keeping of the "accidents" of feeling, intuition, and awe separate from the serious "purposes" of art, business, politics, and human relationships that Lawrence saw as among the central tragedies of his time. And it is precisely a "translation" from one plane to another, a "darkening of all counsel," a "making confusion everywhere" that he attempted as a remedy. When he tried to turn the process into a dogma, he killed it. But the "purposeful accidents" in *Women in Love* are among the many examples of extraordinary poise, wit, and suppleness with which he managed to keep this daring and impossible program alive.

It is tempting to reverse Gudrun's description of Gerald to characterize Lawrence's image of himself as an artist: "He had the faculty of making confusion out of order. Only let him grip hold of a situation, and he would disrupt the inevitable conclusion." But readers of Lawrence will not be fully satisfied with this picture, for without the ordering genius, the disruptive demon has nothing to do. As the narrative of *Women in Love* persistently implies, Birkin needs Gerald as badly as Gerald needs Birkin.

[6]

Lawrence's Lyric Theater:
Birds, Beasts and Flowers

Marjorie Perloff

I

In September 1920, Lawrence was staying at the Villa Canovaia in the hills above Florence. He was alone, Frieda having gone to Germany to visit her family. It is here that he wrote a dozen or so of the poems that were to be collected in what he called his "best book of poems," *Birds, Beasts and Flowers:* for example, "Pomegranate," "Figs," "Medlars and Sorb Apples," the tortoise poems, and the four "Evangelistic Beasts."[1] He was also rewriting the novel begun three years earlier that was to become *Aaron's Rod* (1922). Not surprisingly, similar motifs appear in the novel and in the poems. I want to begin by looking at one such motif as an entrance into the world of Lawrence's poetry, a poetry I construe rather differently from the many critics who have read *Birds, Beasts and Flowers* as late versions of the Romantic quest for otherness, for the unconscious participation in natural process, the life-divine blood being.[2]

[1]See Lawrence to Curtis Brown, 10 February 1923, in *The Collected Letters of D. H. Lawrence*, ed. Harry T. Moore, 2 vols. (New York: Viking, 1962), II, 737. For the dates of composition of Lawrence's writings as well as much useful contextual information, see Keith Sagar, *D. H. Lawrence: A Calendar of His Works* (Manchester: Manchester University Press, 1979).

[2]See Sandra M. Gilbert, *Acts of Attention: The Poems of D. H. Lawrence* (Ithaca: Cornell University Press, 1972), 131–89; and Gilbert, "D. H. Lawrence's Uncommon Prayers," in *D. H. Lawrence: The Man Who Lived*, ed. Robert B. Partlow, Jr., and Harry T. Moore (Carbondale: Southern Illinois University Press, 1980), 73–93; Harold Bloom, "Lawrence, Eliot, Blackmur, and the Tortoise" (1959), in *The Ringers in the Tower: Studies in Romantic Tradition* (Chicago: University of Chicago Press, 1971), 197–206; Joyce Carol Oates, *The Hostile Sun: The Poetry of D. H. Lawrence* (Los Angeles: Black Sparrow Press, 1974), 7–8, 37–57. The place of Lawrence's poetry in the English Romantic tradition is the subject of Ross C. Murfin's recent *The Poetry of D. H. Lawrence: Texts and Contexts* (Lincoln: University of Nebraska Press, 1983).

In chapter 19 of the novel, Aaron Sisson takes a tram to Settignano. He feels a great need to escape all thoughts of the previous night, a night he spent with the Marchesa and his first night with a woman in many months. Although it is he who initiated the love affair, the actual physical contact leaves Aaron feeling "withered," "blasted—as if blighted by some electricity."[3] "He felt an intense resentment against the Marchesa. He felt that somehow, she had given him the scorpion." Hence the need to get away, to be alone in the Tuscan hills:

> He sat for long hours among the cypress trees of Tuscany. And never had any trees seemed so like ghosts, like soft, strange, pregnant presences. He lay and watched tall cypresses breathing and communicating, faintly moving and as it were walking in the small wind. And his soul seemed to leave him and to go far away, far back, perhaps, to where life was all different and time passed otherwise than time passes now. As in clairvoyance he perceived it: that our life is only a fragment of the shell of life. . . . In the dark, mindful silence and inflection of the cypress trees, lost races, lost languages, lost human ways of feeling and of knowing. Men have known as we can no more know, have felt as we can no more feel. Great life-realities gone into the darkness. But the cypresses commemorate. In the afternoon, Aaron felt the cypresses rising dark about him, like so many high visitants from an old, lost, lost subtle world, where men had the wonder of demons about them, the aura of demons, such as still clings to the cypresses, in Tuscany. [*AR*, 257]

The "aura of demons" clinging to the cypresses somehow reassures Aaron: "as he went home in the tram he softened," realizing that his hostility to the Marchesa had been excessive: "She had been generous, and the other thing, that he felt blasted afterwards, which was his experience, that was fate, and not her fault" [*AR*, 257].

It is true, of course, that Lawrence wants us to see the cypresses of this passage as demonic presences, visitants from the dark otherness of a chthonic divinity. But within the context of plot and character relationships, they can be seen, more accurately, as images of displacement, emblematic of Lawrence's longing, particularly acute in these years, to escape the world of threatening human sexuality. It is interesting to note, for example, that the cypresses are imaged in both male and female terms: "rising dark above him," they loom as great phallic figures, yet they are also, somewhat paradoxically, characterized as "soft, strange, pregnant presences."

As such, the cypress imagery seems to reflect Aaron's own sexual

---

[3]Lawrence, *Aaron's Rod* (1922; reprint, New York: Viking, Compass Books, 1967), 255–56. Subsequently cited as *AR*.

ambivalence. He has, we recall, left his wife, even though he says he still "loves" her, because he yearns for "clean and pure division, perfected singleness" (AR, 123). Before long, he falls under the spell of the charismatic Rawdon Lilly and becomes his disciple. After a brief fling with a girl named Josephine, he catches influenza and is nursed back to health by Lilly, who, in a moment of crisis, massages "the blond lower body of his patient" with camphor oil, until "the spark [comes] back into the sick eyes, and the faint trace of a smile, faintly luminous, into the face" (AR, 91). Although Lilly and Aaron later quarrel, temporarily going their separate ways, they meet again in Florence, after the incident with the Marchesa, and in the last chapter, Lilly is once again preaching the "exhaustion of the love-urge" and the need for submission to a strong male leader, in this case himself.

In the poem "Cypresses," written at about the same time as the passage in *Aaron's Rod,* there is no such problematic narrative context. It begins:

> Tuscan cypresses,
> What is it?
>
> Folded in like a dark thought
> For which the language is lost,
> Tuscan cypresses,
> Is there a great secret?
> Are our words no good?
>
> The undeliverable secret,
> Dead with a dead race and a dead speech, and yet
> Darkly monumental in you,
> Etruscan cypresses.[4]

By line 11, the *Tuscan* and *Etruscan* have merged: "the undeliverable secret," it turns out, is that the cypress tree recalls the noble "subtly-smiling" Etruscan male:

> Naked except for fanciful long shoes,
> Going with insidious, half-smiling quietness
> And some of Africa's imperturbable sang-froid
> About a forgotten business.
>
> [CP, 296]

---

[4]*The Complete Poems of D. H. Lawrence,* ed. Vivian de Sola Pinto and F. Warren Roberts (New York: Viking, 1971), 296. I shall hereafter cite this edition as *CP*. Compare the first edition published by Thomas Seltzer in New York (1923).

In the course of the poem, the "vicious dark cypresses. . . , softly-swaying pillars of dark flame," become the "vicious, the slender, tender-footed / Long-nosed men of Etruria." The poet invokes the ghosts of these "spirits of the lost," the "darkly lost." For the Etruscan consciousness, as he argues in *Etruscan Places*, expresses itself through the symbols of phallus and *arx*—"the womb of all the world, that brought forth all the creatures." And it was, so Lawrence posits, the hatred and fear of these two symbols—phallus and arx—on the part of the "puritan" Romans that brought about the destruction of the Etruscan world.[5]

What sort of poem is "Cypresses"? In *Birds, Beasts and Flowers*, says Joyce Carol Oates, Lawrence "honors the unknowable mysteries of other forms of life" (p. 37). This is overtly true: certainly in "Cypresses," the poet tells us, quite openly, that he wants to bring back the dark secret of an alien consciousness. Yet to compare "Cypresses" to Romantic and neo-Romantic poems of communion with nature—Keats's and Shelley's odes or, in our own time, the animistic lyrics of James Wright or Galway Kinnell—is to find more difference than likeness. It is, I think, a question of tone: Lawrence's "I" is not an ecstatic, rapturous shaman, a prophet who must convey, in gnomic fragments, his mysterious vision. Rather, the voice that speaks to us is conversational, hectoring, nervous, energetic, funny, sardonic—the same voice we meet in Lawrence's remarkable letters as well as in such travel sketches as *Sea and Sardinia*, written a year after "Cypresses":

> Tuscan cypresses,
> What is it? . . .
>
> Is there a great secret?
> Are our words no good? . . .
>
> Ah, how I admire your fidelity,
> Dark cypresses!

Einfühlung, one might say, except that Lawrence's speaker knows very well that he is not, so to speak, alone in the room. Having addressed the cypresses as intimate friends ("Tuscan cypresses, / What is it?"), he does a kind of mental half-turn and asks, "Is it the secret of the long-nosed Etruscans?" Or again, "Were they then vicious, the slender, tender-footed / Long-nosed men of Etruria? / Or was their way only evasive and different, dark, like cypress trees in a wind?"

---

[5]Lawrence, *Etruscan Places* (1932; reprint, New York: Viking, 1966), 28–29.

These questions are hardly addressed to the cypresses, nor is Lawrence, on the face of it, arguing with himself. He knows, after all, how he feels about the Etruscans. No, the addressee here, as almost everywhere in the sequence, must be construed as a devoted, which is not to say a like-minded, listener, a close companion, say, or worthy antagonist, as Rawdon Lilly is to Aaron Sisson, or Gerald Crich to Rupert Birkin. Or again, we can posit the audience to be a group of friends in a café or country house, and, beyond this circle, the readership of certain books and journals that "everybody" reads.

Indeed, what makes the poems of *Birds, Beasts and Flowers* so distinctive, so wholly unlike anyone else's flower or animal poems, is, I would argue, their rhetoric, their performative stance. Whereas, in the novels of the middle period, Lawrence's dialogue of self and soul belongs to a set of characters viewed in the third person—Lilly and Sisson, Lilly and Levinson, and so on—the poetry plays brilliant variations on the pathetic argument, the appeal to us to be part of the charmed circle to whom Lawrence is holding forth. Whereas in *Aaron's Rod* the dialogue between antagonists often seems silly and boring, in *Birds, Beasts and Flowers*, Lawrence deflects "realistic" issues (should Aaron go back to his wife? should he take on a new lover?) by granting sexual power only to the vegetable and animal kingdom (or, by fantastic analogy, to a primitive race like the Etruscans) and by making a sorb apple or an almond blossom or a fish the vehicle for his "argument." "The fissure" to be "dared" is no longer the "fissure" of a real woman—say, the Marchesa—but that of a pomegranate or a fig. Accordingly, sexual anxiety is deflected, at least for the moment, and is replaced by a genial exuberance. As W. H. Auden observes in what is, to my mind, the single best essay written on Lawrence the poet:

> Lawrence possessed a great capacity for affection and charity, but he could only direct it toward non-human life. . . . Whenever, in his writings, he forgets about men and women with proper names and describes the anonymous life of stones, waters, forests, animals, flowers, chance traveling companions or passers-by, his bad temper and his dogmatism immediately vanish and he becomes the most enchanting companion imaginable, tender, intelligent, funny and, above all, happy.[6]

This seems to me precisely what happens in *Birds, Beasts and Flowers*. When the scorpionlike Marchesa of *Aaron's Rod* is replaced by the real

[6]W. H. Auden, "D. H. Lawrence" (1948), in *The Dyer's Hand and Other Essays* (New York: Vintage, 1968), 289.

mosquito, bat, or snake, Lawrence's outrage at the bad faith of human beings gives way to a distancing of self or, more precisely, to a theatrical role playing in which the poet alternately adopts the perspective of the plant or animal that happens to be the object of his contemplation and alternatively plays the dark comedian, drawing mock lessons from his careful, almost scientific, observations of plant or animal behavior. To compare cypresses to Etruscan males, for example, is, strictly speaking, absurd, yet the "I" of "Cypresses" convinces us that the analogy makes good sense. But no sooner are we so convinced than the poet abruptly deflates his own metaphor and shifts to a different angle. Indeed, despite his repeated insistence on "the natural *lingering* of the voice according to the feeling. . . , the hidden *emotional* pattern that makes poetry,"[7] the Lawrence of *Birds, Beasts and Flowers* was less an "emotional realist" (A. Alvarez's term)[8] than what we now call a performance artist; his seeming naturalness and spontaneity, his "accuracy of feeling," have a certain theoretical edge. It is this quality I wish to probe further.

II

"Pomegranate," the first poem in the 1923 volume, is paradigmatic of the whole collection:

> You tell me I am wrong.
> Who are you, who is anybody to tell me I am wrong?
> I am not wrong.
>
> In Syracuse rock left bare by the viciousness of Greek women,
> No doubt you have forgotten the pomegranate-trees in flower,
> Oh so red, and such a lot of them.
>
> Whereas at Venice,
> Abhorrent, green, slippery city
> Whose Doges were old, and had ancient eyes,
> In the dense foliage of the inner garden

[7]Lawrence to Edward Marsh, 18 [–20] August 1913, in *The Letters of D. H. Lawrence*, vol. 2, ed. George J. Zytaruk and James T. Boulton (Cambridge: Cambridge University Press, 1981), 61. I shall subsequently cite the Cambridge Edition of the collected letters as *CL*.

[8]A. Alvarez, "D. H. Lawrence: The Single State of Man" (1958), in John Hollander, ed., *Modern Poetry: Essays in Criticism* (New York: Oxford University Press, 1968), 285. Lawrence's poetry, says Alvarez, is notable for its "complete truth to feeling." Further-

Pomegranates like bright green stone,
And barbed, barbed with a crown.
Oh, crown of spiked green metal
Actually growing!

Now in Tuscany,
Pomegranates to warm your hands at;
And crowns, kingly, generous, tilting crowns
Over the left eyebrow.

And, if you dare, the fissure!

Do you mean to tell me you will see no fissure?
Do you prefer to look on the plain side?

For all that, the setting suns are open.
The end cracks open with the beginning:
Rosy, tender, glittering within the fissure.

Do you mean to tell me there should be no fissure?
No glittering, compact drops of dawn?
Do you mean it is wrong, the gold-filmed skin, integument, shown
     ruptured?

For my part, I prefer my heart to be broken.
It is so lovely, dawn-kaleidoscopic within the crack.

                                              [*CP*, 278–79]

It is customary to read this poem as a variant of the Persephone myth, Lawrence (Persephone) "daring the fissure" and eating of the fruit that prepares him for entrance into the dark womb of the underworld.[9] The little prose preface to "Fruits," taken from John Burnet's *Early Greek Philosophy*,[10] supports this reading: "For fruits are all of

more, "The real material of poetry . . . depends on getting close to the real feelings and presenting them without formulae and without avoidance, in all their newness, disturbance and ugliness" (p. 300).

   [9]See especially Sandra M. Gilbert, "D. H. Lawrence's Uncommon Prayers," 81–82. Gilbert argues that the whole volume is "held together by the covert story of a trip underground, a voyage of death and resurrection. . . . But in the *Birds, Beasts and Flowers* narrative . . . , [the poet's] fall is fortunate not because it will enable him, like Milton's Adam, to rise again by his own efforts, but because it is a fall into a hell that he knows is really a darkly radiant heaven, and he may be lucky enough to fall even further, deeper, into the center of all energy" (p. 80).

   [10]Pinto and Roberts, in their notes to the poems, state that "the little prose prefaces to the various sections of the collection were first printed in the illustrated edition of BBF published by the Cresset Press in June 1930. . . . These prefaces contain a number

them female, in them lies the seed. And so when they break and show the seed, then we look into the womb and see its secrets. So it is that the pomegranate is the apple of love to the Arab, and the fig has been a catch-word for the female fissure for ages" (*CP*, 277). However, the paragraph ends with the cryptic sentence "But the apples of life the dragon guards, and no woman gives them," an aphorism to keep in mind as we read "Pomegranate." Indeed, in classical mythology, the pomegranate is not only the fruit whose seeds Persephone fatally eats, thus being condemned to spend part of each year in the underworld, but also the eight-petaled scarlet anemone supposed to have sprouted from the blood of Dionysus. In related myths, the pomegranate tree is that of Tammuz or Adonis, whose ripe fruit splits open like a wound and shows the red seeds inside, thus symbolizing death and the promise of resurrection when held in the hand of the goddess Hera or Persephone.[11] In this variant of the myth, woman is thus the powerful and threatening goddess who controls man's fate. We meet her counterpart in the opening passage of *Sea and Sardinia*, written within a year of "Pomegranate," in which Lawrence, then living at Taormina in the shadow of the great volcano, talks of his need to get away from "Etna, that wicked witch, resting her thick white snow under heaven, and slowly, slowly rolling her orange-colored smoke":

> Ah, what a mistress this Etna! with her strange winds prowling round her like Circe's panthers, some black, some white. With her strange, remote communications and her terrible dynamic exhalations. She makes men mad. Such terrible vibrations of wicked and beautiful electricity she throws about her, like a deadly net! Nay, sometimes, verily one can feel a new current of her demon magnetism seize one's living tissue and change the peaceful life of one's active cells. She makes a storm in the living plasm and a new adjustment. And sometimes it is like a madness.[12]

This passage is complemented, at the end of the book, by the image of a second "witch," this time the puppet witch in a marionette show the narrator attends, with an all male-audience, in Palermo:

> The old witch with her grey hair and staring eyes, succeeds in being ghastly. With just a touch, she would be a tall, benevolent old lady. But

of quotations, chiefly from John Burnet's *Early Greek Philosophy* (3d Edition, 1920). Lawrence seems to have first read Burnet's book (which was given to him by Bertrand Russell) when he was in Cornwall in 1916" (*CP*, 995).

[11]See Robert Graves, *The Greek Myths* (Baltimore: Penguin, 1952), II, 103–11.

[12]*Sea and Sardinia* (New York: Viking, 1948), 1–2 (hereafter cited as *SS*).

listen to her. Hear her horrible female voice with its scraping yells of evil lustfulness. Yes, she fills me with horror. And I am staggered to find how I believe in her as *the* evil principle. Beelzebub, poor devil, is only one of her instruments .... behold this image of the witch; this white, submerged *idea* of woman which rules from the deeps of the unconscious. [*SS*, 203]

When the puppet finally goes up in flames, the little boys in the audience yell with relief. "Would God," thinks Lawrence, "the symbolic act were really achieved. It is only little boys who yell. Men merely smile at the trick. They know well enough the white image endures" (p. 203).

In "Pomegranate," the "white image endures," at least partially, as the rock of Syracuse, "left bare by the viciousness of Greek women"—evidently an allusion to the terrible dismemberment of Pentheus by the Maenads—but, as the poet reminds his silent auditor, the scattering of the dead man's blood on the bare-faced Sicilian rock also spells renewal: it bears the seed of the "pomegranate-trees in flower, / Oh so red, and such a lot of them."[13] And this flowering gives way, in its turn, to the unripe fruit (the "bright green stone" in the Venice garden) and then the ripe "pomegranates to warm your hands at" of Tuscany. But of course once the fruit is ripe, it must be eaten: the poem takes us, in a few quick strokes, from the flowering pomegranate trees of Syracuse to the ripe fruit of Florence and then inside the fissure, where "the setting suns are open," where the seeds ("glittering compact drops of dawn") are inside the "rosy, tender pulp."

This is not to say that the pomegranate functions as a symbol of the female fruit, the womb that the male poet wishes to enter. Lawrence differs from most nature poets, both before and after his time, in allowing for no such consistency of symbolism. Moreover, the rhetorical framing, the foregrounding of the relationship between "I" and "You," makes it impossible to take the description of the fruit, accurate as it is, quite seriously.

The poem opens on a note of argument: the reader is drawn into what seems to be an intense debate between the poet and a close friend, a person, evidently, who regularly engages in dialogue on such subjects—a Rawdon Lilly, say, confronting an Aaron Sisson or a

[13]Here Lawrence evidently conflates Pentheus and Dionysos. In the myth (see especially Euripides, *The Bacchae*), Pentheus is, of course, Dionysos' victim: the Maenads kill and dismember the king at Dionysos' command. For Lawrence's purposes, however, both represent the male, victimized by the devouring female goddess, and hence they can be used interchangeably, just as Syracuse replaces Thebes in his allusion to the Maenads.

Jack Calcott challenging a Lovat Somers. We can take this inference one step further, of course, and say that Lawrence is arguing with himself, and that the "you" who tells him he is wrong is his rationalist alter ego. But "Pomegranate" is not really a convincing *débat*, for there is not the remotest possibility that the poet will be converted by the "you" or that he is even listening to what his antagonist might have to say. It is, rather, a case of buttonholing someone who has to give serious consideration to one's argument; indeed, by the time the "I" asserts loftily, in line 3, that "I am not wrong," the reader senses that this dazzling performer is not going to let anyone—neither his friend nor, for that matter, the reader—challenge him. Thus he plays the role of playful mentor, reminding ("No doubt you have forgotten"), explaining ("Whereas in Venice," "Now in Tuscany"), questioning ("Do you prefer to look at the plain side?"), taunting ("Do you mean to tell me there should be no fissure?"), exulting ("For my part, I prefer").

It is interesting to consider the role that rhythm plays in the creation of Lawrence's performative stance. The so-called free verse of "Pomegranate" is quite unlike, say, Whitman's, in which parallel rhythmic groupings, slow and stately, recur with subtle minor variations. Consider the first three lines:

> Yŏu téll mê I am wróng.
>
> Whŏ are yóu, " whŏ is ánybôdy " to téll mê I am wróng?
>
> Ĭ am nót wróng.

This is the associative rhythm of actual conversation, with its abrupt, choppy phrasing. But this speech rhythm repeatedly crosses a second, more "poetic" line, as in

> In the dénse fóliage of the ínner gárden
>
> Pómegrănates like bright gréen stóne,
>
> And bárbed, bárbed with a crówn.
>
> Ôh, crówn of spiked grêen métal . . .

where heavy stresses on long open vowels cluster together, creating a movement reminiscent of Pound or certain Imagists. But when "Oh, crown of spiked green metal" is followed by the deflationary

> Áctually grówing!

the effect is almost parodic, as if the poet were laughing at his more bardic self. The same thing happens a few lines farther down when the line

Rósy, ténder, glíttering withín the físsure

is followed by

Do yóu méan to téll me there should be nô físsure?

And again, in the final line when the hobby-horse rhythm of

"dáwn"-kaléidoscópic"

follows

It is só lóvely.

[CP, 278–79]

The delicate self-parody of the narrator's rhythms, the comic bullying of his tone, serve, I think, to bring the reader round to the poet's point of view, to adopt his stance toward the successive versions of the pomegranate. Thus the opening image of the flowering pomegranate tree is seen to allude to the Dionysus myth, the transformation of the blood of the dying god into the scarlet flower. It is the flower of male sexuality, just as the bright green stone seen in Venice is a phallic image. For Lawrence, Venice, as opposed to the Syracuse of ancient myth on the one hand and the warm human Tuscany on the other, is always seen as an "abhorrent, green, slippery city," evidently because it is built on water.[14] It is the city of damp canals rather than of fertility; its old Doges with their "ancient eyes," saw nothing, whereas the poet can penetrate "the dense foliage of the inner garden" and discover "pomegranates like bright green stone." These Venetian pomegranates are aggressively masculine ("barbed, barbed with a crown. / Oh, crown of spiked green metal / Actually growing!"), and even though their Tuscan counterparts are fruits "to warm your hands at," they too have "crowns, kingly, generous, tilting crowns / Over the left eyebrow."

The pomegranate is thus first linked to male sexuality. According-

14Compare Lawrence's letter to Cynthia Asquith, 23 October 1913, CL, II, 89: "Did you make your dash to Venice—and did it stink?" And to the same correspondent, he writes a few weeks later, "I am sorry you've got a cold. But what do you expect, after purpling in Venice" (p. 107).

ly, when Lawrence suddenly introduces the line, set off by itself—
"And if you dare, the fissure!"—he has made it impossible for us to
allegorize the object, to relate it to Woman, much less to any particular woman. It is as if the poet finds in himself both aspects of pome-
granatehood, the crowns of spiked green metal, "kingly, generous,
tilting," and the fissure that yields up "setting suns," "glittering, compact drops of dawn." Indeed, in the end it is not the womb that is
ruptured but the heart:

> For my part, I prefer my heart to be broken.
> It is so lovely, dawn-kaleidoscopic within the crack.

The ripe fruit splits open like a wound ("the gold-filmed skin . . . ruptured") and shows the red seed inside.

So tender is the poet's tone, so thoroughly familiar with the life
cycle of the pomegranate that it is easy to downplay the curious nar-
cissism of the final lines. The poet retreats, after all, into the crack of
his own ruptured heart; safe inside, he finds it "lovely" and "dawn-
kaleidoscopic"—one might say "innocent," "pure." But, the poem
implies, its speaker has earned the right to retreat into his own heart
because he has "dared" the fissure, the rupture. Just as the Lawrence
of *Sea and Sardinia* must "dare" the rupture of Etna if he is going to be
at one with the Sicilian landscape, so the "I" of "Pomegranate" understands that only out of intense struggle (the willingness to engage the
Greek women whose viciousness almost prevents the growth of the
flowering tree, the recognition of the crown of spiked green metal,
the daring to look at what is "rosy, tender, glittering within the fissure") can the heart be broken and made new. One thinks immediately of Crazy Jane's aphorism, "For nothing can be sole or whole / That
has not been rent," but Lawrence does not share Yeats's drive toward
Unity of Being; he is willing to accept the universe as decentered, as,
of necessity, contradictory. For who, seeing the "spiked green metal"
crown of the unripe pomegranate, would think that hidden *inside it*
there are glittering drops of dawn?

I have dwelt at what may seem to be unnecessary length on "Pomegranate" because its rhetorical mode raises issues that seem to belie
our usual assumptions about Lawrence's poetry. Much has been written about Lawrence the Orphean Seer, uncovering the secrets of
nature or "expos[ing] a lost and more fundamental discourse that
brings meaning into the present and future."[15] But this is to ignore

---

[15]See Murfin, 197.

the other, more "hard-boiled" or practical side of Lawrence, his stubborn insistence that a flower or animal or bird should be taken for what it *is*.

The central prose text, in this connection, is not the famous "Poetry of the Present" (1918), with its eloquent plea for "instant poetry," the poetry of the "incarnate moment," the *now*, but the 1927 essay called "The Nightingale," in which Lawrence contrasts his own view of the natural world with that of Keats.[16] The fallacy of "Ode to a Nightingale," he declares with mock solemnity, is that the poet thinks he can somehow enter the world of the nightingale, a world actually wholly *other:*

> The viewless wings of Poesy carry [Keats] only into the bushes, not into the nightingale world. He is still outside.

> > Darkling I listen; and for many a time
> > I have been half in love with easeful death. . . .

> The nightingale never made any man in love with easeful death, except by contrast. The contrast between the bright flame of positive pure self-aliveness, in the bird, and the uneasy flickering of yearning selflessness, for ever yearning for something outside himself, which is Keats:

> > To cease upon the midnight with no pain,
> > While thou art pouring forth thy soul abroad
> > In such an ecstasy!
> > Still wouldst thou sing, and I have ears in vain,—
> > To thy high requiem become a sod.

> How astonished the nightingale would be if he could be made to realize what sort of answer the poet was answering to his song. He would fall off the bough with amazement. Because a nightingale, when you answer him back, only shouts and sings louder. [*SLC*, 99]

This is Lawrence the sensible man, the same man who, in real life, could dust a room or bake a loaf of bread with perfect ease. He is also the comedian who delights in taking Keats's lines, "Thou wast not born for death, immortal Bird! / No hungry generations tread thee down," and remarking laconically, "Not yet in Tuscany, anyhow. They are twenty to the dozen" (*SLC*, p. 100).

---

[16]"The Nightingale," in *Selected Literary Criticism*, ed. Anthony Beal (New York: Viking, 1966), 98–101 (hereafter cited as *SLC*). "Poetry of the Present" was the introduction to the American edition of *New Poems* (1918); it is reprinted in *CP*, 181–86.

Accordingly, in "Pomegranate," flower and fruit are not the object of Romantic Einfühlung; they remain stubbornly *other*. Indeed, the poet is less seer than, in W. H. Auden's words, "enchanting companion . . . , tender, intelligent, funny, and above all, happy." In the animal poems, such distancing of self is carried even further: in "Mosquito," for example, the address to the insect as "Monsieur" is repeatedly played off against the precise, scientific knowledge of what a mosquito is and does:

> What do you stand on such high legs for?
> Why this length of shredded shank,
> You exaltation?
>
> Is it so that you shall lift your centre of gravity upwards
> And weigh no more than air as you alight upon me
> Stand upon me weightless, you phantom? . . .
>
> Queer, with your thin wings and your streaming legs,
> How you sail like a heron, or a dull clot of air,
> A nothingness. . . .
>
> Queer, how you stalk and prowl the air
> In circles and evasions, enveloping me. . . .
> I hate the way you lurch off sideways into air. . . .
>
> > [*CP*, 332–33]

And so on. Yet the same observer who knows the mosquito for what it is admits his fear of this "Winged Victory," this devil with its "evil little aura, prowling, and casting a numbness on my mind," this "streaky sorcerer," whose "hateful little trump" is that he "Suck[s] live blood,/ My blood."

As it unfolds, "The Mosquito" can be seen to be a delicately satirical treatment of man's need to triumph over the very smallest and most paltry creatures of the insect world. Thus the "I" alternately displays bravado—"I know your game now, streaky sorcerer"—and cajoles:

> Come then, let us play at unawares. . . .
>
> Why do you do it?
> Surely it is bad policy.

Or again, he waxes philosophical:

> They say you can't help it.

But the most curious twist comes in the final tercet in which we witness man's equivocal triumph over the now-dead mosquito:

> Queer, what a big stain my sucked blood makes
> Beside the infinitesimal faint smear of you!
> Queer, what a dim dark smudge you have disappeared into!
> [*CP*, 334]

As in the case of "Pomegranate," the poem foregrounds the rhetorical situation, the relation of "I" to "you," of manly poet to foppish "Monsieur Mosquito," a relationship characterized by insistent questioning, exclamation, exhortation, aphorism, repetition and hyperbole:

> Such silence, such suspended transport,
> Such gorging,
> Such obscenity of trespass. . . .
>
> Away with a paean of derision,
> You winged blood-drop.
> [*CP*, 334]

Here is man absurdly contemplating his male rival, absurdly needing to "win in this sly game of bluff," to "out-mosquito you." And again, the poem allows Lawrence to handle lightly and humorously what is, in *Women in Love* or *Aaron's Rod,* a deadly contest between male rivals.

A darker version of "Mosquito" is found in "Bat" (September 1921), whose Tuscan setting makes it a fitting complement to "Pomegranate." It begins:

> At evening, sitting on this terrace,
> When the sun from the west, beyond Pisa, beyond the mountains of
>   Carrara
> Departs, and the world is taken by surprise . . .
>
> When the tired flower of Florence is in gloom beneath the glowing
> Brown hills surrounding . . .
>
> When under the arches of the Ponte Vecchio
> A green light enters against stream, flush from the west,
> Against the current of obscure Arno . . . [17]

---

[17]*CP*, 340. The ellipsis points used here and elsewhere in the poem are Lawrence's.

This opening, with its precise setting, time of day, and concrete description of light and color, recalls such Romantic poems as "Tintern Abbey." The suspended "when" clauses follow one another with slow and stately rhythm:

When the tíred *flówer* of *Flórence* is in *glóom* benéath the *glówing* . . .

But this movement (a kind of slow-motion pan of the camera) is intentionally deceptive: Lawrence is setting the stage for the moment of threshold that is his subject, the sudden break between day and night, one state of consciousness and another, the moment when one becomes aware of that which the daylight had obscured. The Romantic opening is punctuated by the decidedly un-Romantic line: "Look up and you see things flying . . . "

Here the second-person address is important. Unlike the countless nature poems in which an "I" communes with the landscape ("I look up and I see"), "Bat" uses perception as a springboard for communication: the poet's experience can be clarified only in the course of talking about it to someone else, in making that other self share one's own angle of vision:

Look up, and you see things flying
Between the day and the night;
Swallows with spools of dark thread sewing the shadows together.

A circle swoop, and quick parabola under the bridge arches
Where light pushes through;
A sudden turning upon itself of a thing in the air.
A dip to the water.

And you think:
"The swallows are flying so late!"

Here the "you" (and, by extension, the reader) is made to share the poet's deception, his assumption that the "things flying" are swallows. Lawrence's description of the bat flight is at once minutely accurate and yet curiously enigmatic in that the geometry of flight (circle, parabola) is divorced from its source; we see, through the poet's eyes, the swoop, the turning, the dip to the water, but the bat who does the turning and dipping remains an absence. Even after the abrupt question "Swallows?" recognition is slow to come:

[123]

> Dark air-life looping
> Yet missing the pure loop . . .
> A twitch, a twitter, an elastic shudder in flight
> And serrated wings against the sky,
> Like a glove, a black glove thrown up at the light
> And falling back.

This is, so to speak, the negative version of the radiant sexuality of "Pomegranate": the "dark air-life looping . . . miss[es] the pure loop"; the "elastic shudder" has neither a perceptible source nor an object. Indeed, in a moment the sexually charged "elastic shudder in flight" collapses like a burst balloon; the profile of "serrated wings" gives way to the image of the inert "black glove thrown up at the light / And falling back."

Only now, twenty-five lines into the poem, is the subject of the poem called by name. It is, of course, the blindness of the bat (its flying into the light) that gives it away:

> Never swallows!
> Bats!
> The swallows are gone.
>
> At a wavering instant the swallows give way to bats
> By the Ponte Vecchio . . .
> Changing guard.
>
> Bats, and an uneasy creeping in one's scalp
> As the bats swoop overhead!
> Flying madly.

So startling is the poet's sudden recognition that he must repeat the word "bat" over and over again (seven times in the last twenty-one lines), gradually distancing himself from their "circle swoops" by turning them into objects: "Little lumps that fly in air and have voices indefinite, wildly vindictive; / Wings like bits of umbrella." Transformed, mechanized, the bats are no longer a threat. The narrator can now regard them with a measure of disdain and bemused tolerance:

> Creatures that hang themselves up like an old rag, to sleep;
> And disgustingly upside down.
> Hanging upside down like rows of disgusting old rags
> And grinning in their sleep.
> Bats!

To call the bats "disgusting" is to neutralize their force; anyone, after all, can deal with a set of "disgusting old rags." It is at this point that the poet can stand up and announce, both to the friend(s) with him on his Tuscan terrace and to the reader, "In China the bat is symbol of happiness." And the subsequent "not for me!" is comically gratuitous.

Indeed, like "Pomegranate," "Bat" has a certain burlesque element; it presents us with a speaker who is less Orphic seer than dark comedian. Confronted by what we most fear, Lawrence seems to be saying, we protect ourselves by metaphorizing the dreaded object: bat becomes black glove becomes little lump, bit of umbrella, disgusting old rag. Dismissed with a comic splutter, the bat can now safely become the topic of polite conversation, "In China the bat is symbol of happiness." Here, at poem's end, is Lawrence, the genial conversationalist, the amusing companion, the delightfully candid friend who admits that, whatever the Chinese may think, the bat is "not for me!"

It is interesting, in this regard, to compare Lawrence's response to the animal kingdom to that of a later poet such as Elizabeth Bishop. When we read, say, Bishop's "The Fish" against Lawrence's "Fish," we are initially struck by the thematic parallel: both poems suggest that the otherness of the fish must be respected, that the act of "catching" a fish bespeaks a mastery more apparent than real. But when Bishop's "I" contemplates the fish she has just caught, there is a clear distinction between subject and object:

> I looked into his eyes
> which were far larger than mine
> but shallower, and yellowed,
> the irises backed and packed
> with tarnished tinfoil
> seen through the lenses
> of old scratched isinglass.
> They shifted a little, but not
> to return my stare.
> —It was more like the tipping
> of an object toward the light
> I admired his sullen face. . . .[18]

Bishop's discourse is characterized by its consistency and narrative continuity; "I looked. . . . It was. . . . I admired . . . . then I saw." Lawrence's poem observes no such decorum; the performing self engages

[18]Elizabeth Bishop, *The Complete Poems* (New York: Farrar, Straus & Giroux, 1969), 49.

in impassioned conversation, sometimes directly with the fish, sometimes with a silent auditor, sometimes with himself. He shifts at will from first to second to third person, now envying the fish's freedom from human, that is to say, sexual, anxieties ("But oh, fish, that rock in water, / You lie only with the waters. . . . No wistful bellies, / No loins of desire, / None."), now standing back and describing the fish's attributes in rapid shorthand:

> Himself,
> And the element.
> Food, of course!
> Water-eager eyes,
> Mouth-gate open
> And strong spine urging, driving;
> And desirous belly gulping.

Or, distancing the fish still further:

> Cats and the Neapolitans
> Sulphur sun-beasts,
> Thirst for fish as for more-than-water;
> Water-alive
> To quench their over-sulphureous lusts.

As in "Pomegranate," Lawrence dissolves perspective: the observer is not located in any one spot, and the poet's canvas becomes, so to speak, a flickering network of multiple stresses, a field of force. Indeed, in its emphasis on the split-second transformation of the object to be examined and in the poet's performative stance vis-à-vis that object, a poem like "Fish" is perhaps closer to Italian Futurism than to the Romantic paradigm that is generally held to be its source.

In a letter to Arthur McLeod (2 June 1914), Lawrence writes:

I have been interested in the futurists. I got a book of their poetry—a very fat book too—and book of pictures—and I read Marinetti's and Paolo Buzzi's manifestations and essays. . . . It interests me very much. I like it because it is the applying to emotions of the purging of the old forms and sentimentalities. I like it for its saying—enough of this sickly cant, let us be honest and stick by what is in us. [*CL*, II, 180]

And the following March, he writes to Gordon Campbell: "Art which is lyrical can now no longer satisfy us: each work of art that is true, now, must give expression to the great collective experience, not to the individual . . . . we have accumulated enough fragmentary data of lyricism since the Renaissance" (*CL,* II, 301).

We must, of course, take such statements with a grain of salt: to express "the great collective experience," whatever that is, is surely impossible for any poet, let alone a poet of the twentieth century. Despite such hyperbole, Lawrence's perception is important; he means that, given the context of the Great War, of the new concepts of space and time and of the machine that so profoundly influenced the Futurists, an *individual* response to nature—the confrontation of an "I" with a skylark or a nightingale or a field of daffodils—is perhaps no longer enough. For Lawrence, there is no longer a distinction between subject and object, consciousness and the external world. Rather, the new space is one in which the mind and its objects are present in a single realm of proximity.[19] Accordingly, it is impossible to know where man ends and "fish" or "bat" or "pomegranate" begins; there is only a charged field of energies, of forces in tension. It is this theater of polarities, this performance arena, we meet in *Birds, Beasts and Flowers.*

Lawrence's debt to the Futurists has often been noted, but always with reference to his novels rather than to his poetry. The famous letter to Edward Garnett (5 June 1914), in which Lawrence cites Marinetti as the source of his new concept of character ("There is another ego, according to whose action the individual is unrecognisable, and passes through, as it were, allotropic states" [*CL,* II, 183]), is regularly quoted and discussed with reference to *The Rainbow* and *Women in Love.* But, ironically, Lawrence's carbon-diamond opposition, his belief that "that which is physic—non-human, in humanity, is more interesting to me than the old-fashioned human element— which causes one to conceive a character in a certain moral scheme and make him consistent" (*CL,* II, 182), a doctrine whose applications in the novels of the 1920s, were to become increasingly problematic, makes good sense when we turn from the fiction to the poetry.

In *Aaron's Rod,* for example, Lawrence cannot quite make up his mind whether the characters do or do not fit into what he calls "a certain moral scheme"; sometimes they behave consistently; some-

---

[19]For an important discussion of this central distinction, see J. Hillis Miller, *Poets of Reality: Six Twentieth-Century Writers* (1965; reprint, New York: Atheneum, 1969), 1–12 and chap. 7 ("William Carlos Williams"). Lawrence is not one of the six writers discussed here, but Miller's thesis about the "new region of copresence," the new space in which "mind is dispersed everywhere in things and forms one with them" (pp. 8–9) seems especially applicable to Lawrence.

times their actions seem to be motivated by what Lawrence, following Marinetti, calls "physiology of matter." The conflict between carbon and diamond, so to speak, remains unresolved. But when, in his role as poet, Lawrence can address a pomegranate or a fish, or when he can mount what we might call his "bat performance," exorcising the black demons that fly in the night, his desire to "purge" the emotions of their "old forms and sentimentalities" finds its proper outlet.

Perhaps we are now in a better position to understand why, for all its brilliance, *Birds, Beasts and Flowers* continues to meet with indifference, if not resistance, on the part of historians and critics of twentieth-century poetry. In their recent *The Modern Poetic Sequence: The Genius of Modern Poetry* (1983), for example, M. L. Rosenthal and Sally M. Gall barely mention Lawrence, even though their study covers lyric sequences from Whitman and Dickinson down to Ted Hughes, Sylvia Plath, Galway Kinnell, and Adrienne Rich.[20] If the exclusion of Lawrence constitutes, as I think it does, the rule rather than the exception, the reason is not far to seek. Lawrence's poetry confounds all our usual categories: modern/postmodern, symbolist/immanentist, romantic/realist, confessional/deep imagist, and so on. If it is not easy to establish a line of precursors for Lawrence, it is even more difficult to determine the nature of his influence on later poets.

Yet there are signs that the marginal status of Lawrence's poetry is changing.[21] Today, with the erosion of the boundaries between lyric poetry and other modes of discourse, with the increasing prominence of performance art, and with the revival of interest in Dada and Futurism, we should be attuned to a poetic voice that, in a poem deceptively titled "Southern Night" (*CP*, 302), commands the moon to "Come up, thou red thing. / Come up, and be called a moon," only to become aware of "The mosquitoes . . . biting to-night / Like memories"—a "sting" that produces the characteristic Lawrencian about-

---

[20]M. L. Rosenthal and Sally M. Gall, *The Modern Poetic Sequence: The Genius of Modern Poetry* (New York: Oxford University Press, 1983). Yeats's sequences are given approximately forty pages, as are Pound's and Williams's. Olson's *Maximus* gets eighteen, Ted Hughes's *Crow*, sixteen.

[21]In "D. H. Lawrence's Uncommon Prayers," Sandra M. Gilbert perceptively remarks that Lawrence is finally a poet's poet. But whereas Gilbert cites Joyce Carol Oates, Robert Bly, Denise Levertov, Ted Hughes, and Adrienne Rich as poets who have followed the Lawrencian model, no doubt because she is primarily concerned with the mythic structure and Orphic symbolism of the poems in *BBF*, I would argue that, as a rhetorician, Lawrence is closer to such poets as Charles Olson, Robert Duncan, Robert Creeley, and Allen Ginsberg—all, incidentally, poets who have written admiringly of Lawrence's lyric.

face: "Call it moonrise / This red anathema?" And of course this challenge makes us want to debate the issue, to come to terms with this "red thing, / Unfold[ing] slowly upwards, blood-dark." As readers, we are *there*—a part of the "Southern Night" and the "Tropic," in which the poet asks:

> What is the horizontal rolling of water
> Compared to the flood of black heat that rolls upwards past my eyes?

[7]

Potent Griselda: "The Ladybird" and the Great Mother

Sandra M. Gilbert

Yea, like bees in and out of a hive, we come backwards and forwards to our woman. . . . we are bees that go between, from the flower home to the hive and the Queen; for she lies at the centre of the hive [and] in her all things are born, both words and bees.
—D. H. Lawrence, Foreword to *Sons and Lovers*

Man has fallen. It would be difficult to point to a man in the world today who is not subservient to the great woman-spirit that sways modern mankind.
—D. H. Lawrence, "The Real Thing"

Beneath every temple to Zeus . . . there was found on excavation without exception, some old cell or cellar or the rough ground-work of some primitive temple to the Early Goddess . . . , the first deity, the primitive impulse, the primitive desire, the first love, Maia, mama, Mutter, mut, mamalie, mimmie, Madre, Mary, *mother*.
—canceled passage from H. D., *The Gift*

This essay is part of a book-length project entitled "Mother Rites: Studies in Literature and Maternity," which evolved from a brief paper that I gave at the Simone de Beauvoir Conference at New York University in the fall of 1979. Over the years, my work on the subject has benefited from the insights of many friends and colleagues, including most especially Susan Gubar, Susan Stanford Friedman, Joanne Feit Diehl, Garrett Stewart, and Elliot Gilbert. In addition, I am grateful to the Rockefeller and Guggenheim foundations for essential support that made this research possible. Epigraphs: D. H. Lawrence, "Foreword to *Sons and Lovers*," in *The Letters of D. H. Lawrence*, ed. Aldous Huxley (London: Heinemann, 1932), 100; D. H. Lawrence, "The Real Thing," in *Phoenix: The Posthumous Papers*, ed. Edward D. McDonald (New York: Penguin, 1978), 196; H. D., unpublished manuscript of *The Gift*, Beinecke Library, Yale University (quoted by permission of Perdita Schaffner).

"The Ladybird" and the Great Mother

"The modern young man is not afraid of being petticoat-ruled," declared D. H. Lawrence in his late essay "Matriarchy." "He is afraid of being swamped, turned into a mere accessory of bare-limbed swooping woman. . . . He talks rather bitterly . . . about matriarchy, and rather feebly about man being master again. He knows perfectly well that he will never be master again."[1] Such an admission from our century's major acolyte of the phallic mysteries and of the lordly "men in whom the gods are manifest"[2] may seem somewhat surprising. Yet as my epigraphs are meant to suggest, the masculinist and often misogynistic Lawrence was oddly close to his quasi-feminist friend the poet H. D. in his presuppositions about the power of female (pro)creativity. Indeed, as perhaps the paradigmatic modernist theoretician of sexuality, he frequently articulated ideas about the primacy of maternity that also represented the views of such equally unlikely contemporaries as Isadora Duncan and James Joyce, both of whom within the same decade expressed almost the same sentiment on what was for these avant-garde revolutionaries a peculiar subject. "*Amor matris,* subjective and objective genitive, may be the only true thing in life," said Stephen Dedalus in *Ulysses* (1922), as if anticipating Lawrence's plaintive "Matriarchy," and through him his creator, James Joyce, also spoke.[3] Five years later, Isadora Duncan, writing in *My Life* (1927), asked a rhetorical question that implied the same speculation. "Is it that in all the universe there is but one Great Cry containing Sorrow, Joy, Ecstasy, Agony, the Mother Cry of Creation?"[4]

Radical and rebellious as they were, neither Duncan nor Dedalus (nor Joyce himself nor H. D. nor Lawrence) can be seen as merely restating typical nineteenth-century verities about Home, Hearth, and Mother. Certainly, naked beneath her Grecian veils, Isadora would seem to have dramatically escaped the decorous cult of True Womanhood, while H. D., living out a liberated expatriatism, could hardly be defined as a hierophant of Mrs. Beeton's Good Housekeeping. Similarly, the mature Joyce and his youthful alter ego, Stephen— both busily inventing fictions of fatherhood—were nothing if not cynical about the claims of the maternal Angel in the House. Stephen, indeed, fantasized his rejection of Catholicism as an act of matricide,

[1]Lawrence, "Matriarchy," in *Assorted Articles,* reprinted in *Phoenix II: Uncollected, Unpublished, and Other Prose Works by D. H. Lawrence,* ed. Warren Roberts and Harry T. Moore (New York: Viking, 1968), 549.

[2]Lawrence, "Benjamin Franklin," in *Studies in Classic American Literature* (1923; reprint, New York: Penguin, 1977), 23.

[3]James Joyce, *Ulysses* (New York: Modern Library, 1934), 205; page numbers in text refer to this edition.

[4]Isadora Duncan, *My Life* (New York: Liveright, 1927), 275.

and Lawrence's gloomy assertion in "The Real Thing" that "man has fallen," together with the rhetoric of fear and resignation that he deploys in "Matriarchy," brings to the surface an anxiety that underlies Joyce's claims, if not H. D.'s or Duncan's. Nevertheless, whether anxious or ecstatic, all four of these figures were shaped by a cultural context that defined motherhood as the ontological fact from which all other facts, fictions, and myths arise.

Why and how did these disparate artists come to create so mystical and metaphysical a definition of female sexuality and more specifically of motherhood? Furthermore, what were the aesthetic implications of such a definition? I will argue here that all were reflecting a general transformation in what Michel Foucault has called the "history of sexuality," a transformation that can be more clearly, if less surprisingly, traced in the treatises of speculative anthropologists from Bachofen to Frazer and Harrison to Briffault, Graves, and Neumann. For women artists—particularly for feminist modernists—this sociocultural change had a number of empowering consequences, as I have suggested elsewhere.[5] For their male (and often masculinist) modernist contemporaries, however, such a change posed crucial problems, implying as it did an important set of unmanning transformations not only in Western culture's biological and anthropological valuation of motherhood but also in those sexual metaphors for creativity through which so many writers have traditionally expressed their deepest feelings about their own nature and the nature of their own art. Because Lawrence's self-analyses were always so frank in their confrontation of the psychodynamics that other poets and novelists only more hesitantly explored, some of his works, and in particular his middleperiod novella "The Ladybird," may allow us clearly to chart both the anxieties induced in men by the newly conceived potency of the "Early Goddess . . . , the first love, Maia, mama, Mutter," and the aesthetic maneuvers through which they defended themselves against such anxieties.

Throughout much of the nineteenth century, of course, as throughout much of Western literary history, the power of the literary artist to create texts was metaphorically equated with the power of

---

[5]In "Potent Griselda: Literary Men, Literary Women, and the Great Mother," a much-expanded version of this essay that was delivered at Mount Holyoke in June 1983, and in "The Long, Long Dances: Modernists, Maenads, and the Great Mother," delivered at the annual meeting of the Modern Language Association in New York City, December 1983; also, in a very preliminary way, in "Literary Paternity," *Cornell Review*, no. 6 (Summer 1979), 54–65.

men to engender children and/or the power of God the Father to generate both the world and the Word, both the Book of Nature and the Book of Judgment. The human author of poems and plays, that is, usually seemed to male writers who worked in the masculinist traditions of what Gertrude Stein called "patriarchal poetry"[6] to be a kind of copy or shadow of that cosmic Author who fathered all things and from whom, ultimately, all authority sprang. Thus there has long been a secret or subliminal sense in which a writer's pen somehow "stood" for his penis (and here a pun may or may not be intended).[7] As recently as 1886, even the withdrawn and submissive clergyman Gerard Manley Hopkins declared that the artist's "most essential quality [is] masterly execution, which is a kind of male gift, and especially marks off men from women, the begetting of one's thought on paper, in verse, or whatever the matter is."[8]

More recently, this idea that, as Hopkins also put it, "the male quality is the creative gift," has been explored by such critics as Jacques Derrida and John Irwin. In particular, both these men, along with many other contemporary thinkers, speculate upon the notion that "the hymen is the always folded . . . space in which the pen writes its dissemination" and that the creative act involves a relationship between "the phallic pen" and "the 'pure space' of the virgin page."[9] In elaborating this argument, moreover, both implicitly allude to the old biological model in which the female is merely a passive vessel upon which and in which the male acts. Acquiescing in male desire, suffering the consequences of man's will, woman, according to this ancient paradigm, is and should be no more than a patient Griselda, like the bizarrely submissive wife of Walter, Marquis of Saluzzo, in

[6]See "Patriarchal Poetry" (1927), in *The Yale Gertrude Stein,* ed. Richard Kostelanetz (New Haven: Yale University Press, 1980), 106–46.

[7]See my "Literary Paternity"; also see Sandra M. Gilbert and Susan Gubar, *The Madwoman in the Attic: The Woman Writer and the Nineteenth-Century Literary Imagination* (New Haven: Yale University Press, 1979), 3–44 (chap. 1).

[8]*The Correspondence of Gerard Manley Hopkins and Richard Watson Dixon,* ed. C. C. Abbott (London: Oxford University Press, 1935), 133.

[9]Hopkins's "the hymen [as an] always folded . . . space" etc. (ibid.) is Gayatri Spivak's succinct summary of the theories presented in Derrida's *La double séance* in her translator's preface to *Of Grammatology* (Baltimore: Johns Hopkins University Press, 1976), lxvi, but for an extended discussion of the point, see Derrida, "The Double Session," in *Dissemination,* trans. Barbara Johnson (Chicago: University of Chicago Press, 1981), especially 209–85; for "the phallic pen" and the "virgin page," as well as a discussion of "the phallic generative power of the creative imagination," see John Irwin, *Doubling and Incest, Repetition and Revenge* (Baltimore: Johns Hopkins University Press, 1975), 163; for a feminist perspective on this material, see Susan Gubar, "The Blank Page and the Issue of Female Creativity," in *Critical Inquiry* (Winter 1981), 243–64.

Boccaccio's and Chaucer's stories, who bears her lord's children only to lose them to his specially defined *droit du seigneur*. Whether she is, as in the current formulation, a blank page, or, as in older terms, an empty vessel, Griselda's story tells us that woman should be humble because she is inert. Man generates life, she receives it; he defines it, she contains it; he imagines it, she embodies it. Familiar notions, for from the fourth century B.C. until at least the eighteenth century, most European medical metaphysicians accepted the "highly influential concept of the relative roles of male and female in development," which Aristotle postulated in his *Generation of Animals:* males were believed to provide "the form, at once formal, efficient, and final cause" and females no more than "the substance, the material cause, for the new organism."[10]

During the seventeenth and eighteenth centuries, moreover, as proponents of the infant science of embryology took up the concept of "preformation"—that is, the notion that, as Seneca had written in the first century, "in the seed are enclosed all the parts of the body of the man that shall be formed"[11]—thinkers such as Dalenpatius, Leeuwenhoek, and Leibniz actually argued that tiny homunculi sprang fully formed from male penises to be lodged temporarily in female bodies, which acted as little more than "homely foster nurses" (to quote Wordsworth) or large incubators.[12] Yet though such an extreme devaluation of even the biological role of the female may now seem absurd, it is, after all, only another version of the famous judgment that Apollo issues at the end of the *Oresteia,* an assertion that has often been seen as one of the founding statements of Western patriarchy: "The true parent is he who mounts, the mother is not the

---

[10]For a summary and discussion of this theory, see Jane M. Oppenheimer, *Essays in the History of Embryology and Biology* (Cambridge: M.I.T. Press, 1967), 121; for a useful analysis of the ways in which "procreation theories" can be seen both "as creation mythemes" and as projective representations of sexual dominance/subordination, see James Hillman, "On Psychological Feminity," in *The Myth of Analysis: Three Essays in Archetypal Psychology* (Evanston: Northwestern University Press, 1972), especially 217–54. For a late and anxiously formulated vision of woman as empty vessel, see Joyce, *Ulysses,* 282, where Leopold Bloom, meditating on his wife's "chamber music," decides that "empty vessels make most noise"; later in the same chapter ("Sirens"), he thinks, "Blank face. Virgin should say: or fingered only. Write something on it: page," and, tellingly, broods that "goddess I didn't see" (p. 285).

[11]Oppenheimer, 130.

[12]Wordsworth's conceit, elaborated in the "Intimations of Immortality" ode, is significant because it implies that Nature, "the homely Nurse," and the "Mother," are comparably inferior "prison-house[s]" when set against the patriarchal God in whom the soul originates and whose generative energy is both "the fountain-light of all our day" and "a *master*-light of all our seeing" (emphasis added).

parent at all."[13] For as Neumann observes, a patriarchate traditionally postulates "that the male seed is the creative element while the woman . . . is only its temporary abode and feeding place."[14] In fact, to translate biological terms back into literary metaphors again, the woman is simply a blank—or in Irwin's phrase "virgin"—page on which the male body inscribes the word made flesh of a new generation.

There is a significant difference, however, between such a metaphor as it is ironically examined by, say, Derrida and Irwin, and the metaphor as it was more confidently expressed by earlier thinkers from Aristotle to Chaucer's clerk to Hopkins. For what intervened between these two sets of theorists was an epoch that became increasingly aware of female power, increasingly conscious that it might be possible to define the female vessel, rather than the male seed, as the actively creative agent both in life and in art, possible to reimagine Griselda as positively potent rather than merely patient.[15] Indeed, it might be possible, as Neumann notes, to describe the male seed as itself no more than a function of the great transformative female vessel. "In the matriarchal world," he declares,

> the woman as vessel is not made by man or out of man or used for his procreative purposes; rather, the reverse is true; it is this vessel with its mysterious creative character that brings forth the male in itself and from out of itself. Bachofen rightly pointed out that in the matriarchate man is looked upon as a sower, but he did not perceive the radical meaning of this image, in which the man is only an instrument of the earth and the seed he sows is not "his" seed but earth seed.[16]

Whether or not it is objectively "true," Neumann's notion that woman as mother goddess might once have been a historically and theologically significant force—that, in Lawrence's phrase, modern generations might be "the embodied ideas of our grandmothers"[17] rather than of our grand*fathers*—was a new idea that developed along with (and no doubt in part because of) the new sciences of embryology

[13]Aeschylus, *The Oresteian Trilogy*, trans. Philip Vellacott (New York: Penguin, 1959), 169–70.
[14]Erich Neumann, *The Great Mother: An Analysis of the Archetype*, trans. by Ralph Manheim, Bollingen Series 47 (Princeton: Princeton University Press, 1963), 63.
[15]Chaucer himself, of course, withdraws in a kind of repugnance from "The Clerk's Tale" in "Lenvoy de Chaucer," where he admonishes "noble wyves, ful of heigh prudence," to "Lat noon humilitee youre tonge naille" and so forth.
[16]Neumann, 62.
[17]Lawrence, "Making Love to Music," in *Phoenix*, 160; Neumann, 62.

and anthropology, as well as the new movements of feminism and Romanticism, in the late eighteenth century and the first half of the nineteenth century, and it is an idea that has had far-reaching implications for literary artists of both sexes. For until that crucial turn of the century, just as physicians imagined the generation of animals very differently from the way in which nineteenth- and twentieth-century embryologists conceptualize the process, so philosophers and scholars imagined prehistory very differently from the way theorists of matriarchy from Bachofen to Harrison, Briffault, and Neumann do. Whether they were "classical" Greeks or Renaissance classicists, their originary age, Golden or Iron, was on the whole as patriarchal as the society in which they lived.[18]

The impulse to question the notion that prehistory was necessarily patriarchal—with patriarchy, indeed, a sort of Platonic form of all society—can no doubt be traced back, first, to the work of speculative anthropologists like Bachofen, Frazer, and Harrison, along with the research of field enthnologists such as Lewis Morgan and Bronislaw Malinowski, who began exploring the differences between both historically and geographically distinct cultures and in doing so revealed that human social structures may be—and may always have been—fluid rather than fixed, unlike rather than like; second, to the work of embryologists such as Wolff and Baer, whose studies of the epigenesis of the fertilized egg emphasized both the power of the female "seed" and the importance of the transformative process that takes place in, and is facilitated by, the female body; and, finally, of course, to the work of Darwin himself, whose large-scale application of the idea of process to all of biological "history" set off, as Gordon Rattray Taylor remarks, "a series of attempts to draw up schemes designed to account for the whole development of human society, [schemes that] represented the application of the idea of evolution . . . to society as a whole."[19]

Taken together, the researches and hypotheses of these thinkers suggested that traditionally patriarchal visions of a fixed prehistory reflecting the modes and fixtures of "modern" society, like the patriarchal biology with which they were (consciously or not) associated, had been in some sense illusory. "The absolute antithesis between our present-day thinking and that of antiquity," wrote Bachofen in the introduction to his massive and groundbreaking *Mother Right* (1861),

[18]For a discussion of this point, see Robert Briffault, *The Mothers,* abridged by Gordon Rattray Taylor (New York: Atheneum, 1977), 27.
[19]Taylor, introduction to Briffault, 10.

"is nowhere so startlingly disclosed as in the field upon which we are entering"—the field, that is, of the relations between, and especially the relative positions of, the sexes.[20] Some forty years later, in her superbly argued *Prolegomena to the Study of Greek Religion* (1903)— about which Joseph Campbell remarks that "if Bachofen's name were mentioned anywhere in its pages [it] might be read from beginning to end as an intentional celebration and verification of his views"—Jane Ellen Harrison observed that, though "our modern patriarchal society focuses its religious anthropomorphism on the relationship of the father and the son," the civilization of pre-Homeric Greece "is quite other than patriarchal."[21] Subversively tracing the evolution of patriarchal Olympus from matriarchal Eleusis, she drew upon the findings of Sir Arthur Evans, who had begun to excavate the ruins of Cretan Knossos, to support her theories, exuberantly exclaiming that "in Crete most happily the ancient figure of the mother has returned after long burial to the upper air."[22] For her, as for Bachofen before her and Briffault after her, the Great Mother, the Lady of the Wild Things—whether in her incarnation as Demeter/Kore, as Isis, as Aphrodite, or as Semele—was in earliest theology the only true and primordially potent parent of everyone.

The work of speculative thinkers such as Harrison and Bachofen was not, of course, in a scientific sense "empirical"; rather, it was based on the painstaking interpretation of what Bachofen himself called "a vast heap of ruins,"[23] and it is questionable whether either the Swiss jurist or the English scholar knew much about the advances in embryological theory that accompanied and in a way offered a counterpoint to their research. Yet it seems more than coincidentally significant that, even among preformationist biologists who believed the human infant to be contained as a tiny homunculus in egg or sperm, the "ovists" had defeated the "animalculists" by the middle of the eighteenth century, that by the end of the century Caspar Friedrich Wolff's theory of ovular epigenesis (substituting active process for static "preformation") had been widely accepted, and that by the end of the nineteenth century, in just the years when Harrison was writing her *Prolegomena*, experimental embryologists like Roux (1888), Driesch (1891), Endres (1895), and Spemann (1901, 1903)

---

[20]*Myth, Religion, and Mother Right: Selected Writings of J. J. Bachofen*, trans. by Ralph Manheim, Bollingen Series 84 (Princeton University Press, 1967), 113.

[21]Campbell, introduction to Bachofen, lv; Jane Harrison, *Prolegomena to the Study of Greek Religion* (New York: Meridian, 1955), 261.

[22]Harrison, 497.

[23]Bachofen, 108.

had established the nature of the cleavage by which the egg/embryo manifests its developmental potency.[24] Clearly, from a medical point of view, such laboratory research definitively superseded the ancient a priori assertions of Aristotle and of Aeschylus' Apollo.

That such research constituted a kind of resonant accompaniment to the mythography of Bachofen and Harrison is made clear from a central symbol studied in Bachofen's first book. *An Essay on Ancient Mortuary Symbolism* (1859), which acted as an overture to *Mother Right*, featured an analysis of "The Three Mystery Eggs" found in an Etruscan tomb. Here, as if intuiting modern embryology's refutation of the Aristotelian reproductive model, the future theorist of matriarchy noted that "in religion the egg is a symbol of the material source of all things . . . which brings forth all life from out of itself," adding that "the phallic god, striving toward the fertilization of matter, is not the original datum: rather, he himself springs from the darkness of the maternal womb" and merely "stands as a son to feminine matter."[25] Similarly, and as if to reinforce the revisionary bio-mythology implicit in this first of Bachofen's interpretive hypotheses, Harrison concluded her *Prolegomena* with a study of the crucial importance of "one characteristic Orphic element, the cosmic egg."[26] Thus, in the very years when Gerard Manley Hopkins, celebrating the "male" creative "gift," defined failed poems as analogous to "hens' eggs that are good to eat and look just like live ones but never hatch,"[27] both mother and egg, womb and womb fruit, were being radically redefined and reempowered. Inevitably, such a drastic reversal of traditional assumptions about the origin and history of physical creativity would seem to have necessitated drastic reversals in just the sorts of metaphors for aesthetic creativity that Hopkins was elaborating.

To be sure, as Terry Castle has shown in "Birth *Topoi* and English Poetics, 1660–1820," a trope of literary maternity had long complemented and supplemented the patriarchal trope of literary paternity.[28] Paradoxically, however, Castle's study illuminates one constant, one term of the childbirth metaphor that did not and could not

[24]See B. I. Balinsky, *An Introduction to Embryology* (Philadelphia: W. B. Saunders, 1960), 14–15.
[25]Bachofen, 25, 29.
[26]Harrison, 626.
[27]*Correspondence of Hopkins and Dixon*, 133.
[28]Terry Castle, "Lab'ring Bards: Birth *Topoi* and English Poetics 1660–1820," *JEGP* 78 (April 1979), 193–208; in "Creativity and the Childbirth Metaphor: A Case Study for Gender Difference in Literary Discourse," an unpublished essay that she has generously shared with me, Susan Stanford Friedman has explored the same material from a more distinctively feminist perspective.

change until the mid-nineteenth century: its underlying assumption that, whether for better or worse, the literal or literary "mother" of a child is merely an inert vessel. But what happened to this view when biology and anthropology conspired to suggest that the energetic darkness of the mother, rather than the apparently commanding lucidity of the father, might be both primordial and primordially authoritative? What happened when it became clear that neither womb nor egg are passive but that instead they, and their bearer, might manifest an ontologically "wise" activity? I would argue that by the end of the century most male artists had begun to approach the childbirth metaphor with a new wariness; furthermore, that in many of these artists and thinkers—and perhaps most clearly in Lawrence—we see a defensive movement toward devaluation of the female expressed not for the most part (like the eighteenth-century satirists' revulsion against witless pregnancy) through an articulation of the physical horror of maternity but rather through a more generalized expression of dread; and that, paradoxically, we see at the same time an acknowledgment of the male subject's dependence on female, and specifically maternal, power.

Not insignificantly, it is among male anthropological and psychoanalytic theorists of maternity that we can first trace such equivocal manifestations of dependency and dread. Bachofen himself, after all, even while excavating and acclaiming the civilizing virtues and primordial authority of "Mother Right," anxiously insisted that this "lunar" stage in human social evolution had necessarily to be replaced by the more spiritual "solar" stage of "Father Right."[29] Similarly, Neumann, following Jung and Briffault, located the "origin and history of consciousness" in the solar hero's separation from, and attack upon, the engulfing darkness of the Great Mother.[30] At the same time, from a different intellectual perspective, but with apparently equal anxiety, Freud, committed archaeologist though he was, managed to construct ontogenetic theories of sexuality that until quite late avoided any recognition of a "Minoan/Mycenaean" matriarchal stage in either culture or the individual while defining the vagina in neo-Aristotelian terms as "nonexistent"—an absence or blank—for much of the young girl's life and as, later, no more than a passive home, refuge, or "asylum" for the aggressively generative activity of the penis.[31]

[29]Bachofen, introduction to *Mother Right,* passim.

[30]See Neumann, *The Origin and History of Consciousness,* and Neumann, "The Negative Elementary Character," in *The Great Mother,* 147–210.

[31]For the "Minoan-Mycenaean" stage in psychosexual development, see Freud, "Female Sexuality" (1931), in *Sexuality and the Psychology of Love* (New York: Collier,

Small wonder, given such theoretical contexts, that the texts of male artists dramatically reproduced the reactions of men like Bachofen, Neumann, and Freud to contemporary discoveries about female reproductive authority. From Henry Adams's nervous assertion that "the proper study of mankind is woman"—the "virgin" who represents "creative energy, the life force"—to Robert Graves's booklength meditation on the often frightening priorities of *The White Goddess* and Philip Wylie's fascinated catalog of the improprieties of "mom-ism," English and American men of letters simultaneously revised, resisted, and rejected theories about female (pro)creativity that put them, as engendered males, in surprising positions.[32] Conceding, with Lawrence, that "we are in for the monstrous rule of women, and a matriarchy," such thinkers often tried to persuade themselves, again with Lawrence, that "Courage! Perhaps a matriarchy isn't so bad after all."[33] But they knew that their situation was radically new, if not "bad." Certainly, for male modernists Bachofen's concept of the Great Mother and her "cosmic egg" implies that the very pages on which supposedly patriarchal authorities inscribe the texts of royal desire, like the vessels presumably possessed by lords like Griselda's Walter, are not only autonomously powerful; they may be text(iles) created by a spinning sisterhood of women, for, as Bachofen observes, in the earliest religions "the spinning and weaving of the great nature mothers . . . represents the creative, formative power of nature."[34] But just as women spin the textiles that clothe and enclose men while creating the bodies men wear, so too they may conceive and give birth to the texts men read. In that case, however, no woman is ever metaphorically a blank or virgin page. On the contrary, every woman is always potentially both the author of the page and of the page's male reader/critic. She is primary; he is secondary; she makes the plot; he enacts it; she delivers both texture and text, he interprets

---

1963), 195; for the vagina as "non-existent," see the same essay, p. 197; for the vagina as "an asylum for the penis," see "The Infantile Genital Organization of the Libido" (1923) in the same volume, p. 175; for a perceptive analysis of Freud's inheritance from such misogynistic precursors as Galen and Aristotle, see Hillman, 238–43.

[32]Adams, *Mont Saint Michel and Chartres*, in Henry Adams, *Novels, Mont Saint Michel, The Education* (New York: Library of America, 1983), 523; (and for a commentary on this subject, see Nancy Schrom Dye, "Clio's American Daughters: Male History, Female Reality," in *The Prism of Sex: Essays in the Sociology of Knowledge*, ed. Julia A. Sherman and Evelyn Torton Beck [Madison: University of Wisconsin Press, 1977], 17); Robert Graves, *The White Goddess* (New York: Creative Age, 1948); Philip Wylie, *Generation of Vipers* (New York: Rinehart, 1955), especially 194–217.

[33]Lawrence, "Matriarchy," 550.

[34]Bachofen, 156.

it. In fact, many a modernist male uneasily decided that, as Lawrence put it, "All this talk of young girls and virginity, like a blank white page on which nothing is written, is pure nonsense."[35]

As I have already observed, Lawrence is the archetype of the male modernist I have been describing here, a literary theorist and metaphorist who implicitly believes in the Great Mother's power even while he explicitly dreads and rejects it. Famously misogynistic and, in rhetoric, fiercely, almost fascistically patriarchal, he is nevertheless the author of books whose very titles—*Sons and Lovers, Women in Love, Lady Chatterley's Lover*—are haunted by female primacy, by the autonomous sexual energy of the goddess. "All women are giantesses in their natures," he once remarked, and though he attacked the role reversals of "cocksure women and hensure men," serious readers of his fiction and poetry must also inevitably conclude that, as one male Lawrence scholar recently quipped, "For Lawrence man is always the second sex." Indeed, it is possible to speculate, as Anne Smith has, that "Lawrence's God was Woman, Woman, moreover, as Magna Mater."[36]

No doubt a number of personal and historical factors contributed to such a position, factors quite distinct from the transformations in biomythology brought about by the researches of nineteenth-century anthropologists and embryologists. Lawrence's own psychosexual development was, after all—as everyone knows but no one more clearly than he—marked and perhaps marred by the long enthrallment to his mother that made him for many years an "Oedipus in Nottingham."[37] In addition, he was exceptionally conscious that he was living in an age of unprecedented feminist emancipation. As he put it, "Perhaps the greatest revolution of modern times is the emancipation of women; and perhaps the deepest fight for two thousand years and more has been the fight for woman's independence or freedom, call it what you will. The fight was deeply bitter, and, it seems to me, it is won."[38] Yet Lawrence's keen awareness of these two points might

[35]Lawrence, "A Propos of 'Lady Chatterley's Lover,'" *Phoenix II*, 490.

[36]Anne Smith, "A New Adam and a New Eve—Lawrence and Women: A Biographical Overview," *Lawrence and Women*, ed. Anne Smith (London: Vision, 1978), 25; a similar point, including a comparable (but very different) reading of "The Ladybird," is offered in Judith Ruderman's *D. H. Lawrence and the Devouring Mother* (Durham: Duke University Press, 1984), a book that has only become available to me since this essay was completed.

[37]See Daniel Weiss, *Oedipus in Nottingham* (Seattle: University of Washington Press, 1962).

[38]Lawrence, "The Real Thing," 196.

have been very differently articulated had it not been shaped and shadowed by an equally keen grasp of the implications of woman's newly defined (pro)creative potency. As Martin Green has brilliantly demonstrated, the young poet-novelist was quite early and quite specifically influenced by the thinking of the circle of German intellectuals who called themselves "Die Kosmiche Runde" when he eloped with Frieda Weekly-Richthofen, whose sometime lover, Otto Gross, was a member of the group. "The Cosmic Circle," notes Green, "stood for life-values, for eroticism, for the value of myth and primitive cultures [and] for the primacy of the female mode of being. The major outside impulse to the development of their ideas came from the Swiss scholar, J. J. Bachofen." In fact, Green argues, "It is surely undeniable that Lawrence was working in the same direction and the same mode of thought as Bachofen," for though the English writer may never have read *Mother Right*, "Frieda's incarnation and enactment of the matriarchal idea" would have been powerfully significant to him.[39] In any case, however, as I have tried to show, the vision of woman as potentially a "giantess" was both new and crucial, so much so that even without the filtering through of specific concepts from Die Kosmiche Runde Lawrence would have been as struck as many other modernists were by a transformed sense of the implications of female sexuality. Thus, in combination with his sense of female domination in both private and public history, it was this vision of woman's primacy that finally determined the nature of the biomyths he himself can be said to have made in response to (and in defense against) all these factors. For as Bruce Clarke observes in a fine meditation on the way in which "Lawrence's sexual affiliations are exquisitely conflicted," this phallic philosopher's "word-demon is a male grasped by a female principle, a logos spermatikos both possessed and empowered by the womb."[40]

Exploring the "female principle," Lawrence wrote a novella not long after experiencing the unmanning trauma of World War I, a work that perfectly illustrates the paradigmatic sexual paradoxes that

[39]For the connections between Lawrence, Die Kosmiche Runde, and Bachofen, see Martin Green, *The Von Richthofen Sisters: The Triumphant and the Tragic Modes of Love* (New York: Basic, 1974), especially 73, 84, 343. Anne Smith also observes that Frieda's principles were consistently matriarchal, quoting her remark in *Not I, But the Wind* that "a man is born twice: first his mother bears him, then he has to be reborn again from the women he loves" as well as her equally important insight that "in his heart of hearts [Lawrence] always dreaded women, felt that they were in the end more powerful than men" (p. 37).

[40]Bruce Clarke, "'The Woman Not Fit to Be Seen': D. H. Lawrence and the Maternal Sublime," 5; I am grateful to Clarke for sharing this interesting essay with me.

he also recorded in many other stories, poems, and essays. "The Ladybird" was first published in 1923 in a volume that included as well "The Fox" and "The Captain's Doll," two more novellas about the relationship between female power and male anxiety or anger. Set in war-torn London around 1918, it is the tale of a mystical and mysterious encounter between a small, dark, "elfish" German prisoner of war named Count Johann Dionys Psanek and a tall blonde English beauty named Lady Daphne Apsley. Because she is Daphne and he is Dionys, because she is flowerlike and pale, while he is dark and lordly with a "devil" of rebellion in his blood, the tale has frequently been read as yet another of Lawrence's "leadership" fictions, and in this light (or darkness) as yet another Lawrencian revision of the ancient myth of the marriage of Pluto and Persephone, a romance with which the author of *The Plumed Serpent* had long been obsessed. And certainly the Pluto-Persephone marriage of darkness, with its mystification of phallic power, is an important motif in "The Ladybird." What is just as important, however, is an exposition of female power, power that is shown as essential for and prior to the Plutonic myth of male energy. In fact, in "The Ladybird" Lawrence clearly, if not consciously, suggests that female power creates male energy.

The story itself can be easily summarized. Daphne's mother, Lady Beveridge, has lost her two sons and her brother in the war, but like a philanthropic "Mater Dolorosa," she persists in visiting a prison-hospital where the "enemy sick and wounded" are incarcerated. There she encounters Count Johann Dionys Psanek, whom she had known before the war, and there she soon brings her daughter, of whom Dionys had once been fond: for Daphne's seventeenth birthday, in fact, Dionys had given the girl a thimble decorated with the Psanek crest, "a gold snake at the bottom, and a Mary-beetle of green stone at the top."[41] Now, however, the imprisoned aristocrat appears to have been fatally wounded, and Daphne herself is ill, her husband Basil "missing in the East," her baby "born dead," and her "two darling brothers dead." Nevertheless, she begins regularly to visit Dionys and, as she does, both slowly recover their strength. Daphne, in particular, who has from the first seemed "looming" by comparison with the delicately formed Count, takes on healing power, so that Dionys begs her to "let me wrap your hair round my hands like a bandage," explaining that "I feel I have lost my manhood for the time being." Finally, reminding her of the gift he had given her when she was a

[41] "The Ladybird," in *Four Short Novels of D. H. Lawrence* (1923; reprint, New York: Viking, 1965), 60. Page numbers in my text refer to this edition.

girl, he asks her to sew him some shirts, using the Psanek thimble. After some difficulty, she does this and then sews some shirts for her wounded husband, Basil, who has now been found and released through a prisoner exchange.

A handsome Englishman, Basil is "the true Dionysos," thinks Daphne, "full of sap, milk and honey, and northern golden wine." When he returns from the war, scarred and strange, she devotes herself to him, though she is somewhat frightened by his worshipful passion. Eventually, however, she takes him to see Count Dionys, and, oddly enough, the two become friends, although, even more oddly, their relationship only prospers when Daphne is in their presence "to complete the circuit" (p. 91). After the armistice of 1918, Dionys is freed, and Basil invites him to visit Thoresway, the ancestral home of Daphne's family. There Daphne hears him crooning ancient songs in his room at night and, drawn irresistibly to "the thin thread of his singing" (p. 100), she goes to him in the dark and they consummate their mystic marriage. At the tale's end, he leaves to return to his homeland but promises her that he will await her in the kingdom of death, for though she is still by day the wife of Basil Apsley, she has become "the night-wife of the ladybird" (p. 109).

Obviously, with what F. R. Leavis calls its tone of "solemn poetic—even prophetic—elevation,"[42] this consciously legendary and carefully symbolic story intends to convey a number of messages. Thus, the shadowy coupling of Daphne and Dionys suggests the mystic marriage of Pluto and Persephone, while the tense friendship of Basil and Dionys functions as a neo-Nietzschean comment on the Apollonian and Dionysian modes of being that the two men incarnate. Glowing and golden, polyandrous Daphne's day-husband is a lucid young man whose way of thinking is purely Apollonian—rational, spiritual, transcendent—so that her temporary identification of him with Dionysos seems ironically mistaken. His name, Basil, means royal or kingly—again, Apollonian—but also associates him with both the medicinal herbs of Apollo and the pot of basil in which Keats's Isabella kept the severed (that is, the disembodied) head of her lover. Conversely, and not surprisingly, if Basil is Apollonian, Dionys is Dionysian. His full name, Johann Dionys Psanek, is one to which he is so intensely attached that the humiliation of defeat causes him to want to change it, and indeed, each part of the name reinforces its almost liturgical significance. "Johann," or "John," for example, recalls both the John who prophesied in the wilderness and the John who envisioned the

---

[42]F. R. Leavis, *D. H. Lawrence: Novelist* (London: Chatto & Windus, 1955), 56.

Bible's Apocalypse. But the Count's other two names tell us that this John is not a prophet of the Law of the Father but of the transformative Rule of the Mother. For "Dionys" does not just recall but literally signifies the darkly demonic fertility god of *The Bacchae,* and "Psanek" means "outlaw" (as Lawrence pointedly tells us), intensifying the air of Dionysian lawlessness and irrational sensual/Satanic energy that clings to this small, "aboriginal"-seeming and somewhat animal-like Middle European aristocrat.

Our sense of Dionys's hellish, anti-Apollonian power is also enhanced by a number of passages that link him with Dracula, the demonic vampire who had long been a Dionysian/Gothic fixture not just in Bram Stoker's novel but also in countless theaters by the time Lawrence wrote "The Ladybird." For instance, besides coming, like Dracula, from "one of those curious . . . aboriginal races of Central Europe," Dionys has "something ages old in his face" (p. 50) and confesses that "I would not mind if they buried me alive, if it were very deep, and dark, and the earth heavy above" (p. 53). Several times, moreover, we are told, as we are about Dracula, that Dionys has "strong white teeth that [seem] a little too large, rather dreadful" (p. 68). And like Count Dracula (whose name is significantly similar to his), Count Dionys belongs by inheritance to a secret society, a night cult that believes "we've got the world inside out. The true living world of fire is dark, throbbing, darker than blood. Our luminous world that we go by is only the reverse of this" (p. 67). Finally, indeed, like both the classical Dionysos and the Victorian Dracula, Count Dionys is a votary of the mysteries of the blood, a prince or priest of what Lawrence was eventually to call "blood-knowledge, the great dark knowledge you can't have in your head."[43]

But as Dionysos's female followers knew, as Frazer, Harrison, and others noted, as the story of Dracula's arrival in England on a ship called the *Demeter* suggests, and as—in spite of his overt phallocentrism—Lawrence shows in "The Ladybird," the mysteries of the blood are female mysteries: they are the rites of female creativity. (In fact, as intellectual categories even the Nietzschean concepts of "Apollonian" and "Dionysian" modes of being are notions borrowed from Bachofen's analysis of "Mother Right.")[44] Thus, behind the screen of masculinist rhetoric with which Lawrence surrounds handsome, Apollonian Basil and pharaoh-dark Dionysian Dionys, "The Ladybird" is a tale of female power, a story of how tall, moon-pale, flower-

[43]See Lawrence, *Studies,* 90.
[44]See George Boas, preface to Bachofen, xx–xxi.

ing Daphne sews both her war-torn husbands together using a thimble whose crest of snake and ladybird symbolizes the archaic transformative energy of the Great Mother.

From the first, Daphne is associated with a strong maternal line. She has lost her two brothers and her uncle, and she frequently appears alone in the company of her "Mater Dolorosa," whose husband, a gloomy and feckless Earl, is always "standing aside, in the shadow" (p. 93). Quite early in the story, too, Lawrence describes "the curious distraught slant of her eyes [that] told of a wild energy dammed up inside her"—the furious energy, we soon infer, of a Maenad, a participant in female mysteries whose powers have been denied outlet in a war-torn, Apollonian/patriarchal society. Later, moreover, Basil calls her—besides Venus, Aphrodite, and Proserpine—Astarte, Cybele, and Isis, a "long, limber Isis with sacred hands." Though there is some indication that Lawrence is trying to undermine Basil by sardonically suggesting that he is a mere woman worshiper, we must ultimately—as Lawrence himself once remarked—trust the tale, not the teller. And this tale tells us that Daphne *is* a kind of Isis, a mothergoddess who, having lost her own child, recreates him in the shape of small, perfectly formed Count Dionys, the demonic scion of the womb of night.

"I have lost my soul, and I can't stop talking to you," cries Dionys to Daphne on one of the occasions when she comes to the hospital to "put" him in the sun. Imprisoned first in her country and later in her ancestral home, he is continually at her mercy throughout the tale. In fact, though he tells Daphne that she almost looks as though "the Evil One" had cast a spell on her, he himself, in his imprisoned passivity, seems like the one on whom a spell has been cast, the one who is inescapably at Daphne's womanly mercy. But most of all he is at her mercy in his need for her to perform the central ritual of sewing by which, and only by which, he is ultimately to be recreated.

"Sew me a shirt that I can wear," he begs Daphne, explaining that "I am a prisoner in other people's clothes, and I have nothing of my own." His urgent, almost prayerful request implies that in "losing his shirt" he has somehow lost both his essential body and his essential identity, his shape and his name. Like Osiris, another ruler of the dark underworld kingdom of whom he is also an avatar, he has been unmanned and fragmented by his enemy; like John the Baptist, as well as Keats's "basil," he has been figuratively speaking decapitated or castrated, and he can only be restored through the creative activity of this moon-luminous woman who is not just Basil's but his own "long limber Isis." She it is who must sew together the scattered pieces, she who must recreate the lost bruised phallus that exists—so the myth implies even if Lawrence refuses to admit it—for her, rather than she for it. For if, like Osiris's Greek parallels Orpheus and Dionysos, or like the prophet who was Salome's victim, Dionys might once have been rended by women (by, for instance, the indifferent wife who left him during the war), he can also only be mended by women. Indeed, Dionys's descriptions of his family make his heritage sound quite as matrilineal and matriarchal as Daphne's, since the chief Psanek (or "outlaw") tradition he mentions is the one in which "my mother sewed for me. And after her, my mother's sister, *who was the head of my house*" (p. 61, emphasis added). No father is mentioned, no brothers, no uncles. Only the mother and the matrilineal aunt, a spinning sisterhood who worked with the *lady*bird, or "Marienbeetle," at their fingers and embroidered that symbol onto the Dionysian young man's shirts.

Interestingly, Dionys describes himself as going like a bride to his marriage with a sort of dowry of sixty shirts, provided by his mother and his aunt. Thus when tall Daphne finally mates with this dark doll of a prisoner, it seems natural to think of him as *her* consort, a son/lover whom she has first birthed and then wed in the tradition of the Great Mother that speculative anthropologists from Bachofen to Neumann describe so well. In this connection, it is significant that Frazer (whose *Golden Bough* might have been one of Lawrence's sources for information about Dionysos) recounts a version of the Dionysos story in which Persephone is the god's *mother,* and another version of the story in which "Demeter, his mother, pieced together his mangled limbs and made him young again."[45] Similarly, Harrison (whose *Prolegomena* might have been another of Lawrence's sources) observes that "an important feature of Dionysiac religion was the rending and death of the god" and notes also that "there was some sort of resurrection of the god, a new birth as a little child," for despite the patriarchal revisionism that was later to describe the infant vine god as reborn from Zeus's thigh, "it is at once a cardinal point and a primary note in the mythology of Dionysos that he is the son of his mother."[46] Taken together, all these allusions and images suggest that Daphne is not Persephone as daughter but Persephone/Demeter/Isis as mother: she is the mother goddess, Dionys is the priest of

[45]Sir James Frazer, *The New Golden Bough* (New York: Mentor, 1954), 420.

[46]Harrison, 461; 403; later Harrison observes, "The interesting thing about Dionysos is that, develop as he may, he bears to the end, as no other god does, the stamp of his matriarchal origin. He can never rid himself of the throng of worshipping women, he is always the nursling of his Maenads" (p. 561).

maternal darkness; she is the Great Mother, Dionys the diabol-
ical/Dionysian child whom the divine woman in her "indomitable"
calm sometimes chooses as consort.

Finally, in fact, this English Isis is not only a revisionary Daphne but
also, just as importantly, a version of Ariadne, the bride of Dionysos
who spins and guards the sacred thread, the clue to the passage of
blood that is the labyrinth of birth and death. Only, as Lawrence
characterizes her, despite (or perhaps because of) his anxiety about
the mother goddess, this Ariadne does not merely rescue the Apollonian Theseus (to whom Basil bears some likeness); she also rescues
Dionysos, rather than being rescued by him. Thus, in their helpless
dependence on her maternal stitchery, both the dark husband and
the light husband, the ruler of the day and the night king, are brothers under the skin. Without her, neither has power. With her to "close
the circuit" of their brotherhood, they are energetic companions. For
like Demeter—about whom Harrison reminds us that "the Mother
herself keeps ward in the *metro*polis of the dead" and therefore "the
Athenians of old called the dead 'Demeter's people'"[47]—Daphne
rules both realms and enables her consorts to see that, in the creative
embrace of the mother, death and eternity might well become, as
Basil says, "the same thing" (p. 109).

What reinforces this argument about Daphne's creative authority is
the fact that, besides the Greek myths that obviously play so important
a part in any consciously literary tale about people named Daphne
and Dionys, another story lies behind or within the plot of "The
Ladybird." Appropriately enough for a novella about a German prisoner of war, it is a Grimm German fairytale entitled "The Six Swans."
And unlike many of the better-known Grimm stories, which are so
often about helpless maidens such as"Snow White" and "Sleeping
Beauty," this one is a story about female power. Specifically, and
centrally, it is about the power of a princess whose six brothers have
been transformed into swans by a wicked stepmother and who alone
has the ability to redeem their humanity by sewing them "six little
shirts of starwort,"[48] which will change them back into princes, a task
that, after many trials, she accomplishes. But "The Six Swans" is also
about other manifestations of female power. Fearing the animosity of
his new queen, for instance, the children's royal father has hidden
them away so deep in the forest that he himself can only find them

[47]Ibid., 267.
[48]See "The Six Swans," in *The Complete Grimm's Fairy Tales*, (1944; reprint, New York:
Random House, 1972), 232–37.

with the aid of a magic ball of yarn given him by a wise woman—an emblem of female knowledge that recalls Ariadne's power over the labyrinth. In addition, the malevolent queen who is the story's villainess manages the first metamorphosis of the young princess by herself sewing magic shirts that turn them *into* swans—a point suggesting that the bodies of the boys have become passive artifacts in a duel between two spinning seamstresses, a good fate and an evil fate.

Finally, then, this resonant German folktale is in some sense an extended meditation on what Bachofen called "the spinning and weaving of the great nature mothers," on the "thread" of life over which the female has ultimate control, and on the primordial authority of the maternal seamstress, from whom, in the view of early religion, all creatures "have the subtle web of their body, which she fashioned with unparalleled mastery in the dark womb of matter."[49] In particular, the central symbolic act of sewing, performed by the swans' sister, is here, as Daphne's sewing is in "The Ladybird," the ultimate sign of female creativity. Like Isis putting her brother/lover Osiris back together again, like Demeter reconstructing her son Dionysos, the swans' sister does for her brothers what all the *King's* horses and all the King's *men* could not do for that sad egg Humpty Dumpty: she brings about a resurrection.

Significantly, moreover, the swans' sister's mode of re-creation is neither passive nor receptive, as woman's sexual/maternal power was traditionally thought to be. On the contrary, while her brothers are helpless in the grip of circumstances, the young seamstress seeks and seizes their salvation, using active transformative energies to make something new and magically alive—new shirts, new bodies—from apparently inert materials. Finally, too, it is significant that even those materials may not be quite as inert as they seem, that they are both biologically alive and uniquely hers. In fact, it seems like still another emblem of maternity that this modest yet potent Griselda creates the boys' fleshly costumes of humanity not from ordinary cloth but from flowers that grow in a forest where women and women alone—she, the wise woman, her stepmother—hold sway.

To be sure, "The Six Swans" does define the swans's sister as a kind of "Griselda"—she must be silent while she sews, she is assaulted by a kind of wicked stepmother, and so on—and thus hedges her round with doubts and fears, anxieties and contradictions, but her power is nevertheless there, crucial, incontrovertible. And to Lawrence such power seemed equally crucial and incontrovertible, though he fre-

[49]Bachofen, 56.

quently tried to seal it off from consciousness or at least to fence it in with deceptively phallocentric rhetoric. Yet that Dionys must beg Daphne to sew his shirts using a thimble crested with a ladybird and a snake, an emblem of the goddess together with the priapic creature that was traditionally her attendant, tells us that, at least in the part of his mind that thought in symbols, Lawrence knew whose power he was confronting in this story. Moreover, there is even some indication that, consciously or not, he may have been thinking not just of the myth of Dionysos but also of the fairytale of "The Six Swans" when he imagined his confrontation of maternal creativity. For toward the end of "The Ladybird," Dionys calls Daphne to him—invokes her, as a priest would his deity—by singing a song about the king of the *swans,* whose bride had left him for a human but who "called her to come back, *or else he would die*" (p. 102, emphasis added), and she is drawn by the "thin thread of *his* singing," a defensive displacement of the female fate symbol that nevertheless suggests he is about to give her another opportunity for re-creative sewing even while it also recalls both Ariadne's thread and the wise woman's ball of yarn in "The Six Swans." Finally, therefore, though the mythic transformations in Dionys's song are different from those in Grimm's story, the theme of the swan's redemption and restoration through the primacy of the ladybird of female potency is exactly the same in both the old fairytale and the modern novella.

Haunted by female primacy, how did Lawrence establish his own personal and literary authority over against the power of the woman upon whom he saw himself as, like all men, dependent for life and limb? To begin with, more than most modernists—perhaps because he had had so famously and for so long to struggle for emotional freedom from both the specter and the reality of his own mother—he frankly revealed his dependency on the creative energy of symbolic mothers such as Daphne Apsley. At the same time, however, he enacted his dread of female power and fought to liberate himself from its threat to his autonomy with special inventiveness and fervor. Thus, no doubt influenced by the real rise in female assertiveness that accompanied the birth of the feminist movement and the entrance of women into the professions, as well as by the work of mythographers like Bachofen, Frazer, and Harrison, he conceded in his late essay on "Matriarchy" that "we are drifting into" a state of "Mother-rule": "No good trying to stem the tide. Woman is in flood." Yet even while he affirmed that "it is nothing but just" if women "form themselves into a great clan, for the preservation of themselves and their children," he also proposed a kind of masculinist separatism brought about through the revitalization of the primitive institution of the men's house, arguing that men need "a new foregathering ground, where they can meet and satisfy . . . deep social needs . . . which can only be satisfied *apart from women*" (emphasis added). The polarities articulated here—on the one hand, a reluctant acquiescence in female authority, on the other hand, a resistant attempt at independence of female authority—were paradigmatic throughout his literary career. For, with Goethe's Faust, Lawrence early knew that the time had come for him, as for most of his contemporaries, to encounter "The Mothers" and their meaning: "The unacceded, / The inaccessible . . . , the never-pleaded" fact of female creative energy. But, also with Faust, he might have almost involuntarily exclaimed, "The Mothers! Still it strikes a note of fear. / What is this word that I am loathe to hear?"[50]

From *Sons and Lovers* through *Women in Love* and *Lady Chatterley's Lover*, therefore, Lawrence enacted a profound ambivalence toward both real mothers and Great Mothers. The Paul Morel who devoutly promises his mother that "I'll never marry while I've got you"[51] is paradoxically identical, after all, with the Paul Morel who achieves his (and her) "release" from the matriarchal bonds of their love by feeding her a "bitter" draught of poisoned milk. Similarly, the Lawrence who, in a curious inversion of Hopkins's vision of infertile "hens' eggs," wrote to Gordon Campbell in 1914 that "there is no getting of a vision before we get ourselves *fertilized by the female*"[52] (emphasis added) is the same novelist who was, a year later, to create the dramatic scene in which Rupert Birkin, his surrogate self in *Women in Love*, passionately stones the reflection of the moon in Willey Water, muttering "Cybele—curse her! The accursed Syria Dea!"[53]

But it is in later, more overtly allegorical or mythic works that Lawrence's anxieties achieve both their fullest expression and their most imaginative resolution. In "The Captain's Doll," for instance, a novella that appeared in the same volume with "The Ladybird," he told in different terms and with a different emphasis another story about the "shock and fear" that the very name of "the Mothers" inspired in so many modernists. In this tale, however, female creative power is more bitterly described, and it is definitively defeated. The

---

[50]Goethe, *Faust*, pt. 2, act I, ll. 6223–24, 6265–66.

[51]Lawrence, *Sons and Lovers* (New York: Random House, 1922), 288.

[52]*The Collected Letters of D. H. Lawrence*, ed. Harry T. Moore (New York: Viking, 1962), I, 291.

[53]Lawrence, *Women in Love* (New York: Penguin, 1978), 238.

doll of the story, for instance, is not a soldier's girlfriend, as the title may suggest. Rather, it is a playful miniature effigy that Hannele— Countess Johanna zu Rassentlow, an aristocratic German doll-maker—has made of Alexander Hepburn, a Scottish officer with whom she is in love. Hepburn is married to a domineering but genteel little woman very much like Mrs. Morel in *Sons and Lovers* or Law-rence's own mother. When this woman discovers the doll in the Countess's shop, she tries to buy it. Thus the love triangle in which the two women are engaged in a struggle for possession of the captain soon becomes also a triangle in which these sinister "mothers" battle for the doll to which they have reduced him.

By the end of the story, however, Hepburn's wife is dead ("fallen" from a third-story window under suspicious circumstances) and Hannele has lost the doll. In a ritual climb up a very female-sounding glacier not unlike the Swiss "Mer [*Mère*] de Glace," Hepburn tri-umphs over the "gills" and clefts, the "immense depths" and crevices in the "huge body of the soft-fleshed ice," the body, so it seems, of the "Terrible Mother." And informing the repentant Hannele that he now wants "a sort of *patient Griselda* [emphasis added], I want to be honoured and obeyed. I don't want love," he exacts her promise that she will go with him to Africa. There he is, significantly enough, planning to "do a book on the moon" that will no doubt be a scientific attempt to murder the mother goddess by dissecting her.[54]

Rather differently, but with a similar intent, two poems from Law-rence's great middle-period collection, *Birds, Beasts and Flowers,* deal specifically but defensively with the Eleusinian mysteries and with "the female mystery" of the "ripe womb." In the first, "Purple Anem-ones," the flowers of "Sicily, on the meadows of Enna," are charac-terized variously as "hell-hounds" or "little hells of colour" that have "risen in pursuit" of the "husband-snared hell-queen," Persephone, who is trying in vain to return to her mother.[55] Revising Eleusis to update it, the poet describes "Madame Ceres" and her daughter as "two enfranchised women" and warns them that "the enemy is upon you." Clearly, despite the concessions he was later to make in his essay on "Matriarchy," he has not the slightest sympathy here for "Poor Persephone and her rights for women." At the same time, however, he is almost feverishly aware how vigorous a defense he himself, and the male "husband-blossoms" that he makes into his agents, must

---

[54]Lawrence, "The Captain's Doll," in *Four Short Novels*, 262, 264.
[55]"Purple Anemones," in *The Complete Poems of D. H. Lawrence,* ed. Vivian de Sola Pinto and Warren Roberts (New York: Viking, 1964), I, 307–309.

conduct against the "Mother Right" that these two goddesses represent. *"At 'em, boys, at 'em! . . . Smell 'em, smell 'em out!"* he snarls, his words italicized as if to emphasize the strenuousness that must mark the male hunt for patriarchal authority in a possibly matriarchal new age.

Again, with the same fervor but with an even deeper acquiescence in the transformative "secret" implicit in the "inward" flowering of the "ripe womb," he writes in "Figs" of that fruit's "symbolic" power, its "covert nakedness, / where," as if in an illustration of the discoveries of nineteenth-century embryologists, "everything happens invisible, flowering and fertilisation and fruiting."[56] Yet here, too, he has to defend himself against the secret, sacred power of the "female mystery," and he does so by predicting the inexorable corruption implicit in that mystery. When the fig is "over-ripe," "she" bursts "to give up [her] ghost," and becomes a kind of "prostitute . . . , making a show of her secret." Worse still, like that emblematically female fruit, modern women, with their demands for matriarchal power, have "fallen over-ripe" and "bursten into self-assertion." But, insists Lawrence, "ripe figs won't keep," so by analogy, assertive women, like their matriarchal foremothers, are doomed to a rottenness in which their rule will inevitably be superseded by the less fleshly, more transcendent state that Bachofen called "Father Right" and that Jacques Lacan has more recently called "the Law of the Father."

Finally, however, Lawrence could not remain content with purely polemical defenses like those he mounted in "Figs" and "Purple Anemones" and, to a lesser extent, in "The Captain's Doll," for his sense of the primacy of female power was too haunted and haunting to allow him, given the aesthetic honesty that characterized so much of his writing, to escape for long into rhetorical rationalization. Thus, in the complex of late works constituted by *The Escaped Cock, Lady Chatterley's Lover,* and *Etruscan Places,* he affirms matriarchal authority more humbly than ever before while definitively creating the only theology that he can imagine to oppose it: the religion of the phallus. "The goddess is great," concedes the risen "Jesus" of *The Escaped Cock* on his first encounter with the priestess of Isis who will resurrect his fallen manhood, and later "Great is Isis!" he exclaims. "In her search she is greater than death. . . . All men praise thee, Isis, thou greater than the mother unto man."[57] Yet this story, which celebrates "the

---

[56]"Figs," in *Complete Poems,* I, 282–84.

[57]Lawrence, *The Escaped Cock,* ed. Gerald M. Lacy (1929; reprint, Santa Barbara: Black Sparrow, 1978), 41, 45. Page numbers in the text refer to this edition.

mysterious fire of a potent woman" (p. 52) and the "fulness of the woman . . . , the soft white rock of life" (p. 57) was also, according to Earl Brewster, called *The* Escaped *Cock* (emphasis added) because it was inspired by "a little shop, in the window of which was a toy white rooster *escaping* from an egg"[58] (emphasis added). For Lawrence, obviously, that "toy" cock became a triumphant phallus that, anxiously asserting (with "the man who died") that "I am risen," he set against what he really believed to be the primal power of the womb.

Indeed, it might even be said that, for Lawrence, the phallus almost always functions as a kind of substitute baby, in an ironic reversal of Freud's dictum that for women the baby functions as a kind of substitute phallus. Miniature but autonomous, it is "his" mysterious product even while it has its own separate life, its own separate and nameable identity ("John Thomas"). As "Jesus" punningly cries "I am risen" in *The Escaped Cock*, he feels, just as punningly, "his own sun [son] daw[n], and sen[d] its fire running along his limbs" (p. 57). Similarly, in *Lady Chatterley's Lover*, where the paralyzed Clifford Chatterley has been definitely immobilized by the seductions of the Magna Mater in the person of Ivy Bolton, the sexually victorious Mellors croons to his John Thomas as a woman might to her child. "Ay, ma lad," he murmurs, "tha'rt theer, right enough. Yi, tha mun rear thy head! Theer on thy own, eh? an 'ta'es count o' nob'dy?" reminding his baby/phallus of "his" origins ("tha's dipped me in again") even as he nurses "his" individuality ("Art boss of me?").[59] At the end of that novel, moreover, when Connie is left, like the priestess of Isis in *The Escaped Cock*, satisfyingly pregnant, the book's hero can do no more than ask her to meet him at an allegorical tavern hopefully called "The Golden Cock in Adam Street."

Finally, in *Etruscan Places*, viewing and reviewing the very tombs that had inspired Bachofen's ideas about "The Three Mystery Eggs" less than a century earlier, Lawrence perfunctorily acknowledged the powers of the womb ("the ark of the covenant, in which lies the mystery of eternal life"),[60] the egg ("the egg of resurrection, within which the germ sleeps as the soul sleeps in the tomb" [p. 45]), and the egg-like "*patera* or *mundum*" ("the plasm . . . of the living cell, with its nucleus, which is the indivisible God of the beginning and . . . which yet divides and subdivides" [pp. 29–30]) but devoted his closest atten-

[58]Quoted by Lacy in *The Escaped Cock*, 136.

[59]Lawrence, *Lady Chatterley's Lover* (The Hague: Heinemann, 1956), 193.

[60]Lawrence, *Etruscan Places*, in *D. H. Lawrence and Italy* (New York: Viking, Compass Books, 1972), 14; page numbers in the text refer to this edition.

tion to the phallus, which he saw as both born from and standing against these female symbols. Unlike Bachofen—almost, in fact, as if responding to Bachofen—he declared that "the thing that impresses one in the very first five minutes . . . in an Etruscan necropolis [is] the phallic symbol" (p. 13), and as he journeyed deeper into the tombs, he saw that symbol manifested in divine creatures like the dolphin ("carrying the fiery spark of procreation down into the wet darkness of the womb" [p. 53]) and the "hot, soft, alert duck" ("symbol of a man's own phallus and phallic life" [p. 54]) as well as, more grandiosely, in the Etruscan kings "who are gods by vividness, because they have gathered into themselves core after core of vital potency from the universe" (p. 51) and the Etruscan institution of the "*Lucumo . . .* , sitting very noble in his chariot driven by an *erect* charioteer" (emphasis added, p. 59), the Lucumo who was "divine . . . within another world of power." That last phrase, indeed, is a crucial one, for Lawrence ultimately and rather desperately opposed to the authoritative "Ladybird" of female creativity "another world of power" whose source was fictive and whose trappings were elaborately fictionalized. In that gesture, conceding the primacy of the "second sex" and the secondariness of the "first sex," the authority of the female and the otherness of the male, he formulated a defense against the Great Mother that male modernists from Yeats and Joyce to Eliot and Stevens also attempted to raise.

Certainly Yeats, despite (or perhaps because of) his years of ambivalent devotion to the powerful Maud Gonne, raised such defenses even while making similar concessions. Throughout his middle and late career, of course, he consistently drew upon the metaphysical "system" of *A Vision,* which, as if anticipating the Celtic matriarchalism of Graves's *The White Goddess,* he had based upon the "phases of the moon." But particularly in a late poem called "The Crazed Moon," he analyzed the specifically maternal primacy of *his* white goddess, describing the contrast between a rotting matriarchal age (like the world of Lawrence's "Figs") in which "Crazed through much child-bearing / The moon is staggering in the sky" so that her male as well as female subjects are "moon-struck by the despairing glances of her wandering eye," and the days of the moon/woman's primordial authority, when "in all her virginal pride" she "trod on the mountain's head" and "every foot obeyed her glance!"[61] Again, in "To Dorothy Wellesley," a poem from almost the same period, Yeats

[61]W. B. Yeats, "The Crazed Moon," in *The Complete Poems of W. B. Yeats* (New York: Macmillan, 1955), 237; page numbers in the text refer to this edition.

assured a woman writer whose work he much admired that she should await a visit from (in a phrase echoing the revisionary evaluations of the *Oresteia* formulated by Jane Harrison) "that great family / Some ancient famous authors misrepresent, / The Proud Furies, each with her torch on high" (pp. 301–302).

At the same time, however, Yeats was as ambivalent as Lawrence about the resurrection of the Furies. If his Cuchulain was at one point redeemed by the matriarchal energies of his motherly wife, Emer, that hero was also destroyed by the insidious intentions of Terrible Mothers like the warrior Queen Aoife and the crow-headed death goddess, the Morrigu. Furthermore, for his own daughter Yeats famously wished nothing more than that she should become a "flourishing *hidden* tree" (emphasis added), a beautiful but modest Daphne without the primally regenerative creativity of "The Ladybird's" Daphne Apsley. Imagining moments of annunciation and impregnation, moreover, he wishfully transformed virgin mothers into the inert vessels for male authority ("Did she put on his knowledge with his power / Before the indifferent beak could let her drop?") that Apollo had claimed they were in the *Oresteia,* so that not egg but phallus engenders the sexually burning towers and broken walls of history. Finally, and perhaps at his most defensive, he assumed the creative authority of maternity into an ostensibly androgynous but essentially male divinity, celebrating in "Supernatural Songs" the "He"/God who "holds him from desire, all but stops his breathing lest / Primordial Motherhood forsake his limbs" (p. 285).

That last maneuver—the imagining of a sacred male motherhood—is one Lawrence apparently never thought of, but it was an obvious resort for Yeats, who, despite his sense of Leda's dumb passivity, always brooded on the question of the virgin mother's power, wondering "What sacred drama through her body heaved / When world-transforming Charlemagne was conceived?" (p. 286). For his countryman James Joyce, moreover, such a maneuver was almost a first resort. The very Stephen Dedalus who asserts in *Ulysses* that "*Amor Matris* ... may be the only true thing in life" is, after all, merely an older version of the Stephen Dedalus who, at the end of *A Portrait of the Artist as a Young Man*, gives birth to a villanelle conceived in "the virgin womb of the imagination" as if to propose a specifically modernist revision of the old trope of literary maternity.[62] As Joyce's surrogate self, moreover, he is also simply another version of the Richard Rowan who, in a canceled passage from *Exiles*, gives birth to

[62]James Joyce, *A Portrait of the Artist as a Young Man* (New York: Viking, 1969), 217.

his wife and "character" Bertha, and he is an alter ego, too, of the "new womanly man" Leopold Bloom, who, comically exclaiming "O I so want to be a mother," manages in "Nighttown" to bear "eight male yellow and white children . . . with valuable metallic faces" (p. 494) and then is burned as a witch. Finally, in the sense that such fantasies suggest a desire not only to have a womb but to be in a womb, they are associated with characters who share the desire for regeneration not just *as* but *in* the female body that the young James Joyce expressed in a 1909 letter to Nora Barnacle: "O that I could nestle in your womb like a child born of your flesh and blood, be fed by your blood, sleep in the warm secret gloom of your body!"[63]

As Richard Ellmann observes, such an ecstatic vision of a return to the warm stasis of the womb, where the growth of the "manchild" could be facilitated (but not threatened) by the mother's nurturing autonomy, foreshadows Joyce's later subtextual metaphor of Stephen Dedalus as "an embryo," with *A Portrait* being the account of "the gestation of a soul,"[64] and it also prefigures the author's description of Leopold Bloom, returned to Molly's bed, as "the childman weary, the manchild in the womb" (p. 722). At the same time, moreover, it predicts the obsession with embryology that seized the author of *Ulysses* as he labored on the "Oxen of the Sun" section of that novel. As Ellmann notes, and as the physician J. B. Lyons has extensively documented, Joyce intended this episode, set in the Dublin Lying-In Hospital, to suggest that human ontogeny recapitulates linguistic phylogeny by displaying a parallel between the evolution of English style and the development and birth of the "manchild" who is delivered from the prostrate body of one Mina Purefoy at the end of the chapter. Thus he took elaborate notes from a textbook of embryology in order to produce a "gestation chart," which he "kept before him" during the writing of the section; declared that "the art" of the episode was medicine, while its "organ" was the womb; and explained to Frank Budgen that "Bloom is the spermatozoon, the hospital the womb, the nurse the ovum, Stephen the embryo," adding, "How's that for high?"[65] And certainly, in the intensity with which he pursued the conceit of linguistic evolution as embryological growth, Joyce would seem to have carried the trope of literary maternity to new "heights." Implicit in his heightening of that metaphor, moreover, would seem to have been the kind of profound "womb envy" that

[63]James Joyce, *Selected Letters*, ed. Richard Ellmann (New York: Viking, 1975), 169.
[64]Richard Ellmann, *James Joyce* (New York: Oxford University Press, 1982), 297.
[65]Ibid., 475.

Robert Graves, in *Goodbye to All That*, attributes to the nameless Frenchman of whom Graves's mother reported that he "died of grief because he could never become a mother."[66]

Yet even while, like Lawrence, he expressed his dependence on the literary as well as the literal implications of woman's newly empowered biology, Joyce, again like Lawrence, defended himself vigorously against that biology. Unlike Lawrence, he did not set a phallus/baby against the woman's baby/phallus, but as if himself recapitulating the evolution Bachofen postulated for all human society, he did implicitly oppose a "higher" fiction of paternity to the "lower" factuality of maternity. "The progress from the maternal to the paternal conception of man forms the most important turning point in the history of the relations between the sexes," declared Bachofen in his introduction to *Mother Right*, adding:

> Standing in no visible relation to the child [the father] can never, even in the marital relation, cast off a certain fictive character. Belonging to the offspring only through the mediation of the mother, he always appears as the remoter potency [and] discloses an immateriality over against which the . . . nourishing mother appears as matter [so that] the triumph of paternity brings with it the liberation of the spirit from the manifestations of nature.[67]

These words seem almost to gloss, and may well stand behind, the famous meditation on paternity as "a mystical estate, an apostolic succession . . . , a legal fiction" (p. 207) with which Stephen Dedalus introduces his theories about Shakespeare in the "Scylla and Charybdis" section of *Ulysses*. But the assumptions they embody also underlie almost all of Joyce's manifestations of "womb envy," for in every case this neo-Homeric Irishman subverts (as Homer himself might have) what would seem to have been his own inclination to celebrate the principles and powers of Mother Right.

The poem that is "made flesh" in the "virgin womb" of Stephen Dedalus's imagination is, after all, a banal and sentimental villanelle, a parody of some of Yeats's more mannered early works, written in praise of a neoSwinburnian femme fatale. Soon after writing this pastiche, moreover, the artist-hero realizes he must leave both mother and motherland, and, escaping like Lawrence's cock from the egg of his former life, calls upon the proper deity—"old father, old ar-

[66]Robert Graves, *Goodbye to All That* (New York: Doubleday, Anchor Books, 1957), 31.

[67]Bachofen, 109.

tificer"—to "stand" him "in good stead" (pp. 262–63). Similarly, the Bertha whom Richard Rowan conceives and bears in the womb of *his* imagination is a character whose contrived faithlessness attests to his own perversity, in particular his own perverse desire for emasculation. Again, Leopold Bloom's childbearing is almost immediately followed by his scornful juxtaposition of the phrases "Laughing witch!" and "The hand that rocks the cradle" (p. 500), and it is set in the context of a whorehouse ruled by a Circe who is a decidedly Homeric and horrifying temptress, though she might once have been a fertility goddess and her subject pigs might once, as Harrison shows, have been *pharmakoi,* sacred sacrificial animals. Finally, and perhaps most tellingly, Joyce's excursion into embryology in the "Oxen of the Sun" issued in what was perhaps his most powerful defense against female power, for in his schema of literary childbirth—"Bloom . . . the spermatozoon, the hospital the womb, the nurse the ovum, Stephen the embryo"—there was, paradoxically enough, no room whatsoever for Mina Purefoy, the laboring mother, whose son, English literary history, emerges to cheers of "Hoopsa Boyaboy Hoopsa" into the "Allfather's air" (and as the Allfather's heir) with the Carlylean comment that his only begetter, Theodore Purefoy, is "the remarkablest progenitor barring none in this chaffering allincluding most farraginous chronicle" (p. 423).

These virtually simultaneous assertions of dependency and dread exhibited by male modernists like Lawrence, Yeats, and Joyce could easily be traced in the works of many of their contemporaries. Certainly T. S. Eliot revealed a characteristic ambivalence toward the metaphor of literary maternity, and toward the Great Mother whose newly defined potency informed that metaphor, when he replied to Conrad Aiken's praise of his 1920 *Poems* with a page torn from the *Midwife's Gazette* on which were underlined the words "blood, mucus, discharge, purulent offensive discharge,"[68] and certainly he expressed the same ambivalence when he rewrote the *Oresteia* in *The Family Reunion* to force his Harry, Lord Monchensey, to be haunted by the horror of the matriarchal Furies even while, in the same years, he struggled in "Ash Wednesday" to free himself from the sensual seductions of the mother goddess's "brown hair across the mouth blown" and to find a transcendent Mother's "Garden / Where all Love *ends*" (emphasis added). Similarly, Eliot's American antagonist William Carlos Williams seems to have had to cope with an equally

---

[68]Quoted by Conrad Aiken in *Ushant* (New York: Duell; Boston: Little, Brown, 1952), 233.

fierce ambivalence toward female sexual potency. As a practicing physician, after all, he knew as much as any man could about the deliveries and deliverances of birthing women, yet his "Paterson," like Blake's "Albion," is a male spirit of place created in the image of a Father God-like giant.

But perhaps the motions of the mind that marked the work of one apparently unlikely modernist poet can serve to summarize the equivocations of all these men. With his celebrated proclivity for "musing the obscure" and tracing the ambiguities of the relationship between the "blue guitar" of the imagination and the ontological "rock" of reality, Wallace Stevens would seem to have been a philosopher-poet purely detached from the exigencies of sexuality. Yet even while he shaped a paean to the power of the muse, "the one of fictive music" whom he defined as "sister and mother and diviner love," and even while he prayerfully praised the creative authority of a deific woman singing on the shore at Key West ("She was the single artificer of the world / In which she sang"), Stevens gradually began to express ever intenser anxiety about the Great Mother's primal energy, so that, moving through a famously fearful assertion in "Sunday Morning" that "Death is the mother of beauty / Within whose burning bosom we devise / Our earthly mothers, waiting, sleeplessly," he finally arrived, in an extraordinary late poem called "Madame La Fleurie," at a vision of the earth/mother's *vagina dentata* not unlike that expressed in Robert Bly's more recent description of "The Teeth Mother Naked At Last."[69] Dying and returning to the womb/tomb of the figure whom Neumann, before Bly, called "the Terrible Mother," Stevens's poet recognizes that "His grief is that his mother should feed on him, himself and what he saw, / In that distant chamber, a bearded queen, wicked in her dead light" (p. 507). Against such a neo-Bachofian vision of primordial female authority (and female eschatology), he set, like Joyce and like Bachofen himself, a transcendent masculine construct, a "Supreme Fiction" of the (male) poet whose simultaneous alienation from and reimagining of that "fat girl" (p. 406) the sensible world made him explicitly into "major man" (p. 388) and implicitly into a masterful Apollo who represented, like Bachofen's primal father, "the liberation of the [male] spirit from the [female] manifestations of nature."

[69]*The Collected Poems of Wallace Stevens* (New York: Knopf, 1955), 507 and elsewhere as noted in my text; Robert Bly, "The Teeth Mother Naked at Last," in *Sleepers Joining Hands* (New York: Harper, 1973), 18–28.

Because Lawrence was never convinced, as Stevens was, of "The Pure Good of Theory," he never defended himself with such openly metaphysical abstractions against the "Madame La Fleurie" whose hegemony he also acknowledged. Yet his self-preserving maneuvers can be seen as analogous to the American poet's more disguised celebrations of aesthetic "virility." Concretely described, vitally embodied, the Etruscan king toward whom he nostalgically yearns paints himself "vermilion like the throat of dawn" until he is so "red and utterly vivid" that he has become not just, as Lawrence declares, "god's body" but more specifically god's phallus, a phallus whose power to re-engender the ancient texts and textures of the world would seem to offer some hope of reducing Griselda's new potency to passive patience and reachieving the old "mastery that man must hold."[70] At the same time, though, possessed by (rather than possessing) the womb, Lawrence ultimately and explicitly concedes—as Stevens, Yeats, and even Joyce more covertly do—that he must acquiesce in its power. More, if he finally implies that, as he says in "Matriarchy," "man will never be master again," he hints, after much internal struggle, that such a change may be for the best. In one of his last and most poignant poems, in fact, he reimagines himself as a Dionys even weaker and needier than the dark hero of "The Ladybird." Invoking the primal creative energies of the Great Mother, he addresses her lunar avatar—"Moon, O Moon, great lady of the heavenly few"—and begs her to

> give me back my lost limbs
> and my lost white fearless breast
> and set me again on moon-remembering feet
> a healed, whole man, O Moon![71]

To him, as to H. D., Isadora Duncan, James Joyce, and so many other major modernists, it must often have seemed that in the end only "the first deity . . . , the first love, Maia, mama, Mutter" could both cure the body and recreate the soul.

---

[70]Lawrence, "The Woman Who Rode Away," in *The Complete Short Stories*, II, 581.
[71]Lawrence, "Invocation to the Moon," in *The Complete Poems*, II, 695–96.

[8]

He Do the Polis in Different
Voices: Lawrence's Later Style

AVROM FLEISHMAN

A nonspecialist coming to D. H. Lawrence studies must be moved
by the intensity with which his ideas are debated but surprised at how
little is made of his stylistic achievements.[1] When attention is paid, it is
usually to deride or defend the universally acknowledged *badnesses*—
the purple passages, the swatches of slack dialogue and careless narration, the lapses into self-indulgent vituperation. These traits are
occasional flaws in his masterpieces, the great novels of the 1910s, but
in the 1920s, they become endemic, from the labored anathemas of
Aaron's Rod, through the matey sketchings of *Kangaroo* and the mystical mumbo-jumbo of *The Plumed Serpent,* to the explosion of sentimental and sexual explicitness in *Lady Chatterley's Lover.* The local
defenses that are thrown up to blunt these attacks do little to defend
the central position: that Lawrence is a master of English prose,
whose style reaches a new plateau in the 1920s, on which it moves in a
number of exploratory directions after a breakthrough in narrative
art. It is my present purpose to locate this breakthrough as precisely
as possible in time, place, and text and to exhibit its fulfillment in one
novella, *St. Mawr,* yet an adequate study of these developing resources
would justify extended and ongoing treatment.

It is no accident that the great change in Lawrence's style—a dif-

---

[1]An exception is Michael Ragussis, *The Subterfuge of Art: Language and the Romantic
Tradition* (Baltimore: Johns Hopkins University Press, 1978), 172–225. Alan Wilde,
"The Illusion of St. Mawr: Technique and Vision in D. H. Lawrence's Novel," *PMLA* 79
(1964), 164–70, summarizes the state of critical disapprobation of the narrational style
as of its date; unfortunately its own categories for stylistic description (nn. 6 and 10) are
too crude to advance the discussion greatly. It calls due attention to the great change of
style in describing the ranch landscape but misses its opportunities in characterizing the
final ironies.

ference in kind as well as in degree of deviation from standard fictional proprieties—came in the 1920s: not so much because this was a
time of enthusiastic experimentalism in the general shake-up following the first modern holocaust, but because this was the moment of
Lawrence's personal shake-up, following prosecution and persecution
during the war years, which he acted out in self-exile and wandering
for the decade remaining to him. Yet the breaking of the vessels in
life-style and prose style emerges as no simple parallelism or overflow
of life into art; it can be traced more precisely in the languages that
Lawrence spoke and read and in the texts in which he played upon
those languages.

It is well known that he first settled in Sicily (1920), traveled in
Sardinia and returned to Sicily (1921), then took ship for Ceylon,
Australia, Mexico and New Mexico (1922ff.). Another activity of
these years has also been remarked, Lawrence's reading and translating of the fiction of Giovanni Verga: *Mastro-Don Gesualdo* (begun in
Sicily and finished en route to Ceylon, 1922), *Little Novels of Sicily*
(begun in Ceylon and finished in Australia, 1922), and *Cavalleria
Rusticana and Other Stories* (begun in 1922 but finished much later, in
1927).[2] The interest in this literary conjunction has been largely confined to Lawrence's theory and practice of translation, the Italianists
and the Lawrencians staking out predictable positions;[3] meanwhile,
Verga's reputation has risen from that of a period-bound naturalist to
that of a powerful innovator in modern fiction.[4] But the rich poten-
tialities of Verga's technical example for Lawrence—the narrational

[2]See Keith Sagar, *The Art of D. H. Lawrence* (Cambridge: Cambridge University Press,
1966), 118, for a chronology of these writings, later expanded in a separate volume.
Two recent studies of these years are: Leo Hamalian, *D. H. Lawrence in Italy* (New York:
Taplinger, 1982), and Jeffrey Meyers, *D. H. Lawrence and the Experience of Italy* (Philadelphia: University of Pennsylvania Press, 1982).

[3]The poles of the translation controversy may be represented by Giovanni Cacchetti,
"Verga and D. H. Lawrence's Translations," *Comparative Literature* 9 (1957), 333–44,
which deplores Lawrence's cockney equivalents, and G. M. Hyde, *D. H. Lawrence and the
Art of Translation* (London: Barnes & Noble, 1981), which admires his use of his native
Nottingham dialect (p. 41). The ultimate wisdom in this affair is contained in Lawrence's remarks to Elizabeth Mayer, paraphrased in H. T. Moore, *A D. H. Lawrence
Miscellany* (Carbondale: Southern Illinois University Press, 1959), and cited in Hyde:
"Lawrence's advice, . . . therefore, was to avoid both cheap solutions ["to translate the
dialect of the original into another dialect" or "simply verbally to reproduce his dialect"] and try to *invent* a new dialect, . . . preserving the flavour of some sort of relaxed,
uncitified, untutored mode of speaking" (p. 40).

[4]For a useful review of Verga criticism, see Gregory L. Lucente, "Critical Treatments
of Verga and *Verismo:* Movements and Trends (1950–1980)," *MLN* 98 (1983), 129–38.
See also Lucente's *The Narrative of Realism and Myth: Verga, Lawrence, Faulkner, Pavese*
(Baltimore: Johns Hopkins University Press, 1981) for close studies of texts by these
intertextualists.

influences on Lawrence's *fiction*, which go beyond the language experiments of his translations—have not to my knowledge been explored. It is my contention that Lawrence learned something crucial
about narrative method from Verga, that he was linguistically enriched from his translating activities and from living in a meridional
speech community, and that these experiences effect a major transition in his fictional style. In what is perhaps my most questionable
claim, I believe it possible to demonstrate these stylistic changes with
reference not to the lexical and syntactic evidence (although better
qualified linguists will find much to pursue there) but to the level of
narrative voice alone.

Verga's narrational advances, particularly in the novel *I Malavoglia*
(the English translation is called *The House by the Medlar Tree*), have
been thoroughly described by Italian scholars and more recently by
linguistically oriented critics in other countries. Sophisticated studies
have been made of Verga's adaptations of free indirect style to create
a narrator who speaks the collective wisdom of the village that wit-
nesses the protagonists' rise and fall—a communal viewpoint that has
been called a "choric voice."[5] Less recondite but equally fruitful is the
long-standing awareness of the novel's robust employment—also present in the stories that Lawrence translated—of Sicilian folk speech,
producing an ironic copresence of the point of view of the local
culture and the detached stance of the tragic-visioned author. To sum
the matter up, one linguistically informed critic has remarked, "It is
clear that the homology between narrator and narrated on the ideological, psychological and spatio-temporal levels is partly the result of
a lack of differentiation between the two on the phraseological level.
It is this lack of differentiation on the phraseological level which
creates the impression, much commented upon in Verga criticism,
that in *I Malavoglia* there is no narrator who narrates but that the
story seems to narrate itself; that the 'choric voice' of the village takes
the place of the narrator."[6] This emphasis on narration in (or by
incorporating) folk idiom goes beyond the superficial delights of
reading Verga's warmly humorous and sardonically judgmental peasant language. It reveals the underlying medium that produces both
the reader's sense of immediacy (somewhat distorted by calling it
narratorless narration) and the ultimate disjunction that allows him to

[5]Leo Spitzer, "L'originalità della narrazione nei 'Malavoglia,'" *Belfagor* 11 (1956),
43ff.
[6]Michal Peled Ginsburg, "*I Malavoglia* and Verga's 'Progress,'" *MLN* 95 (1980), 82–
103; the passage quoted is from p. 94.

grasp Verga's transcendence of the peasants' mentality while intimately portraying their tragic fate. Yet it does not indicate the modes of discourse by which these effects are accomplished, nor does it seem aware that these modes—and their affective consequences—are already at work in the speech habits of the very society in which the tales are set.

As Leo Spitzer described the habits, they are inveterately conversational, in the double sense that each speaker in a conversation is inclined to incorporate into his discourse the words and phrases of the other, and sometimes those of third parties, in the spirit of mimicry, sarcasm, or other jocular or aggressive ends. I quote Spitzer on the form of incorporation:

> When we reproduce in our own speech a portion of what our conversational partner said, a change of tone inevitably occurs if for no other reason than that the addressers have been shifted around: the words of the "other" in our mouths always sound like something foreign, very often with a mocking, exaggerated, or derisive intonation . . . . we often resort, not only to grammatically incorrect, but even to very daring, sometimes completely impossible constructions for the sole purpose of somehow repeating a part of our partner's speech and giving it an ironic twist.[7]

Do we find ourselves by this detour on the verge of Lawrence's Vergian style, perhaps on the doorstep of his very-bad style? The first prose of his to bear the full marks of his Mediterranean residence is the travel book *Sea and Sardinia* (written and published in 1921).[8] We find there an extended series of reported conversations with Sicilians and Sardinians, in which the appropriation of the "other's" words occurs at a double level: in Lawrence's report and in the conversations themselves. Some examples follow.

> Fortunately or unfortunately [a Sardinian woman's] inquisitiveness got the better of her, and she fell into her native Italian. What were we, where did we come from, where were we going, *why* were we going, had we any children, did we want any, etc. After every answer she nodded her head and said Ahu! and watched us with energetic dark eyes. Then she ruminated over our nationalities and said, to the unseeing witnesses: Una bella coppia, a fine couple. . . . And she said that on a sea voyage

---

[7]Leo Spitzer, *Italienische Umgangssprache* (Bonn: K. Schroeder, 1922), 175; I quote the translation given in the Bakhtin essay cited below, n. 10.

[8]Lawrence, *Sea and Sardinia* (New York: Viking, 1963); page numbers in text below refer to this edition.

one must eat, one must eat, if only a little. But—and she lapsed into
Italian—one must by no means drink wine—no—no! One didn't want
to, said I sadly. Whereupon the grim [steward], whom, of course, we had
cheated out of the bottle we refused to have opened for us, said with a
last sarcasm that wine made a man of a man, etc., etc. [P. 32]

[The ship's carpenter says:] The coal—il carbone! I knew we were in for
it. England—l'Inghilterra she has the coal. And what does she do? She
sells it very dear. Particularly to Italy. Italy won the war and now can't
even have coal. Because why. The price. The exchange! *il cambio.* Now I
am doubly in for it. [P. 48]

The bus-driver, the only one with an earnest soul, was talking of the
Sardinians. Ah, the Sardinians! They were hopeless. Why—because they
did not know how to strike. They, too, were *ignoranti.* But this form of
ignorance he found more annoying. They simply did not know what a
strike was. If you offered them one day ten francs a stint—he was speaking now of the miners of the Iglesias region.—No, no, no, they would
not take it, they wanted twelve francs. Go to them the next day and offer
them four francs for half a stint, and yes, yes, yes, they would take it.
And there they were: ignorant—ignorant Sardinians. [Pp. 114–15]

These passages are typical of the entire work, rich in Lawrencian
ruminations on the passing scene and on his own daemons but also
richly inclusive of the speech of the people he encounters.

The first of these passages runs through all the modes of citing
another's speech: free indirect style ("What were we": marked as such
by the pronoun and tense changes from the original "What are you");
direct discourse ("Ahu!"); indirect discourse ("she said that on a sea
voyage one must eat"). Still more interesting in this passage, as we
shall discover, is the mélange of polyglot conversation: the quoted
Italian ("Una bella coppia"); the indications of switching back and
forth from Italian to the speaker's Sardinian French ("she fell into her
native Italian . . . , she lapsed into Italian"); the English texture of the
narrator's prose, foregrounded at moments when the French or Italian it represents is less vivid than his English equivalents ("One didn't
want to"; "wine made a man of a man"). In the second of the above
passages, extended direct discourse is made more salient by the absence of punctuation indicators and by interspersed remarks of the
first-person narrator; more important, the carpenter's discourse takes
the form of a conversation in which he plays both roles ("And what
does she do? She sells it very dear. . . . Because why. The price."). In
the third of these passages, we reach the situation described by
Spitzer: the bus driver not only conducts a dialogue with himself

("Why—because they did not know how to strike"), but also mocking-
ly incorporates the purported expressions of those whom he describes
("No, no, no . . . yes, yes, yes"). We find, throughout *Sea and Sardinia*,
Lawrence orchestrating a multitude of voices, each one of which is
capable of itself becoming such an orchestrator. Where shall we find a
stylistic terminology adequate to this polyphonic dissonance, one
more enlightening than the musical metaphors presently in play?

A bridge toward such a terminology is provided by the Verga critic
who hears most acutely the doubled voices of his narrators: "The
narrator, I have said, speaks the language of his characters. His narration is *skaz*, in the sense that Bakhtin gave to the word, that is to say
not simply an orientation towards oral discourse, but a discourse with
an orientation towards a foreign word. In the very act of using a
language which is not his own ('foreign word'), Verga dissociates himself from the world he describes, representing it as linguistically, cul-
turally, socially, different from himself."[9] These remarks may be ap-
plied, pari passu, to Lawrence's stance in *Sea and Sardinia*, but it
remains to see whether they extend to his fiction. For that more
complex undertaking, we need the full range of narratological distinctions made by Mikhail Bakhtin, Ginsburg's authority.

For Bakhtin, skaz is only one in a range of narratorial variations
that he groups as "double-voiced": "In all of them discourse maintains a double focus, aimed at the referential object of speech, as in
ordinary discourse, and simultaneously at a second context of discourse, a second speech act by another addresser."[10] These combina-
tions of speech-about-objects and speech-about-speech Bakhtin calls
"dialogical," defining the term in a way that includes what Anglo-
Saxon critics have described in speaking of the "reflector," "unrelia-

---

[9]Ginsburg, 100–101. An instance of Verga's method—in Lawrence's translation—
may be given briefly: "They know how to read and write—that's the trou-
ble . . . . they're made of flesh and blood like their fellow-men, and . . . they've got to go
out and watch to see that their fellow-man doesn't rob them of his time and of his day's
pay. But if you have anything to do with them, they hook you by your name and your
surname . . . , and then you'll never get yourself out of their ugly books any more,
nailed down by debt" ("The Gentry," in *Little Novels of Sicily* [New York: Thomas
Seltzer, 1925], 183; the peasant narrator speaks in his own voice and slang and also
sarcastically incorporates the homiletic voice of the gentry whom he describes ("they're
made of flesh and blood like their fellow-men"). By the combination of the two sets of
clichés, the authorial stance emerges as distinct from both.
[10]"Discourse Typology in Prose," in *Readings in Russian Poetics*, trans. L. Matejka and
K. Pomorska (Cambridge: MIT Press, 1971), 176. I quote the much-cited anthologized
version (to which page numbers in text below refer); the full text of Bakhtin's *Problems
of Dostoevsky's Poetics* has been translated by R. W. Rotsel (Ann Arbor: Ardis, 1973); this
section appears on pp. 153–68.

ble narrator," and other mediated narrations: "The ultimate conceptual authority (the author's intention) is brought out, not in the author's direct speech, but by manipulating the utterances of another addresser, utterances intentionally created and deployed as belonging to someone other than the author" (p. 179). The dialogical varieties include stylization: "The stylizer makes use of another speech act [that is, style] as such and in that way casts a somewhat objectified tint over it . . . . as a consequence, it becomes conventional" (p. 181); skaz: "In the majority of cases skaz is brought in precisely for the sake of a different voice, one which is socially distinct and carries with it a set of viewpoints and evaluations . . . . it is a storyteller who is brought in, and a storyteller is not a literary man; he usually belongs to the lower social strata . . . , and he brings with him oral speech" (p. 183); parody: "Here, too, as in stylization, the author employs the speech of another, but, in contradistinction to stylization, he introduces into that other speech an intention which is directly opposed to the original one. . . . Speech becomes a battlefield for opposing intentions" (p. 185); parodic skaz: "*Skaz* in contemporary literature for the most part has parodic coloring . . . . one speaker very often repeats literally an assertion made by another speaker, investing it with a new intention and enunciating it in his own way" (p. 186: at this point Bakhtin quotes Spitzer on conversational Italian, as cited above); hidden polemic: "Besides its referential meaning, the author's discourse brings a polemical attack to bear against another speech act. . . . That other utterance is not reproduced; it is understood only in its import; but the whole structure of the author's speech would be completely different, if it were not for this reaction to another's unexpressed speech act" (p. 187); and hidden dialogue: "Imagine a dialogue between two persons in which the statements of the second speaker are deleted, but in such a way that the general sense is not disrupted. . . . We feel that this is a conversation of the most intense kind, because each uttered word, in all its fiber, responds and reacts to the invisible partner" (p. 189).

The distinctions may seem plausible and familiar enough, stylization being a standard narrational approach in which the speaker assumes a professional or conventional voice, as in Thackeray or Turgenev (Bakhtin calls this technique, in fiction, "narrator's narration"); skaz was studied by the Russian Formalists in O. Henry and Mark Twain as well as in Gogol and Leskov; parody and parodic skaz are, as Bakhtin says, hallmarks of contemporary literature, ranging from Kafka to Nabokov and taking in most of *Ulysses* and *Finnegans Wake*. "Hidden polemic" and "hidden dialogue" may be more difficult to localize, but it is not necessary to follow up Bakhtin's copious examples in Dostoyevsky to call them to mind: a close study of Lawrence will reveal that *all* of these double-voiced, dialogical situations are in play in his later prose.

It is my larger contention that Lawrence is a grand master of the oral, dialectical, parodic, and polyglot manner that Bakhtin has established for Dostoyevsky and that Lawrence creates in normal English diction an equivalent of the narrational heteroglossia distinguishing encyclopedic authors from Rabelais to Pynchon. Indeed, in at least one text, *St. Mawr,* Lawrence manages an extended construction in what Bakhtin calls "dialogized heteroglossia," the interchange and opposition of competing languages or linguistic registers.[11] Although the canonical instances of this phenomenon occur from antiquity down through modern times, in periods of social change, racial interaction or national convergence, such logomachies as *Gargantua and Pantagruel, Don Quixote,* and *Ulysses* or *Finnegans Wake* suggest that fiction participates in and dramatizes acute cultural-historical transitions. In this context and given its historical moment, Lawrence's worldwide questing and his experiments in sifting and synthesizing various languages in his narration may be seen as an engaged campaign to engender a new language—to answer the question, how shall mankind speak when all the languages have been debased?

"Lou Witt had had her own way so long, that by the age of twenty-five she didn't know where she was. Having one's own way landed one completely at sea."[12] Who speaks these deathless words? Surely not the D. H. Lawrence who could rain down anathemas on Lou's class and on most other stylish moderns. The voice of that very class speaks here and elsewhere in *St. Mawr,* but this is not the only linguistic register to be articulated, nor is this the only mode in which the narrator allows it to appear. His method of imposing a distinctive style on a fictional narration may be called "stylization," with Bakhtin, or even as a case governed by the "Uncle Charles Principle,"[13] in which narration is modulated not by a literary style but by a personal one, the character's. The specific style in question is unique neither to Lawrence nor to *St. Mawr;* Katherine Mansfield's stories of the preceding decade had made much of the society tone and the girlish

[11]Mikhail Bakhtin, "Discourse in the Novel," in *The Dialogic Imagination: Four Essays,* trans. M. Holquist and C. Emerson (Austin: University of Texas Press, 1981).

[12]Lawrence, *St. Mawr and Other Stories,* ed. Brian Finney (Cambridge: Cambridge University Press, 1983), 21; page numbers in text refer to this edition.

[13]Hugh Kenner, *Joyce's Voices* (Berkeley: University of California Press, 1978), 15ff.

clichés in evidence here, similarly creating the effect of identifying with, yet standing beyond, the minds of her characters. This initial and dominant style in *St. Mawr* may be labeled the cosmopolitan style and may be used as a base line from which to measure subsequent modulations and alternative styles.

Almost immediately, an initial modulation is heard: "To be sure for a while she had failed in her grand love affair with Rico . . . . they were a charming married couple. He flirted with other women still, to be sure. He wouldn't be the handsome Rico if he didn't. But she had 'got' him. Oh yes!" (p. 21). These are no longer benign clichés such as "didn't know where she was" or "landed one completely at sea" but the smarmy rhetoric of "grand love affair," "charming married couple," and "she had 'got' him"—even the inoffensive "to be sure" is lowered to an affectation by repetition. From its opening stylization, the narrative discourse turns to *parody*—unless the text is to be considered a pseudonarration by a gossipy habitué of the smart set, in which case we would have parodic skaz. The text suggests as much, inserting a passage in italic type that represents a "society columns" report of Lou and her mother riding in Hyde Park, citing the remark of "somebody," evidently worth heeding, that Lou "might be on the movies" and aligning Lou with these fashionable speakers: "She simply luxuriated in the sun of publicity" (p. 26)—not merely ascribing the attribute but parodying the terms in which she/they would express it.[14]

In the third paragraph, the impression of overhearing a society gossip columnist is accentuated in an extended personal assessment of Lou, one that is particularly attentive to appearances:

> She, with her odd little *museau*, not exactly pretty, but very attractive; and her quaint air of playing at being well-bred, in a sort of charade game; and her queer familiarity with foreign cities and foreign languages; and the lurking sense of being an outsider everywhere, like a sort of gipsy, who is at home anywhere and nowhere: all this made up her charm and her failure. She didn't quite belong. [P. 21]

The class clichés and relaxed colloquialisms are still in evidence, but a new stress is given to the consonance of the social report and Lou's

---

[14]Gossip may seem to stand low in Lawrence's scale of values for discourse, yet it is compared, not unfavorably, with the novel (or the contemporary novel is reduced to its level) in *Lady Chatterley's Lover*, chap. 9 (1928; reprint, New York: Modern Library, n.d.): "The gossip was humiliating. And for the same reason, most novels, especially popular ones, are humiliating too. . . . Nevertheless, one got a new vision of Tevershall village from Mrs. Bolton's talk . . . . it sounded really more like a Central African jungle than an English village" (p. 113).

subjective point of view: for example, "the lurking sense of being an outsider everywhere" (this internal point of view is detectable from the outset, if "didn't know where she was" is taken as a feeling, not a judgment). We gather that the reporting voice is not totally divorced from the character it describes, that its modish clichés as well as its judgmental epithets accord with Lou's dissatisfied sense of herself, and that we are being treated to a superimposition of voice upon voice: the author yielding to the narrator and the latter adopting the style of the prevailing speech community, all the while catching the personal tone of the representative character. All are speaking at once yet are subtly distinguishable in their own right; we shall see these effects magnified in the grand finale. This combination of choric harmony and ironic diversity is foregrounded in the key phrases of the language that describes Lou: she is both "well-bred" and playing at being so, manifesting both "familiarity" and unfamiliarity, both insider and "outsider," both charmingly attuned to and a "failure" in her milieu. "She didn't quite belong"—the theme of alienation is sounded early, in such a way as to specify the careful class distinctions ("not quite") that mark both the character's situation and the prose that describes it. This language is Lou's and her class's, yet "foreign," "gipsy"; the narration is in their linguistic register, but like her it is "odd, quaint, queer"; Lou is a representative of her world but at home "anywhere and nowhere."

In presenting the theme of the half-alienated individual in a false society—the stuff of fiction from the picaresque to the Bildungsroman—in the familiar/unfamiliar diction of that society it-self, Lawrence is not attempting merely the Vergian effect of empa-thy *cum* distantiation. He is also providing the materials from which his tale fashions its dramatic progression, and locating the medium of character change as well. Both the narrative performance and the mimesis of personal growth are to be conducted in the same breath, as it were, and that breath is a set of variations on the cosmopolitan style. To put the claim less abstractly: Lou Witt is to learn a new language in the course of gaining a new consciousness of the world, and the action in which she does so is conveyed in a series of narrative styles that follows a parallel course of development.

In running through a sequence of styles in *St. Mawr*, Lawrence has in view not merely the formalist norm of commensurability of form and content; he enacts the drama of growth in his narrator's activity as well as in his character's career, modifying his modes of discourse to achieve a comparable development in his own voice. The opening paragraphs of this novella, which can be faulted for their tinsel and casualness in the way that much of Lawrence's late prose has been faulted, are redeemed from badness in much the same way that Lou is redeemed—through subtle change to something better. The employment of all the Bakhtinian varieties of storytelling is, therefore, not simply the tour de force of a crafty stylist, but also a way for him to participate in the processes he traces in his imagined world. By joining his authorial voice with the voices of his narrator and character, yet remaining distinct from them—capable of judging their limitations, capable also of leaping out *in propria persona* and filling the air with his private wrath and anguish—Lawrence reenacts the Vergian dialogical in behalf of his own regeneration.

The force that changes Lou's sense of life is, of course, materially embodied in St. Mawr, but we may consider its influence as taking the form of a linguistic shift, one that broadens her language as well as her perspective. For her first perception of the horse's power, the ordinary equestrian categories will no longer serve, and the narrator switches to religious expressions to convey her response: "mysterious," "brilliant" (repeated), "vision," "great darkness," and "demonish" form a metonymic chain leading up to the summative phrase: "his great body glowed red with power" (pp. 30–31). At this point the narrator calls on free indirect style to perform its favored role of implicating both internal and external focalization (to use Gérard Genette's terms), both characterized and omniscient points of view: "What was it? Almost like a god looking at her terribly out of the everlasting dark, she had felt the eyes of that horse; great, glowing, fearsome eyes, arched with a question, and containing a white blade of light like a threat. What was his non-human question, and his uncanny threat? She didn't know. He was some splendid demon, and she must worship him" (p. 31). The question-and-answer form serves not only to summarize Lou's bewildered state of mind but also to reproduce her mental sentences (following the convention of interior-monologue, if not of stream-of-consciousness texts, that the mind works in sentences). "She didn't know" is not merely a narratorial statement about her state of mind but also a transposed form of her presumed sentence, "I don't know," in answer to her own self-question, "what is his . . . uncanny threat?" Yet this passage goes beyond the normal free indirect style of grammatical transformations and dual-voice effect;[15] it also operates on the level of *hidden dialogue*, in

---

[15]The considerable literature on free indirect style leads me to focus on the following: on the history of its scholarship and literary practice, Roy Pascal, *The Dual Voice: Free Indirect Speech and Its Functioning in the Nineteenth-Century European Novel* (Manchester: Manchester University Press, 1977); on its linguistic markers, Roger Fowler,

Bakhtin's terms. Beyond the mental questions and answers that structure the prose is a deeper layer of challenge and response—spiritual-erotic challenge by St. Mawr and commensurate response by Lou. This dialectic is nonverbal, of course, and is only suggested by the questions and answers in Lou's mind and the narrator's prose, but its working is real enough to be described explicitly: "It haunted her, the horse. It had looked at her as she had never been looked at before: terrible, gleaming, questioning eyes arching out of darkness, and backed by all the fire of that great ruddy body. What did it mean, and what ban did it put upon her?" (p. 31) Here the challenge is described as "questioning" and is immediately represented in the form of questions in free indirect style ("What did it mean?"). The question is not merely about the horse; it is the horse's question.

Lou's further inquiries into St. Mawr's nature—which are her responses to his inquiries—are not confined to the level of hidden dialogue but are dramatized in the form of foregrounded linguistic discussions. One instance of explicit dialogue about the hidden dialogue that goes on sotto voce is Lou's conversation with her mother about the nature of man. Mrs. Witt is declared a rationalist not only by her name and manners but also by her distinctive vocabulary, running to terms like "mind," "intelligence," "think," and other items in the philosophical lexicon. Lou systematically questions these and related terms:

> "Man is wonderful because he is able to *think*."
> "But is he?" cried Lou, with sudden exasperation. "Their thinking seems to me all so childish. . . ."
> ". . . no matter what you say, Louise, lack of mind makes the commonplace."
> Lou knitted her brows nervously.
> "I suppose it does, mother.—But men's minds *are* so commonplace. . . ."
> ". . . nevertheless, I shall never alter my belief, that real mind is all that matters in a man, and it's *that* that we women love."
> "Yes mother!—But what *is* real mind? . . . Why can't men get their life straight, like St. Mawr, and then think? Why can't they think quick, mother: quick as a woman: only farther than we do? Why isn't men's thinking quick like fire, mother?" [Pp. 60–61]

Linguistics and the Novel (London: Methuen, 1977), 102f.; and on its fusion of voices of narrator and character, Ann Banfield, "Narrative Style and the Grammar of Direct and Indirect Speech," *Foundations of Language* 10 (1973), 1–39 (later elaborated in *Unspeakable Sentences: Narration and Representation in the Language of Fiction* [Boston: Routledge & Kegan Paul, 1982]).

Here dialogue in direct discourse is at the service of larger interests than those of the cut and thrust of repartée; there is a *hidden polemic* at work in this and other portions of the narrative, in which Lawrence sets about his sustained demolition job on the governing assumptions of Western civilization. These redefinitions are not, to be sure, incorporated into the narration so as to fulfill Bakhtin's requirements for double-voiced discourse but are sufficiently dialogical to serve with other stylistic modes in the process of changing Lou's mind.

A similar dialogue in direct discourse furthers the goals of foregrounding language systems and leading Lou to question and revise them. Here an alien vocabulary is brought into play by the mystic Cartwright (modeled after Frederick Carter, whom Lawrence had encountered with mingled interest and amusement). Cartwright's idiolect includes the previously heard terms "mystery," "hidden" (four times in one passage) and "God," while introducing such novel items as "Pan within the thing" and "third eye" (pp. 65–66). The character and his doctrines are treated with the mingled attention and irony that correspond to Lawrence's response to Carter (indeed, Cartwright is allowed a measure of self-irony in his playful remarks on his goat-like appearance). But the larger enterprise here is to introduce alternative conceptual terms for dialogical resounding. Curiously enough, it is Mrs. Witt who plays the largest role in their echoing and examination; she asks Lou, "You, you *get* something from what Mr Cartwright said, about seeing Pan with the third eye? Seeing Pan in something?" (p. 66), and the terms become part of the dialogical activity of the text as a whole. They have their place in Lou's language learning as well, although her mother's giant strides leave her temporarily behind ("Do you understand what I mean? Unfallen Pan!" "More or less, mother" [p. 67]).

Another infusion of alien language is provided for Mrs. Witt by Lewis, and its effect is to shock her into a most unladylike proposal of marriage. Lewis's idiolect is that of the Welsh folk, and he makes the most of his opportunities:

"They say that ash-trees don't like people. When the other people were most in the country—I mean like what they call fairies, that have all gone now—they liked ash-trees best. . . . But when all these people that there are now came to England, they liked the oak-trees best, because their pigs ate the acorns. So now you can tell the ash-trees are mad, they want to kill all these people. But the oak-trees are many more than the ash-trees." [Pp. 107–108]

The diction is simple and self-consciously archaic ("what they call fairies") and gains distinctiveness from its rhythms more than from its arcana. The intrusion of yet another idiom, if not a language or dialect, creates the situation Bakhtin calls *dialogical heteroglossia*, not from the mere presence of foreign words but because of their active competition. The unorthodox systems of thought and language of Cartwright and Lewis challenge the dominant styles of Mrs. Witt's rationalism and Lou's cosmopolitanism—challenge them not only in their thinking but in their speech as well.

As we recall from the opening paragraphs, the cosmopolitan style is heavily laced with gallicisms, as befits not simply the international set (the skaz narrator's class) but the heroine in particular, whose family is from Louisiana and who has been educated in France. Along with *museau*, quoted above, we have *gamine* (p. 22), *ménage* (p. 24), *Apache*, *grand monde* and *beau monde* (p. 25), *tableau vivant* (p. 27), *Belle-Mère* and variations on it (p. 48), and so forth. Although the playing on French persists into the later pages of the novella—"plus ça change" and other phrases (pp. 129, 132), "Merci, mon cher" (repeated p. 137)—it gradually gives way to Spanish terms, in keeping with the change of scene to New Mexico and with the turn to a new consciousness. The key term that emerges at the close is the name of Lou's ranch, Las Chivas (she-goats or kids, never translated in text), and I shall have more to say about it below. For the moment it is sufficient to note the series: *padres* (p. 143), *mariposa* (p. 149, re the lily), *arroyo* (p. 152), *pueblo* (p. 152), and so forth as well as the full sentence "Quien sabe!" (p. 138).

The interplay of these varied languages and the systematic progression of the heroine's learning must tend to dampen any salient authorial presence in the narrator's prose, and the series of modulations on the cosmopolitan style might be expected to make a prophet as articulate as Lawrence occasionally impatient. So he seems at the dramatic climax of *St. Mawr*, the much discussed passage in which the horse shies from a dead adder in his path, throws and cripples Rico, and precipitates a marital breakdown and change of scene. Beyond the symbolic cruxes involving the imagery of horse, snake, and fish—revising the power hierarchy of horse and man and placing both in subjection to a larger force, universal evil—there is a striking shift in narrative mode that demands comment. Lou's observation of the débacle leads to a passage in free indirect style that conveys her shock mingled with the narrator's outrage: "What did it mean? Evil, evil, and a rapid return to the sordid chaos. Which was wrong, the horse or the rider? Or both?" (p. 79). Not content to express these questionings from the point of view of the protagonist, in dialogical relation with the author's concerns, the narration turns to a simpler form of utterance: "The evil! The mysterious potency of evil. She could see it all the time, in individuals, in society, in the press. . . . And as soon as fascism makes a break—which it is bound to, because all evil works up to a break—then turn it down. With gusto, turn it down. Mankind, like a horse, ridden by a stranger, smooth-faced, evil rider" (p. 79). I have quoted only the main phases of a passage that continues at some length, at a point where we can see the transition clearly. From echoings of Lou's voice and careful statements about her thoughts, the narrator turns to unascribed judgments and a political jargon of his own, without any attempt to ground them in the character's mental processes. From the dialogical, the prose turns monological, from hidden polemic it becomes mere polemic; this kind of "authorial intrusion" has called down critical anathemas on Lawrence. By setting the phenomenon in the context of dual-voiced narration, we do not excuse the faults but see more clearly the point of its departure from more arresting utterances. We may also judge that the infraction represents less a bad style all its own than a deviation in the course of developing a complex and commanding style, the double-voiced mode of Lawrence's later writings.

The major activity of bringing about Lou's new vision and its commensurate language continues after this flare-up of Lawrencian vehemence. I shall not detail the multiple strands by which the education is conducted, for they include minor actions at a number of simultaneous levels: language learning, for example, Phoenix instructing Lou in Spanish tree names—important preparation for what follows (p. 86); renewed interrogation ("What was real? What under heaven was real?": p. 132); writing exercises, like Lou's packet of letters to her mother, keenly describing her milieu (pp. 113–14; some of these letters include extended passages in direct discourse, quoting other speakers); and renewed dialogical interplay between characterized and authorial prose, for example, the extended disquisition on Phoenix's and other dark males' "sexual rat-holes" (pp. 135–37). Finally, the ranch is reached, with an amusing echo of Joseph Smith's Mormonish declaration, "This is the place" (p. 140). The breakthrough that occurs at this second climax is an accession to Dionysian wisdom in a landscape of barren, brutal, indifferent nature, marked by the life force as repeated patterns of bristling energy in pines, goats, ridges and lightning. It is also a fulfillment of the dialogical mode, in a passage that brings its resources into the foreground.

In fact, the dialogical here becomes trialogical or tetralogical, if the neologisms may be forgiven. Not only does an omniscient narrator (and perhaps the protagonist, who is learning what he knows) speak in the key passage; the New England woman who precedes Lou at the ranch is also heard echoing the New England theological rhetoric in which she was bred:

> The rivers of fluid fire that suddenly fell out of the sky and exploded on the earth near by, as if the whole earth had burst like a bomb, frightened her from the very core of her, and made her know, secretly and with cynical certainty, *that there was no merciful God in the heavens.* A very tall, elegant pine-tree just above her cabin took the lightning, and stood tall and elegant as before, but with a white seam spiralling from its crest, all down its tall trunk, to earth. The perfect scar, white and long as lightning itself. And every time she looked at it, she said to herself, in spite of herself: *There is no Almighty loving God. The God there is shaggy as the pine-trees, and horrible as the lightning.* Outwardly, she never confessed this. Openly, she thought of her dear New England Church as usual. But in the violent undercurrent of her woman's soul, after the storms, she would look at that living seamed tree, and the voice would say in her, almost savagely: *What nonsense about Jesus and a God of Love, in a place like this! This is more awful and more splendid. I like it better.* [Pp. 147–48]

A full linguistic analysis of this passage would require careful attention to the technique of internal quotation (in italics rather than with punctuation), which includes both direct and indirect discourse forms. A full semantic analysis would relate its images of lightning and scarred trees to Frazer's widely influential lore on the golden bough, which he identified with mistletoe, taken by the ancients as mana-laden divine power and associated by them with lightning, congealed on trees where it had touched earth.[16] Lou and the New England woman find their golden bough and use it to follow Nietzsche's path beyond a Christian ethical metaphysics to the Dionysian world view (accompanied by a strong measure of weariness with consciousness and of drift toward death).

These thematic revelations should not lead us to overlook the stylistic breakthrough that accompanies—shall we say, accomplishes?—the climactic vision. Lawrence's narrator succeeds in pronouncing the tenets of the outmoded religion in the course of articulating the new; he superimposes the avatar of his heroine upon her and though she is

[16]Sir J. G. Frazer, *The Golden Bough: A Study in Magic and Religion,* abridged ed. (London: Macmillan, 1950), 658ff., 703ff.

not literally present, Lou is filled by the same vision and doctrine; and he does so while speaking highly charged, characteristically Lawrencian prose that nevertheless bears the idiomatic marks of the particular speakers who are engaged in it. Here we may speak no longer of hidden dialogue or hidden polemic, of skaz or stylization, but of the choric voice that has been found in Verga. It is a chorus of disparate voices, some of them even antithetical to the ideology that Lawrence fosters, yet we have the impression not merely that this or that individual speaks here but that the world of nature and man itself utters its barbaric chords, its Yahvistic self-pronouncement.

We cannot be sure that the fourth participant in this chorus, the protagonist Lou, is as articulate a voice as the omniscient narrator, the New England woman he quotes, or the religious rhetoric she cites in order to negate it. The passage is given in the course of an extended intercalated narrative (pp. 140–51), designed to fill in the ranch's prior history, from which Lou is entirely absent—it is not even clear that she ever learns the story. Yet she may be found participating in this chorus, if only empathically, when we consider the language that surrounds her immediately before and after the passage. Approaching the place, she is described as thinking in much the same terms: "It seemed to her that the hidden fire was alive and burning in this sky, over the desert, in the mountains. She felt a certain latent holiness in the very atmosphere, a young, spring-fire of latent holiness. . . . 'For me, this place is sacred. It is blessed'" (pp. 139–40). Such terms are tied to the linguistic register of biblical religion that the ranch teaches the New England woman and Lou to transcend. Since Lou's initial language of the numinous resembles that of the New Englander, despite their differences of upbringing, we gather that she experiences the same kind of metaphysical revision that the latter does— that she participates in a like transvaluation of values.

In her final speech to her mother on the ranch's meaning for her, Lou remains at this pitch of intensity but purges her diction of terms like "holiness," "sacred," and "blessed." Instead she generates a religious terminology from elements such as "spirit," "wild" and "mission": "It's my mission to keep myself for the spirit that is wild, and has waited so long here: even waited for such as me. . . . And I am here, right deep in America, where there's a wild spirit wants me, a wild spirit more than men. And it doesn't want to save me either" (pp. 154–55). After this afflatus, the required decrescendo is provided by Mrs. Witt, speaking along the lines of the skeptical interlocutor who ironically punctures the tall tales of the Southwest: "How much did you say you paid for Las Chivas?" (p. 155). But Lou's "surprised" response naming the figure does not mark the last word; Mrs. Witt has one more comic line: "Then I call it cheap, considering all there is to it: even the name!" The literal sense, that Lou has acquired a linguistic property as part of her purchase, must guide us here; we have seen from the outset that language is not merely the medium of *St. Mawr* but in large measure its message. The modulations of the narrative voice have gone hand in hand with the heroine's acquisition of a new personal style as, following the Wittgensteinian dictum, the limits of her world expand with the limits of her language. In this final appropriation of the Spanish name along with the material assets of her ranch, Lou comes to possess or be possessed by its presiding spirit, for to command the name of a god is, according to long tradition, to command or communicate with him as well.

This final access to right language is not an epiphenomenon of *St. Mawr* but part of a concerted movement in Lawrence's later fiction. The long ritual poems that Kate Cipriano hears and reads in *The Plumed Serpent,* the initiation into sex talk side by side with sex in *Lady Chatterley's Lover,* these are not embellishments on their themes: the language is largely what those novels are about. Much the same conclusion is already widely acknowledged in Lawrence criticism; in the present contribution, I have sought to adduce only that artful style is still at the master's command in these late works and that his innovations in narrative technique are in behalf of his wider goals in life and language.

[9]

D. H. Lawrence
and Mexico

CHARLES ROSSMAN

D. H. Lawrence made three trips to Mexico between March 1923 and April 1925, spending altogether some eleven months in various parts of the country. His reactions were intense, extreme, and above all, sharply ambivalent, embracing both exquisite sympathy and strident hostility. Like Aldous Huxley, Graham Greene, and Malcolm Lowry, who made their own pilgrimages from England to Mexico over the ensuing fifteen years, Lawrence found the country, by turns, irresistibly appealing, deeply unsettling, and ultimately nightmarish.

Mexico became for Lawrence a potent symbolic landscape, an exotic and dangerous world that exacerbated the extremes of corruption and potential renewal. As intellectual catalyst and ideological muse during Lawrence's tormented "leadership phase," Mexico was more provocative to him than either Italy or Australia. Mexico struck Lawrence's fertile imagination as a battleground upon which was fought a Manichaean contest for the future of humanity. It is as such a symbolic battlefield that Mexico figures in works like "The Woman Who Rode Away," the most disquieting of Lawrence's short fictions, *Mornings in Mexico,* the most ideological of his travel books, and *The Plumed Serpent,* at once the most shocking and the most artistically successful of his "leadership novels."

Lawrence wrote prolifically during each of his sojourns to Mexico, often blending accounts of personal experience with searching assessments of the country's postrevolutionary circumstances and prospects. During his first trip, for instance, in March 1923, his impressions seem to have boiled from his pen starting the very moment that the train left El Paso. (Those impressions reached print as "Au Revoir, U.S.A.") Before that first trip of four months ended, Lawrence completed a draft of *Quetzalcoatl,* as he called *The Plumed Serpent* in manuscript. The early chapters of the published novel offer near-transcripts of Lawrence's experiences and attitudes in Mexico City during April 1923, while the later chapters fancifully amalgamate his perceptions of Lake Chapala, the Sayula of the novel, with his vast readings in Mexican history and mythology and with his idealized vision of Mexico's future.

Lawrence's second trip to Mexico, in late September of 1923, was a two-month forage by train, car, and horse through the wilds of the Pacific coast in search of a suitable site for his long-dreamed-of utopian community, Rananim. During the journey, Lawrence revised Molly Skinner's manuscript "The House of Ellis" and fashioned from it their coauthored novel, *The Boy in the Bush.* Mexico does not figure directly in the novel. Yet the ideas and moods nourished by Lawrence's confrontation with Mexico—particularly his rejection of European civilization, his investigation of irrational and primitive religions, and his fascination with strong male leaders—leave their imprint from the first chapter to the last.

Less than a year later, Lawrence made his third and final visit to Mexico, this time to Oaxaca in the deep south. There he finished *The Plumed Serpent* and wrote four of the essays in *Mornings in Mexico.* As with Lawrence's previous writings about Mexico, these four essays vividly reflect his intimate experiences. They draw immediately on his daily life in Oaxaca, describing, respectively, the activity in Lawrence's patio; a walk through the Oaxacan countryside; Lawrence's servant, Rosalino; and a shopping trip in the open market of Oaxaca.

Ineluctably a reader turns from Lawrence's writings about Mexico to the antecedent experiences that so thoroughly pervade them. The persistent obtrusiveness of Lawrence's recognizably personal perspective, coupled with the sheer intensity of his feelings about Mexico, both tempt us to investigate the complex relationship between Lawrence's life and his art. It is Lawrence's art, of course, that gives significance to his life. The creative power of the artist provokes us to read his letters, chart his travels, probe his ideas and attitudes, and scrutinize his personal relationships. But concern for the details of Lawrence's life is more than idle prying into the private life of a public artist. We turn to the life because the art is somehow incomplete in itself. In so doing, we follow Lawrence's own suggestion.

Lawrence repeatedly stressed the intimate link between his life and his writing. He once confessed, for instance, that "one sheds one's sicknesses in books—repeats and presents again one's emotions, to be master of them."[1] Another time he declared: "I always say, my motto is 'Art for my sake.'" Similarly, his Foreword to *Women in Love* describes that novel as "a record of the writer's own desires, aspirations, struggles; in a word, a record of the profoundest experiences of the self." He would doubtless have said much the same thing about *The Plumed Serpent*, which he once described as "nearer my heart than any other work of mine" and called his "most important novel so far." More so than with most writers, then, Lawrence's life provides a legitimate interpretive context for his creative works. The life and art intermingle and inform one another.

What follows seeks to explore Lawrence's life and his art together, to trace through both the chronology of his passionate involvement with Mexico—the record of his "desires, aspirations, struggles" during the excruciating years when he wrote some of his most lovely and disturbing works. Lawrence did not always distinguish between the United States and Mexico when he used the word "America." Moreover, his experience of Mexico was an extension of his prior (and continuing) experience of the North American Southwest, with its aborigines, its primitive religions and rituals, and its wild, magical landscape. My account of Lawrence's involvement with Mexico begins, therefore, with his decision to come to America.

Lawrence and Frieda arrived in Taos, New Mexico, on 11 September 1922, his thirty-seventh birthday. They had been enticed to the New World by Mabel Dodge, a wealthy and willful American *Kulturträger* who wanted Lawrence to write about the "powerful spirit that hovered over the Taos Valley" that she had adopted.[2] Mabel Dodge had written Lawrence in Sicily, after she had been inspired by his vivid and potent descriptions in *Sea and Sardinia*, to invite him to Taos. She described the Indians, the lofty and isolated mountains, the clear air that seemed, she said, almost to hum with music, and the pristine beauty of the landscape. In her letter she included three items that she believed carried Indian magic that might convince Lawrence to accept her invitation: a necklace for Frieda, a few leaves of desachey (a perfume), and a medicinal root known as *osha*.

The magic worked. On 5 November 1921, the same day that he received this invitation from a stranger to visit a place that he could

---

[1]Lawrence makes this declaration in a letter from 1913. See Harry T. Moore, ed., *The Collected Letters of D. H. Lawrence*, 2 vols. (New York: Viking, 1962), 234; hereafter cited parenthetically in the text as *ML*. The quotation in the following sentence of my text is from Aldous Huxley, ed., *The Letters of D. H. Lawrence* (London: Heinemann, 1932), 86.

[2]Mabel Dodge Luhan, *Lorenzo in Taos* (New York: Knopf, 1932), 4.

not even say for sure that he had previously heard of, Lawrence responded with enthusiasm. He wrote that he had "smelt the Indian scent, and nibbled the medicine" (*ML*, 671). "Truly," he said, "I would like to come to Taos."

He was especially intrigued by the Indians. "Are your Indians dying out," he asked, "and is it rather sad?" The Indians appealed to him as a possible source of renewal for the white European civilization that he regarded as desiccated and withering. "One must somehow," he declared, "bring together the two ends of humanity, our own thin end, and the last dark strand from the previous, pre-white era." He was tantalized by the thought that Taos might offer a cyclical return to the past that could liberate the future. "I want to leave Europe," he wrote to Mabel Dodge. "I want to take the next step. Shall it be Taos?"

Mabel Dodge's invitation must have struck Lawrence as the work of destiny. He had been preparing himself to seize such an opportunity for years. As early as January 1913, nearly nine years before Mabel Dodge's letter from out of the blue, he had described his "great religion" as a "belief in the blood, the flesh, as being wiser than the intellect," and he had already begun to associate "intellect" with white European, especially English, civilization (*ML*, 180). His novels had explored, from the beginning, the relationship between the blood's wisdom and culture's (or mind's) intervention. Gradually he came to the conclusion that England and all of Europe were moribund, a feeling aggravated by the Great War, and he began to look yearningly toward primitive cultures.

Lawrence articulates his growing attraction for primitive societies, for example, in the first version of "Herman Melville's *Typee* and *Omoo*," written in 1918 before the armistice and containing none of the rancor or stridency that torments his writing over the next few years. Lawrence describes Melville's adventures in the South Pacific as the acting out of a dream of escape from modern Atlantic civilization and hence from Melville's own "European self, ideal and ethical as it is, chain-bound."[3] Lawrence does not dismiss Melville's dream as mere escapist fantasy. Quite the contrary, he regards it as a quest for a pristine civilization that is both vastly more ancient than Europe and yet "nascent with a new world . . . , latent with all the unborn issues of the coming world of man." Moreover, Lawrence identifies intimately with Melville's quest. Melville nearly found, Lawrence writes, "what every man dreams of finding: a perfect home among timeless, un-

---

[3]Lawrence, *The Symbolic Meaning*, ed. Armin Arnold (New York: Viking, 1964), 202. Page numbers in text refer to this edition, hereafter cited as *SM*.

spoiled savages. There, in Nukuheva, the European psyche, with its ideals and limitations, had no place" (*SM,* 202).

Lawrence fled England within months after the war ended. He did not follow Melville to the South Pacific—he would do so later—but headed straight for Italy, where he and Frieda had spent a happy winter before the war and which appealed to him as the one European country that kept alive warmth of feeling. The Lawrences arrived in Italy in mid-November 1919 and remained until the end of February 1922, leaving the country only to spend a few months in Germany and Switzerland during the summer of 1921. Clearly Italy partially satisfied Lawrence's personal yearning for "what every man dreams of finding," even if he despised Sardinia and sometimes felt profound disillusion with the whole of Italy. But that satisfaction was only partial, and Lawrence soon began to look further abroad for an ancient civilization "nascent with a new world." Early on, America struck him as a likely possibility.

In "America, Listen to Your Own," written in Florence in September 1919, Lawrence advised Americans to ignore the "monuments of our European past" and to "catch the spirit of [their] own dark, aboriginal continent."[4] It was an ironic sentiment to formulate in one of the European cities most filled with "monuments of our European past," and it hints at the restlessness that Lawrence would inevitably feel no matter where he lived over the next decade. Nevertheless, "America, Listen to Your Own" articulates some of Lawrence's most urgent desires at that time. Americans, he argues, must recognize "that which was called the Devil, the black Demon of savage America" because it "hides the Godhead which we seek." He asserts that Americans "must take up life where the Red Indian, the Aztec, the Maya, the Incas left it off." Employing the strand image to which he would return fourteen months later in his reply to Mabel Dodge, he writes that modern Americans "must pick up the life-thread" that ended with the red Indians. As he elaborates his argument, Lawrence increasingly identifies himself with the white Americans whom he exhorts. "We," he says—and the "we" is crucial—"we must start from Montezuma." Ostensibly lecturing Americans about the ignored but potent mysteries in their collective past, Lawrence declares *his own* desire to confront the dark, aboriginal American past: "the pulse of the life which Cortes and Columbus murdered," as he puts it.

[4]Lawrence, *Phoenix: The Posthumous Papers of D. H. Lawrence,* ed. Edward D. McDonald (London: Heinemann, 1936), 90.

D. H. Lawrence and Mexico

When Mabel Dodge's invitation to join her in Taos reached Lawrence in Sicily, then, he was already well disposed to visit America. He hoped to recover there the ancient life of passion and instinct that the European invaders had suppressed. What is more, and what is especially valuable for our understanding of Lawrence's version of Mexico, he had already developed an intellectual habit that permeates this whole period of his life: the tendency to read history in terms of his own fears and aspirations, his own frustrations and demands. This quality of Lawrence's thought manifests itself frequently after the war, not only in "America, Listen to Your Own," but also in the early versions of the essays later published as *Studies in Classic American Literature,* in *Psychoanalysis and the Unconscious,* in *Education of the People,* and in *Movements in European History,* which offers a notorious example in the solemn declaration from its final paragraph: "The will of the people must concentrate in one figure, who is also supreme over the will of the people."

In these works, Lawrence often regards his theories and ideas as "laws of life." Although as always an acute observer of the external world, with the ability to bring it vividly to life for his readers, Lawrence during this period writes increasingly from his will, bending his perceptions to serve a thesis or an attitude. By the time that Lawrence wrote the descriptions of Mexico in *The Plumed Serpent* and *Mornings in Mexico,* his perceptions of Mexico had become difficult to separate from his projections onto Mexico. The line between the two is all the more obscured by Lawrence's vacillating and ambivalent assessment of the New World. His vacillation and ambivalence not only complicate the narrative perspectives of his writings about Mexico but are also a fundamental and recurrent aspect of his entire experience with the New World.

Lawrence began to vacillate about America as soon as it became a concrete possibility for him rather than a mere theory. For example, in the flush of enthusiasm during the month following Mabel Dodge's invitation, Lawrence wrote S. S. Koteliansky, E. H. Brewster, and Mary Cannan of his plans to go to Taos. To his friend Koteliansky, in particular, he aggressively affirmed his intentions. Europe, he wrote, "is a dead dog which begins to stink intolerably. Again I entertain the idea of going to America" (*ML,* 673). But as the departure date drew near, he abruptly changed his plans—and his direction. He went east to Ceylon rather than west to America. He had planned to sail for America in January or February 1922, and he wrote Brewster in Ceylon as late as January 2, sending the Taos address. Yet he did not set foot on American soil until nine months later, after extended visits to Ceylon and Australia and after sailing through Melville's South Pacific.

Lawrence's ambivalence toward America becomes apparent in one of the first pieces that he wrote after arriving in Taos, "Indians and an Englishman." On his fourth day in New Mexico, Lawrence went with a small group on a five-day trip to the Jicarillo Apache Indian Reservation north of Taos. "Indians and an Englishman" is an account of that outing and records Lawrence's experiences of the first real "Red Indians" that he had seen. Despite the self-inclusive "we" in his call to Americans to "listen to your own," Lawrence feels like a distinct outsider during his five-day encounter with American aborigines. The concrete reality of red Indians—New Mexico's Apaches—appeals to him less than had its theoretical possibility—the "black Demon of savage America" that he conjured up while in Florence.

Lawrence begins the essay by depicting himself as a "lone lorn Englishman, tumbled out of the known world of the British Empire onto this stage" (*Phoenix*, 92). He treats both Mexicans and Indians with mocking irony. "It is all," he writes, a "masquerade," "rather like comic opera" or "various troupes in a circus." He feels like someone who "fell onto the moon, and found them talking English." The Southwest is not at all, he says, "like the proper world."

Lawrence finds danger as well as comedy in the whole show. He describes how, his first night on the reservation, he wrapped himself up to the nose in a red serape and went to visit the Indian chanters, passing through the "dark air" "thick with enemies." Even the horses "jerk aside" as he passes, while the "dark Indians passing in the night peered at me. The air . . . had a jeering, malevolent vibration in it."[5] For all his eagerness to encounter the "black Demon" in aboriginal America, Lawrence regards darkness as especially ominous. He emphasizes the darkness repeatedly: "dark air," "dark face," "dark Indians," "night." And for all his theoretical interest in a radically non-European civilization, he experiences such "otherness" as hostile: the looks of the Indians are jeers, their silence is malevolence. Laughter and play go on all around him, but he is immune to their spirit. The playfulness of the Indians strikes him as "ridicule," as a "comic sort of bullying" with "a sort of unconscious animosity." In the laughter of

---

[5]To Lawrence's credit, he acknowledges that his own reactions to the "wild and wooly" comic opera are suspect and that his own feelings might be merely fearful projections. "I know less than nothing," he abruptly confesses. Indeed, he concedes that his entire response "may just be the limitation of my European fancy" (*Phoenix*, 93, 96).

the cowboys and cowgirls, Lawrence detects "an inevitable silent gibing."

The final paragraphs of "Indians and an Englishman" describe how Lawrence, drawn by the beating drums through the hostile darkness, "stumbled down to the kiva," an enclosure of cut Aspen trees within which the younger Indians squatted round a fire, chanting and drumming, while an old man in their midst recited, hour after hour. The old reciter—a "mask-like, virile figure . . . with his eyes as if glazed in old memory"—touches Lawrence deeply. Suddenly he declares himself "no enemy of theirs; far from it." Lawrence abruptly drops his mocking tone and confronts with sympathy the old man and his chant. The old Indian strikes him as fathomlessly ancient, as the living representative of the primeval human connection with the "living red earth" and of "far-off tribal understandings." A reader who has also read Lawrence's letter to Mabel Dodge, which speaks of picking up "the last dark strand from the previous, pre-white era," or who recalls Lawrence's injunction to Americans to "listen to your own," might expect this encounter in the dark on an Apache reservation to satisfy, partially at least, the promptings that brought Lawrence to America.

Not so. Lawrence responds to the old reciter as a "voice out of the far-off time [that] was not for my ears." The old man's chant emerges from the "bristling darkness of the far past." Lawrence discovers that that dark past, whatever its previous attractions, "was not for me." "I knew it," he concludes. As Lawrence stands on the edge of the kiva's flickering firelight, he repudiates the old reciter. "My way is my own, old red father; I can't cluster at the drum any more."

To stress the difference between Lawrence's anticipation of America and these initial experiences among the Apaches is not, of course, to expose him as merely a supercilious English tourist fretting about dark skins and "proper" worlds. Lawrence came to America on a religious pilgrimage. He did not expect to find, ready made and awaiting him, "a perfect home among timeless, unspoiled savages," as he put it in the essay on Melville's *Typee* and *Omoo*. Yet he longed to hear ancestral voices of relevance to a modern European, hoped to "pick up the life-thread" that would lead back to "the Godhead which we seek," in order to move forward as a new kind of being in a new kind of civilization. The differences between Lawrence's expectations of New Mexico and his first impressions exposes the painful gap between his most passionately held ideals and the prospects for their implementation.

During the first months after arriving in New Mexico, Lawrence worked over the essays written in 1917–18, and already revised once in Sicily in 1920, on "classic American literature." Most of the essays underwent substantial changes in both subject matter and tone, as Lawrence cast them in their final form. The changes in the essay on *Typee* and *Omoo* pointedly reflect Lawrence's experiences among the New Mexican Indians, as well as his earlier experiences in Ceylon, the South Pacific, and Australia. There is a new hardness of tone, a brittle, flippant quality altogether absent in the first version of the *Typee* essay. Lawrence respects both Melville and primitive cultures much less than he had four or five years before. In the first version, he depicted Melville as a visionary on a quest of enormous importance to any sensitive descendent of European culture. Melville's failure to remain among the primitives is depicted, in the first version, as understandable, even inevitable, yet also as something of a failure to transcend his past. In the later, published version, Melville and his quest both suffer radical diminution. Melville is now motivated by a hatred of human life and of the world. He sought an impossible dream, a paradise regained. Although Lawrence treats Melville's experience rather cavalierly, he agrees with his departure from the South Pacific. One cannot, Lawrence writes, "go back" to the savages. "I know now I couldn't."[6] The word "now" reveals a significant change in Lawrence's outlook since writing the first essay on *Typee*, and since leaving Italy. Lawrence's repudiation of the old Apache chanter was a fundamental decision, a redefinition of self that dictated a change in future direction. Lawrence's convictions about the contemporary value of America's primitive civilizations have been seriously weakened.

Yet Lawrence does not abruptly abandon his American quest for the lost "life-thread." He continues to believe that although "we can't go back to the savages: not a stride," we can nonetheless "take a great curve in their direction, onwards," as she puts it in the final version of the *Typee* essay (p. 130). Disappointed, frustrated, angry, yet determined, Lawrence turns his attention southward once more—this time to Mexico.

Six months after arriving in New Mexico, Lawrence and Frieda boarded a train in El Paso for the journey to Mexico City. They departed El Paso on 21 March 1923, and reached the Mexican capital

---

[6]D. H. Lawrence, *Studies in Classic American Literature* (London: Heinemann, 1964), 129, hereafter cited in text as *SCAL*.

on 23 March. After trying a large American-style hotel for a night, they moved into a more modest hotel run by an Italian family, the Hotel Monte Carlo. They were joined there about a week later by Witter Bynner, an American poet they had met in New Mexico, and his companion, Willard (Spud) Johnson. Bynner and Johnson moved into the Hotel Monte Carlo to be near the Lawrences. Prior to their move, Bynner and Johnson had spent two days at a German hotel, where they were disconcerted to learn that their room had been occupied some months before by an acquaintance, Wilfred Ewart, who had been killed on the room's balcony, the victim of a random bullet during a street fiesta. Ewart's death reminded all four travelers that Mexico, whose revolution was barely a decade old, had ample potential for violence.

Lawrence read voraciously about Mexico during his first weeks in the country. In March, he read Prescott's *The History of the Conquest of Mexico*. In April, he devoured *Life in Mexico* by Calderón de la Barca, *Viva Mexico!* by Charles Flandrau, *The Mexican People: Their Struggle for Independence* by Gutierrez de Lara and Pinchon, and Thomas Terry's *Terry's Guide to Mexico*, which Lawrence had begun in New Mexico and later found maddeningly unreliable. Some time during this period he also read Bernal Diaz's classic *The True History of the Conquest of New Spain* as well as *Fundamental Principles of Old and New World Religions* by Zelia Nuttall. Zelia Nuttall was an American archeologist living in Mexico at the time of Lawrence's visit. She invited the Lawrences to a tea party at her home in Coyoacán, later offered a part of her house to the Lawrences during their stay in the capital, and ultimately figured as the prototype of Mrs. Norris in the second chapter of *The Plumed Serpent*.

All the while, Lawrence and his group traveled widely throughout the capital and the surrounding area, with Lawrence functioning as extraordinarily well informed guide, thanks to his wide reading. In the capital itself, Lawrence absorbed the major churches and government buildings, went to see various frescoes then being painted by Rivera, Orozco, and others, watched the pilgrims prostrate themselves at the Basilica of the Virgin of Guadalupe, and attended the bullfights on April Fool's Day. He also took in such nearby sights as the canals of Xochimilco, the ruined abbey of El Desierto de los Leones, and the pyramids of San Juan Teotihuacán, then in an early stage of excavation.

Lawrence's first letters after arriving in Mexico City register his favorable impressions. To Bessie Freeman he wrote, "The city [is] pleasant—much more like S. Italy than America. . . . I think we are going to like it."[7] To Ada Lawrence he wrote: "Mexico just warm enough and very free and easy, like Naples—to me much pleasanter than U.S.—we shall probably stay at least a few months" (Nehls, 212). These first warm feelings no doubt derived in part from the atmosphere of the Hotel Monte Carlo, where the Forte family had contrived to duplicate a little bit of Italy, complete with ravioli, spaghetti, and Chianti served in straw-covered bottles.

Despite the warmth of the Monte Carlo, Lawrence soon tired of the capital. Both the city and its citizens began to oppress him. Religious rituals like those at the Basilica of the Virgin of Guadalupe, or like those during the Day of the Dead or during Holy Week, struck him as grisly and morbid impositions of decadent European Christianity upon native Indian culture. He found the bullfights cruel, repulsive, and hateful, an especially bloody European intrusion on native culture. He regarded the new frescoes being painted as crude and ugly propaganda that simultaneously idealized and exploited the Indians for political ends. Soon eager to escape the capital, Lawrence began to lead his group into the surrounding country. They took, first, an excursion to Cuernavaca. Then they went on a nine-day trip to several towns east of Mexico City, including Puebla, Orizaba (which Lawrence found evil and deathly), Cholula, and Atlixco.

Witter Bynner describes Lawrence's temperament as extremely volatile during the weeks in Mexico City and environs. According to Bynner, Lawrence was interested in everything but satisfied by nothing. He was critical of the architecture, the art, the religion, the government, the peasants, and the aristocrats. Bynner depicts Lawrence as fascinated by the dark-skinned Indians yet fearful of them. Bynner says that Lawrence often described Mexico in extreme terms, like "evil" or "destructive" or "a land of death."[8] He was given to unpredictable spasms of anger, such as when he demanded that the whole group leave Orizaba because he could feel the evil exuding from the ground and creeping in the air or when he stormed out of the office of the progressive minister of education, José Vasconcelos, because Vasconcelos had kept him waiting too long for an appointment (Bynner, 27, 38).

Lawrence's letters from these weeks reflect his shifting moods and judgments. On 11 April, for instance, he wrote Bessie Freeman a note

---

[7]Edward Nehls, ed., *D. H. Lawrence: A Composite Biography* (Madison: University of Wisconsin Press, 1958), 212; hereafter cited in text as Nehls.

[8]Witter Bynner, *Journey with Genius* (New York: John Day, 1951), 38–40; hereafter cited in text as Bynner.

that both acknowledges his recent discontent with Mexico and claims that he now feels more positive: "I am liking Mexico better—think now of finding a house to live [in] some months—in the country for preference" (Nehls, 218). The same day he wrote to Knud Merrild: "I want to find a house. . . . Spit on Taos for me" (Bynner, 23). But then, only nine days later, his mood changes. He wrote Merrild, "I've had about enough of this country and continent. Think we shall sail at the end of this month" (Nehls, 226). The following day, Lawrence decided that the United States had not been so bad, after all: "I really didn't dislike the U.S.A. as much as I expected" (Nehls, 227). Within a week, he felt good about Mexico once again and spoke of staying: "I like Mexico, and am still uncertain of my movements. . . . I may stay the summer here and write a bit" (Nehls, 227).

Bynner reports that Lawrence's revulsion against Mexico City increased after he witnessed the bullfight on 1 April. But the experience that finally drove him from the city appears to have been the aborted meeting with José Vasconcelos, on 26 April. Only two days later, Lawrence went by train to Lake Chapala, via Guadalajara, leaving Frieda behind with Bynner and Johnson. He wanted to give Mexico "one last chance," Bynner says (Bynner, 59). He also wanted to find a place to settle down and write. On 2 May, Frieda received a telegram from Lawrence: CHAPALA PARADISE. TAKE EVENING TRAIN (Bynner, 79). Frieda, Bynner, and Johnson caught the evening train, barely. The last of their party did not leave Chapala until the ninth or tenth of July, some nine weeks later. During the interim, Lawrence produced the first draft of *The Plumed Serpent*.

"Au Revoir, U.S.A.," the first piece that Lawrence wrote after heading south from El Paso, offers one clue to the welter of apparently conflicting attitudes and judgments that Lawrence felt on his first visit to Mexico. At the same time, "Au Revoir, U.S.A." illuminates the ideological structure of both *The Plumed Serpent* and *Mornings in Mexico*. The essay implies three relevant points. First, the United States failed to offer the source of renewal that Lawrence had sought in the New World, largely because the North American Indian suffers from what Lawrence calls the "great paleface overlay" of white European culture upon the indigenous culture. "In the United States," Lawrence writes, "the gods have had their teeth pulled, and their claws cut, and their tails docked, till they seem real mild lambs" (*Phoenix*, 106). Second, although Lawrence finds the "paleface overlay" abundant in Mexico, too, he regards it as a mere veneer: "The great paleface overlay hasn't gone into the soil half an inch. The Spanish churches and palaces stagger, the most rickety things imaginable. . . . And the peon still grins his grin behind the Cross. . . . He knows his gods" (*Phoenix,* 105). It follows that, third, Mexico might still offer what the U.S.A. did not—the life-renewing link with primitive, dangerous, "pyramid-building," pre-European forms of consciousness.

Lawrence went to Mexico City, then, in a spirit of recoil against the United States, just as he had come to the United States in recoil against Europe. For a while, he was intrigued by the new experiences in an exotic capital, especially one that surprised him with the fortuitous hint of Italy that he found in the Hotel Monte Carlo. But as a man in search of ancestral voices that might speak to his most urgent desires, Lawrence soon grew impatient of playing the tourist. Moreover, he seems quickly to have concluded that the "paleface overlay" affected the capital much more profoundly than he had anticipated. The art, religion, commerce, and social and governmental organization of Mexico City all struck him as the Mexican embodiment of American and European influences, a relentless imposition of ideal, foreign culture upon a preexisting, instinctual culture. To Lawrence, an Indian in a European business suit seemed a travesty; an Indian selling fruit on a streetcorner seemed a betrayal of vital cultural inheritance. As had happened previously in Europe, Ceylon, Australia, and the United States, much of the tangible, mundale reality surrounding Lawrence in Mexico began to disappoint and irritate him. Finally, the gap between his imagined ideal and the daily reality of Mexico City became too much to endure. He fled the capital in the same mood of recoil that he had departed the United States.

When Lawrence reached Chapala, he was no longer intrigued with the mere investigation of the concrete, contemporary Mexican reality. He had made his investigation and his assessment, and it was largely negative. He was now ready to write his "American novel." That is, he was prepared to settle into comfortable domestic routines, enjoy as much of his immediate environment as possible while enduring what he did not approve, and turn his attention inward to confront the ideal Mexico of his imagination. That pattern of experience—from the repudiation of the particulars of Mexico City to a contemplation of the world of ideals—is replicated by Kate Leslie in *The Plumed Serpent.*

The first three chapters of *The Plumed Serpent* establish the ugliness and degeneracy of Mexico City, which becomes a symbol for the repudiated Mexican present that is transcended in the remainder of the novel. Each of these chapters draws in detail on Lawrence's experiences in Mexico City during the first month of his stay there. Chapter 1, "Beginnings of a Bull-Fight," derives from the bullfight that Lawrence, Frieda, Bynner, and Johnson attended on the first of April. Chapter 2, "Tea-Party in Tlacolula," records with "extraordinary fidelity" a tea party given the group in Coyoacán by Zelia Nuttall (Bynner, 22). Chapter 3, "Fortieth Birthday," draws on several visits that Lawrence made with the Mexican artist Miguel Covarrubias to examine the aggressively political frescoes then being painted on public buildings by Diego Rivera and others. But even though these early chapters depict real places, use real street names, and mention real persons, their goal is not to give a mimetic account of Mexico City. Rather, Lawrence offers a consciously contrived *interpretation* of the city. Much of that interpretation is voiced by Kate Leslie, the middle-aged Irish protagonist who blends the robust presence of Frieda with the mind and opinions of Lawrence himself. Kate's interpretation is corroborated by the judgments and perspective of the narrator, whose opinions, like Kate's, are not easily distinguishable from Lawrence's own.

The opening chapter is unrelenting and unqualified in its criticism of Mexico City. Even seemingly incidental descriptions present the city negatively. During the first two pages, for instance, Kate and her party (Kate's American cousin, Owen, based on Witter Bynner, and his traveling companion, Villiers, based on Willard Johnson) buy their tickets for the bullfight from "an unpleasant individual." To make their way to the arena, they pass up the "frightful little Ford omnibuses" that cause Kate to feel a "sudden dark feeling," and they elect instead to travel by private taxi—a "busted car" that careens through the "wide dismal street" past the stone buildings that "in Mexico have a peculiar hard, dry dreariness." They arrive at the "huge, ugly stadium," where they find "in the gutters, rather lousy men" selling sweets and "greasy food." Finally, after "a real gutter-lout" checks their tickets, they take their seats in the "big concrete beetle trap" of a bullring.[9]

The entire chapter documents the horrors of contemporary Mexico City. It is not merely that Kate and Lawrence despise the bullfight, although the novel depicts the bullfight as irredeemably brutal and repugnant. Rather, the bullfight is a synecdoche for the whole of Mexico City and, indeed, for all of postrevolutionary Mexico that tries to modernize itself, as we see if we look past the gored horses and the terrified bull and examine the description of the crowd. "The au-

[9]D. H. Lawrence, *The Plumed Serpent* (New York: Vintage, 1954), 4–5; hereafter cited in text as *PS*.

dience was," Kate thinks, "a mob. . . . How I detest them" (*PS*, 6–7). Moreover, the "mob" is not merely a particular group that is fond of Sunday bullfights. It represents "the People," the "degenerate mob of Mexico City" that thrills to its newly acquired, revolution-based power. Individuals in the audience are "fattish town men" who wear "shoddily-fitting black" clothes, and who are uniformly ill mannered and threatening. Kate regards them as "mongrel men of a mongrel city" (*PS*, 18). The occasional women in the audience strike her as "fat mammas in black satin that was greasy and grey at the edges with an overflow of face powder." The bullfight amounts, for Kate, to a vision of hell: "She had been in many cities of the world, but Mexico had an underlying ugliness, a sort of squalid evil" (*PS*, 19). As the chapter draws to a close, she reiterates that the whole of Mexico reeks with a contagious "crawling sort of evil." "I do think," she tells General Viedma, who finds her a taxi when she runs from the bullfight in outrage, "Mexico City is evil, underneath" (*PS*, 21).

Chapter 2 begins the evening of the bullfight, and it continues to heap up negative images of Mexico City. Kate remains so disturbed by her experience of the afternoon that she cannot fall asleep. She dwells on "the strange, grisly fear that so often creeps out on to the darkness of a Mexican night" when the hidden "evil came forth" (*PS*, 27–28). Interestingly, Kate fears Mexico, as Lawrence often does, but she does not describe her fear as a subjective experience. Instead, the "fear" is an objective quality in the environment, something that "creeps out" by night. In the morning, Kate receives an invitation from Mrs. Norris (based on Zelia Nuttall) to a tea party, an invitation that contains its subtle, implicit contempt of Mexico. Mrs. Norris informs Kate that among the guests will be two Mexicans who are both charming men—which makes them "both entirely the exception among Mexicans" (*PS*, 28).

Thinking about the general who will be at the tea party, Kate broadens her criticism of the Mexican population to include more than the "mob." She dismisses Mexican generals—"as a rule, a class to be strictly avoided" (*PS*, 29). She asserts that Mexicans holding political office are also to be avoided, like "the lice that creep on the unwashed crowd." Nevertheless, she and Owen "bumped out to Tlacolula" to attend the party. Once more, the passage through the streets of Mexico City is a somber experience. The outskirts of town are "squalid." The soil in the open country is "strange, dry, blackish, artificially wetted, and old." The buildings along the way are either "new and alien" or "cracked and dilapidated." The people in the streets are mostly "men with blackened faces," as though darkness

were, in itself, an evil, or "blank dark natives in dirty cotton clothes."
Street vendors seem more animal than human, "squatting on the
ground, selling fruits or sweets." When Kate and Owen reach Mrs.
Norris's house, they find it "ponderous, as if dead for centuries" (*PS*,
31).

The conversation at the tea party drifts casually until Mrs. Norris
asks how Kate likes Mexico. "It strikes me as evil," Kate replies moral-
istically. Following Kate's remark, the conversation turns to a free-
wheeling condemnation of many aspects of contemporary social and
political life in Mexico. The revolution, the masses, the Indians, the
army, the president, the workers, and the political parties all come in
for their share of scorn. The dominant tone of the white foreigners'
conversation is fear and loathing. At last, General Cipriano Viedma
and Ramón Carrasco arrive. They are superior in tact, sensitivity, and
intelligence to any of the other guests. Nevertheless, Don Ramón
confirms Kate's opinion that Mexico is oppressively deathly. "When-
ever a Mexican cries Viva!" he says, "he ends up with Muera!" (*PS*,
40).

In terms of the novel's ideological development, the conversation at
the tea party makes several points, some overt and some implicit.
First, it converts the visceral repudiation of Mexico heretofore felt by
Kate into conceptual terms. Second, the Mexican reality is broadly
condemned by everyone present, including even the two distinguished Mexicans. Third, the satire at the tea party cuts so many ways, and
so deeply, that it demolishes virtually all orthodox political and social
solutions to the problems of Mexico. Lawrence thus sets the stage for
the development of the unorthodox solution that will be offered by
Don Ramón and Don Cipriano later in the book—the resurrection of
an ancient religion as the basis for a new social order.

Another essential issue developed in this chapter is Kate's deeply
ambiguous feelings about the dark-skinned Indians and mestizos.
Like Lawrence, she both fears them and finds them intriguing. Kate
says of "the peons" that "their eyes have no middle to them." To her
this means that the men are selfless: "They aren't really there. They
have no center, no real *I*. Their middle is a raging black hole" (*PS*,
40). At this point in the novel, Kate has not even spoken with an
Indian and has only observed them at a distance. Her judgment, then,
is impetuous in the extreme, a mere projection of her own ignorance
and fear onto the silent and distant darkness of the Indians. Interestingly, Kate's attitude and imagery parallel those expressed by
Lawrence in a letter from Ceylon on 10 April 1922, some two weeks
after he arrived there and saw "dark people" in large numbers for the

first time. Lawrence reaffirms his desire to see the North American Indians but only "if one is sure that they are not jeering at one. I find all dark people have a fixed desire to jeer at us" (*ML*, 700). Like Kate, Lawrence experiences the dark otherness of the Ceylonese as threatening. Also like Kate, Lawrence finds the eyes of the natives particularly disturbing. The natives, he asserts, "seem to be built around a gap, a hollow pit. In the middle of their eyes, instead of a man, a sort of bottomless pit." As the essay "Indians and an Englishman" makes clear, Lawrence felt that the "dark people" of New Mexico also jeered at him, and he found them potentially dangerous. Now, in Mexico, he finds the Indians more dangerous still, yet somehow attractive. For instance, as Kate leaves the tea party and observes a group of natives, the sort with centerless eyes, she responds with both fear and sympathy: "She was a bit afraid of the natives . . . , but stronger than her fear was a certain sympathy with these dark-faced, silent men. . . . Anyhow they had blood in their veins: they were columns of dark blood" (*PS*, 48).

Chapter 3 begins with Kate awakening on the morning of her fortieth birthday. By now in the novel, Mexico has been so thoroughly transformed into a symbol for the states of mind of the protagonist and her creator that even the famous volcanoes Popocatépetl and Ixtaccíhuatl strike her as part of the general evil. The volcanoes seem like "two monsters" watching over a "lofty, bloody cradle of men." They are "alien, ponderous" mountains that emit a "sound of dread," quite unlike the "soaring or uplift or exaltation" of the "snowy mountains of Europe." The actual Popocatépetl and Ixtaccíhuatl that Kate sees from her rooftop are, of course, blankly white and utterly silent. The "sound of dread" is an echo of her own mind. Nevertheless, gazing at them she concludes that "the spirit of place" in Mexico is "cruel, down-dragging, destructive." "Why," she wonders, "had she come to this high plateau of death?" (*PS*, 50–51).

Kate goes that afternoon to examine the frescoes by Diego Rivera at the University of Mexico. Her first impression is that, although Rivera "knew his craft," the basic impulse behind his work was that "of the artist's hate" (*PS*, 53). She recognizes the "sympathy with the Indian" in the frescoes, but dismisses that sympathy as a forced and tendentious political ideal. She regards the "flat Indians" of the frescoes as "mere symbols in the great script of modern socialism." As Kate passes from the work of Rivera to that of lesser artists, she finds their treatment increasingly deliberate and crude. The images impress her as ugly and vulgar caricatures of the capitalists and the church.

García, a young Mexican admirer of the frescoes, defends them on the grounds that they merely reflect ugly social facts. Although Kate and García quarrel about the technique of the frescoes, they quickly agree on the hopeless ugliness of the antecedent Mexican reality that the frescoes represent. Their conversation turns to the political means available to change that reality. García is bitter about the foreign exploitation of Mexico, despises capitalism as the enemy, and embraces socialism as the only solution. Kate regards both capitalism and socialism as alien European ideologies, equally inappropriate to the Mexican reality. As with the discussion at the tea party, everyone concedes that Mexico is in dire need of salvation. Only the question remains: What can be done?

At this point in the novel, the case against modern Mexico has been thoroughly made. It is a squalid, lice ridden, oppressive, evil, and deathly place. The Indians are uncreated beings without centers. Politics of all varieties is a futile exercise dominated by pompous self-seekers. Foreign ideas, like Catholicism and capitalism, have overwhelmed and destroyed the indigenous culture. Granted, in making this assessment Lawrence may have exaggerated his personal feelings to serve the dialectical needs of his novel—to prepare the way for Ramón and Cipriano and their redemptive religion. Nevertheless, in shaping his novel, Lawrence has offered a relentlessly negative portrait of the modern Mexico City of his own experiences.

For the purposes of this discussion, the early chapters of *The Plumed Serpent,* which reveal Lawrence's repudiation of the actual, historical Mexico City that he visited, are more important than the later chapters that detail Lawrence's imagined, alternative reality and its implementation. What is essential to recognize about the rest of *The Plumed Serpent* is that the Mexico presented there derives less from Lawrence's perceptions than from his imagination. These chapters contain vivid, powerful, and sympathetic descriptions of landscapes and people, to be sure. But they are suffused and transvalued—redeemed—by the myth of the resurrected Quetzalcoatl, concocted in Lawrence's mind. The early chapters of *The Plumed Serpent* draw on Lawrence's experiences of Mexico City—his attendance at a bullfight and a tea party, his visit to the frescoes of the university—in all their richly textured detail, *for the purpose of evaluating them.* If the nights in Mexico City creep with fear or the mountains emit a sound of dread, that is the way that Kate/Lawrence experienced them. But when the peons of Sayula respond to the drummer in the plaza, naked to the waist and majestic in his confidence and dignity, by joining him in dance and song, Lawrence's imagination is creating a Chapala/Sayula that did not exist outside the novel. Lawrence's invented reality, based on the legends and mythology of the Indians of pre-Columbian Mexico, and on the dances of contemporary Indians of New Mexico, supplants the reality of Mexico City that Lawrence experienced.

Ironically, *The Plumed Serpent* is yet another "paleface overlay," one more white man's version of what Mexico should be. Like the frescoes that the novel attacks, it is a socially and politically tendentious version of Mexico. Whatever the novel's pretensions to reclaiming a lost Mexican past, and whatever value individual readers might discover in that project, *The Plumed Serpent* represents an imported ideology as surely as does capitalism, socialism, or Catholicism. Moreover, the characters in the novel who effect the Quetzalcoatl revolution either are themselves foreigners or bear the deep influence of foreign culture. Cipriano may be a pure Indian, but he spent years at school in London, afterward trained to be a priest in Oxford, and speaks British English impressively well. Ramón is described as "almost a pure Spaniard" (*PS*, 67), and he studied anthropology at Columbia University in New York. Kate, who eventually becomes a modern Mexican goddess, is Irish, pure and simple. Under the guise of resurrecting the Mexican "Gods of Antiquity," *The Plumed Serpent* documents, and is itself the agent of, the most recent instance in Mexico's long history of cultural imperialism.

Lawrence and Frieda left Chapala on 9 or 10 July 1923. They went first to Mexico City, then north through Texas, New Orleans, and Washington to New York, where they arrived on 19 July. Lawrence's letters indicate that he planned to return to Europe, reluctantly, with Frieda. But he expected to be disappointed by Europe, and he also speaks in the letters of returning to Mexico. Some two weeks before leaving Chapala, for instance, he wrote Knud Merrild, a Danish painter he had known in Taos, "If I can't stand Europe we'll come back to Mexico and spit on our hands and stick knives and revolvers in our belts—one really has to—and have a place here" (*ML*, 748). He wrote Merrild again on 15 July, from New York: "I am not very keen even on going to England. I think what I would like best would be to go back to Mexico. If we were a few people, we could make a life in Mexico."[10] By a few people making a life in Mexico, Lawrence had in mind his dream of Rananim, a small colony of like-minded friends.

Finally, Lawrence could not yet face the prospect of Europe. In August, Frieda sailed for England, and Lawrence returned to Mexico. Traveling with Kai Gotzsche, another Danish painter and friend of

[10]Huxley, 572.

Knud Merrild, Lawrence made his way down the rugged west coast of Mexico, from the California border to Guadalajara. The weather was mercilessly hot, the trains maddeningly slow, the hotels primitive. After Mazatlán, where the railroad track ended, they continued their journey by car and, for two days, on muleback. Given the demands of the trip, the barrenness of the countryside, and the fact that Lawrence was traveling without Frieda, and no doubt grieving over her absence, it is hardly surprising that Lawrence did not find a place to found Rananim. As Ronald Walker points out, Lawrence was less than enthusiastic about settling in western Mexico, even when given the opportunity.[11] Lawrence explains to Merrild in a letter from Sonora:

> On the whole, the west coast is a little *too* wild—nothing but wildness. . . . One wants a bit of hopefulness. These wild lost places seem so hopeless. But a man said he'd *give* me six or eight acres of land near Guaymas, near the sea, in a very wild, very strange and beautiful country, if I'd only build a house on the place. . . . But one feels so out of the world: like living on Mars. As if the human race wasn't real.—I don't know what effect it would have on one in the end. [*ML* 754]

In a letter written to Bynner the same day, Lawrence remarked that "this West is much wilder, emptier, more hopeless than Chapala." Beneath the blazing sun and a "vast hot sky" are "lonely inhuman hills and mountains," with occasional "little towns that seem to be sliding down an abyss." As Lawrence had so often felt before about Mexico, he found the West deathly. He regarded a dead dog lying in the midst of the public market in a "once lovely little town" called Alamos, for instance, as emblematic: the entire town seemed to him to have "a sentence of extinction written all over it" (*ML,* 755–56).

Kai Gotzsche reports that Lawrence grew irritable and extremely tense during their trip, chiefly because of Frieda's absence. At one point, Lawrence became so difficult that Gotzsche maintained a distance between them: "I am avoiding Lawrence as much as possible at present, because, considering all things, he is really insane when he is as now" (Nehls, 266). Gotzsche describes Lawrence's disappointment during a one-day return to Chapala. Lawrence had not wanted to visit the lake without Frieda but had been deeply moved when he and Gotzsche nevertheless went out for the day. Lawrence thought the lake very much changed. "Somehow it becomes unreal to me now," he told Gotzsche. "I don't know why. . . . The life has changed somehow,

---

[11]Ronald Walker, *Infernal Paradise: Mexico and the Modern English Novel* (Berkeley: University of California Press, 1978), 54.

has gone dead" (Nehls, 264). Gotzsche's theory about why the lake seemed unreal and dead to Lawrence is very penetrating. "He is always so concerned about the 'spirit' of the place," Gotzsche writes, "that he isn't aware . . . that it is he, himself, his own mood or frame of mind, that determines his impressions of the moment, or the landscape." Gotzsche understood that, for all Lawrence's keenness of perception and his ability to give life to a landscape in language, the "spirit of place" was more often than not a projection of Lawrence's moods, fears, and hopes. The bleakness and inhospitality of the Mexican West, like the unreality and deadness of Chapala during his one-day return, reflect Lawrence's own isolation and hopelessness as he traveled without Frieda in a willful effort to keep the ideal of Rananim alive.

Despite the disappointments during his second trip, Lawrence also kept alive the ideal of Mexico as the place where the lost life thread might be found, where Rananim might flourish. On 17 October, he wrote Catherine Carswell from Guadalajara that "Mexico has a certain mystery of beauty for me, as if the gods were here." He goes on to express the wish that he could "start a little center" in Mexico, a ranch "where we could have our little adobe houses and make a life, and you could come" (*ML*, 757–58). Lawrence wrote Willard Johnson the next day expressing a moderated version of the same sentiments. "The country is quite lovely in the autumn," he says. But he is less grand in his hopes for the future than he had been with Carswell: "Don't suppose I shall stay long." To Johnson, Lawrence's ideal on a ranch is not to "make a new life," but merely "to go on a ranch somewhere here for the winter" (*ML*, 759). Lawrence wrote his most aggressive affirmation of Mexico during this period to Middleton Murry. England, he proclaims, must "pick up a lost trail," and, he continues, "the end of the lost trail is here in Mexico" (*ML*, 759). This letter is filled with Spanish phrases, as though to demonstrate to Murry how far apart their consciousnesses were, and is written in short, confident, staccatolike declarative sentences. Clearly, Lawrence's determined affirmation of Mexico in this letter is equally a repudiation of Murry and the England that he represented to Lawrence.

Lawrence wrote with less posturing and bravado to Frieda during the trip. Writing from Guadalajara on 10 November, he describes Mexico as "still very attractive and a very good place to live in: it is not tame" (*ML*, 762). Recalling his one-day visit to Chapala without her, he comments, "I like the plain round Guadalajara, with the mountains here and there around. I like it better than the lake." He adds, "I still wish I was staying the winter on a ranch somewhere not far from this city." Lawrence makes it apparent that his heart is not in the quest for Rananim, without Frieda: "But I'll come back to England to say how do you do! to it all." Despite his deliberate declaration of enthusiasm for Mexico in these letters to Carswell, Murry, and others, Lawrence was, on balance, an unhappy man during his second trip to Mexico. Rananim was an abstract ideal that seemed with each passing day less likely to be fulfilled. As Gotzsche wrote, "to have a ranch here will not mature, I can see that" (Nehls, 266).

Lawrence sailed for England and Frieda from Vera Cruz on 22 November, 1923, bringing to an end the first phase of his New World adventure a bit more than thirteen months after his arrival in Taos. He and Frieda spent Christmas and New Years in England, then moved on to France and Germany before returning to Taos in late March 1924. They remained until early fall at a ranch north of Taos presented to Frieda as a gift by Mabel Dodge. After a wearying and dismal experience in Europe, springtime in the mountains of New Mexico, coupled with his reconciliation with Frieda, lifted Lawrence's spirits. He did not return to the "Quetzalcoatl" manuscript written the previous June in Chapala. Apparently, he felt that he could continue work on it only while actually residing in Mexico. But Lawrence wrote prolifically during these months. He wrote "The Woman Who Rode Away," *St. Mawr,* and "The Princess," as well as several essays. Three of the essays—"Indians and Entertainment," "Dance of the Sprouting Corn," and "The Hopi Snake Dance"—are among the most sympathetic accounts of Indians that Lawrence ever wrote. All three were eventually included in the second half of *Mornings in Mexico.*

Despite his contentment and productivity in Taos, Lawrence soon yearned to return to Mexico. There is little evidence that he still felt the magnetic appeal of Mexico as the place for rediscovering the lost life thread. No doubt that motive lingered in his mind. But his letters suggest that he felt something like a migratory instinct. He wanted "to go south," as he puts it in several letters, almost as though he were a roving bird that changed continents with the seasons. And he also wanted to write, to finish the "Mexican novel." On 20 October 1924, the Lawrences and Dorothy Brett, who had accompanied them from Europe, left El Paso for Lawrence's third and final sojourn to Mexico. They paused more than two weeks in Mexico City, which Lawrence found extremely unpleasant, and then continued south to Oaxaca. Lawrence's first impressions of Oaxaca were favorable: "Oaxaca is a very quiet little town, with small but proud Indians. . . . It is very peaceful, and has a remote beauty of its own" (*ML,* 817).

Within a week, however, the "wildness" of the Indians and the political turbulence began to qualify his judgment. On 15 November, he wrote Middleton Murry praising the beauty of the countryside but complaining about the people: "The Indians are queer little savages, and awful agitators pump bits of socialism over them and make everything just a mess" (*ML*, 820). He concludes, with resignation, that he will stay and try to finish "my *Quetzalcoatl*." Two days later, Lawrence wrote Clarence Thompson in the same vein: "We are way down here in the South of Mexico—marvellous sunshine every day, but rather stupid people" (*ML*, 820). He believes that he will probably remain in Oaxaca for "a month or two," in order to finish the novel, "though I'm wishing I'd gone to Europe instead of coming here." Lawrence remarks condescendingly that he called on the provincial governor at his palace: "He was an Indian from the hills, and an Indian in a Sunday suit! *Dio benedetto!* What a fool's world altogether!" Lawrence could not accept dark-skinned Mexicans in anything but idealized primitive surroundings, like those in the Sayula section of *The Plumed Serpent* or those in "The Woman Who Rode Away." An Indian in modern dress, or merely an Indian in a modern urban setting, inevitably seemed to Lawrence somehow a lie, a fraud, or a forfeiture—pathetic or foolish at best, dangerous or evil at worst.

By 19 November, Lawrence had settled into a house and had begun his revision of *Quetzalcoatl*. In mid-December he paused to write four essays that would become the first half of *Mornings in Mexico*. These were: "Friday Morning," published as "Corasmin and the Parrots"; "Saturday Morning," published first as "The Gentle Art of Marketing in Mexico" and in book form as "Market Day"; "Sunday Morning," published first as "Sunday Stroll in Sleepy Mexico" and in book form as "Walk to Huayapa"; and "Monday Morning," published as "The Mozo."[12] Given Lawrence's impatient mood and his general experiences of Oaxaca as wild and frightening, while also more than a little absurd, these four essays are remarkably sympathetic toward Mexico. They also have their condescending and hostile moments.

The task of anyone seeking to understand Lawrence's attitude toward Mexico in the essays, and therefore his feelings about the country in the final months of his last visit, is to assess the relationship of sympathy and hostility and to discern which attitude, on balance, is dominant. Two valuable critical studies of *Mornings in Mexico* have

[12]Lawrence assigned titles mentioning days of the week to the essays while they were in manuscript. The published versions had new titles and, in the volume *Mornings in Mexico,* were reordered without regard to the days of the week shown on the original manuscripts.

already addressed these issues: the first by Thomas R. Whitaker in 1961, the second by Ronald Walker in 1978.[13] Whitaker rejects the obvious conclusion that *Mornings in Mexico* is a casual assortment of four travel sketches of Mexico plus some tacked-on pieces written earlier, as Richard Aldington, for example, implies in his introduction to the published volume. Whitaker regards the wide range of attitudes and judgments that Lawrence displays in the four essays— ranging from jeering hostility to respectful sympathy—as part of a careful design. Lawrence's various points of view on Mexico are arranged, in Whitaker's opinion, as stages in a journey, a vacillating progression of attitudes that culminates in a salutary total acceptance of the initially alien Mexican otherness. Lawrence's four essays recount, Whitaker argues, a successful spiritual quest for transcendence of the isolated ego. Ronald Walker accepts Whitaker's basic notion that the four sketches portray the gradually deepening insight of the speaker, Lawrence himself. But Walker dwells on Lawrence's hostility and fearfulness more than Whitaker. He regards Lawrence's attitudes as, at times, frankly virulent. And Walker is not convinced that the venting of such virulence accomplishes more than temporary and partial amelioration.

"Corasmin and the Parrots," the first essay in the published version of *Mornings in Mexico,* opens with a description of the spot where Lawrence writes—the patio of a "crumbly adobe house."[14] The sun is shining. The smells of flowers and cote wood mingle with those of coffee. The cocks crow in the distance. The servant, Rosalino, sweeps the patio with a twig broom. A dog, Corasmin, stretches out in the sun or shade, depending on the temperature. And a pair of parrots whistle and squawk overhead. Lawrence is keenly aware that he describes uniquely private experiences and that to generalize them into "mornings in Mexico" is a bold, possibly distorting, aggrandizement of the particular.

Lawrence dwells on the mimicry of the parrots, who whistle like Rosalino, "only more so," who imitate the human voice that calls the dog, and who imitate the bark of the dog in response. Lawrence is amused by the parrots. They seem to him to be mocking Rosalino, Corasmin, and all humans who call dogs. Lawrence then sketches his version of Aztec cosmogony, in which the universe undergoes a se-

---

[13]Thomas R. Whitaker, "Lawrence's Western Path: *Mornings in Mexico,*" *Criticism* 3:3 (1961), 219–36; and Walker, 61–70. The two works are hereafter cited in text as Whitaker and Walker.

[14]D. H. Lawrence, *Mornings in Mexico* (London: Heinemann, 1956), 1, hereafter cited in my text as *MM*.

quence of creations and destructions. Each new creation takes the superior creatures of the previous creation down a peg, because it introduces fresh "superiority" into the order of things. Each displaced "superior" being saves face by mocking his successor. Yet each being exists in an absolutely unique dimension of time, and each is divided from every other by an invisible and unbridgeable gulf. That gulf separates the creatures on Lawrence's patio. The parrots exist in one dimension, Corasmin in another. Similarly, Lawrence and Rosalino occupy different dimensions of reality. Thinking of Rosalino, Lawrence writes: "Between us also is the gulf of the other dimension, and he wants to bridge it. . . . He knows it can't be done. So do I" (*MM*, 8).

"Corasmin and the Parrots" adumbrates the themes that will recur throughout the remaining essays in *Mornings in Mexico:* the gulf that separates individual beings; the yearning to bridge the gulf; the temptation to jeer at those who are different, as though difference necessarily implied inferiority; and the dangers inherent in generalizing about the other on the basis of one's limited experience. Thomas Whitaker regards Lawrence's articulation of these issues, especially his recognition of the gulf between him and Rosalino, as evidence of Lawrence's "humility" and of his acceptance of "his limits." More grandly still, Whitaker understands that acceptance as signifying that Lawrence "opens himself to the tide of continual creation" (Whitaker, 221). But there are difficulties with this extremely positive reading of the essay. To begin with, for Lawrence to accept the absolute otherness of Rosalino and celebrate creativity is not quite the act of growth that Whitaker believes. Rather than the ends of a long process, these attitudes are the departure points of *Mornings in Mexico.* Indeed, they have been données of Lawrence's work from the outset of his career. Lawrence has always celebrated "new life" in the abstract, however much he may have despised given individuals. And he has always had a horror of what he called "merging." He even posited this horror, in his essay on "Edgar Allan Poe," as a "law of life." "The central law of all organic life," he wrote, "is that each organism is intrinsically isolate and single in itself" (*SCAL*, 62). To "accept" the gulf between him and Rosalino, then, is not a hard-won victory, and may even be a *repudiation* of Rosalino. Lawrence notes, for example, that Rosalino "wants to bridge" the gulf, but Lawrence insists on it. Finally, Lawrence's tone of amused tolerance (not "light humility," as Whitaker describes it) seems to presume that he represents a later stage of creation that has superseded Rosalino. *His* perspective and *his* understanding are superior by implication.

The second essay in *Mornings in Mexico,* "Walk to Huayapa," describes a Sunday walk that Lawrence, Frieda, and Rosalino took to a nearby village (actually Huayapan) on the morning of 21 December 1924. Both Whitaker and Walker regard the essay as depicting Lawrence's progress from the perspective of mocking outsider to sympathetic observer. There is much to be said in favor of their reading. Lawrence as speaker undertakes the outing with reluctance, spurred on by his "better-half." He feels annoyed by the dullness of Rosalino, particulary his mindless repetition of "como no, Señor" as the ready answer to all questions. As the trio marches through the dusty countryside, Lawrence feels acutely that both the landscape and the people are foreign to him. But as the essay draws to its conclusion, Lawrence has accepted Rosalino, yet again, and has made his peace with the Indians near Huayapa, several of whom he finds beautiful. He concludes the essay in a mellow mood: "*mañana es otro día.* Tomorrow is another day."

So goes the positive reading, in brief. The trouble is that it overlooks the central issue of the essay—Lawrence's intense frustration in his efforts to find fresh fruit in Huayapa. He goes from shop to shop and from yard to yard, asking if there is fruit for sale. Even though he sees fruit growing on the trees, he can find no one who will readily sell it to him. Like Rosalino's mechanical "como no, Señor," the people respond, over and over, "no hay frutas," "there is no fruit." Earlier, Lawrence had thought that Rosalino was a "dumb-bell." Now, the whole village of Huayapa seems crowded with dumbbells. Lawrence describes the people gathering in the streets as "gangs." He mocks a political rally as a farce. The musicians playing at a fiesta willfully render unrecognizable the tunes they play. When at last a woman gives him some fruit in exchange for an empty bottle, it turns out to be full of worms. Lawrence shows some self-irony in recounting all these frustrations—he describes himself, for example, as a member of the "ruling race," as he boldly enters yet another yard demanding fruit. But Lawrence can hardly be regarded, in these passages, as embracing the otherness of the people of Huayapa. It never occurs to him, for example, that "no hay frutas," might mean "we have fruit but not for sale today" or "we have fruit but not for sale to *you.*" It never occurs to him that the village might resent his intrusion into its Sunday life. All he knows, at the time, is that he is hot, thirsty, and hungry, and surrounded by dumbbells. Without question, the essay includes its moments of appreciation of the beauty of certain Indians, those bathing in a stream below the spot where Lawrence's party finally picnics. But the overall mood of the essay's conclusion is not so much sympathy as resignation. "Tomorrow is another day" ironically formulates the attitude of the people of Mexico that surround Lawrence. It is Lawrence's shrug of the shoulders, not his embrace.

"The Mozo," the next essay in the sequence, examines Rosalino in comparison to his entire race of Mexican Indians. Rosalino differs from the rest, Lawrence says, because he does not "stare with a black, incomprehensible, but somewhat defiant stare" (*MM*, 23). Lawrence then turns to ancient Aztec mythology, as he had in "Corasmin and the Parrots," to help define the Mexican present. The Aztec goddess of love, he explains, is a "goddess of dirt and prostitution." When she conceives, she brings forth not a child, but a razor-edged obsidian knife to be used to cut the heart out of sacrificial victims. Forgetting altogether his own earlier warning about the dangers of basing generalizations on limited personal experience, Lawrence derives from the Aztec myth one of his most hostile assessments of Mexico: "And to this day, most of the Mexican Indian women seem to bring forth stone knives. Look at them, these sons of incomprehensible mothers, with their black eyes like flints, and their stiff little bodies as taut and as keen as knives of obsidian. Take care they don't rip you up" (*MM*, 24).

Although Rosalino is an exception to his race, he wavers (Lawrence continues) between the dangerous otherness of the obsidian knife and the servile mimicry of the parrots. Lawrence complicates this division between defiance and compliance, without attempting to resolve it, with an account of Rosalino's past. Rosalino had refused to join the revolutionary soldiers who tried to recruit Indians from the hills. The soldiers had beaten him badly, injuring his back. The injury explains to Lawrence why Rosalino would not carry a bit of furniture for him on the day that he and Frieda moved into their Oaxaca house, a refusal that had seemed to Lawrence at the time to be the first evidence that Rosalino was a dumbbell. More than that, Rosalino's defiance of the revolutionaries establishes, in Lawrence's mind, a kinship between him and Lawrence. "He is one of those, like myself, who have a horror of serving in a mass of men" (*MM*, 33). Lawrence has discovered a small plot of common ground between him and Rosalino. But it does not cause Lawrence to modify his judgment of the race of obsidian knives, the rest of Rosalino's people who might, this essay suggests, be expected to have personal stories that make them individuals, too.

"Market Day" is the last of the Mexican essays in *Mornings in Mexico*. It is the purest and most uncomplicated acceptance of daily life in Mexico that Lawrence wrote. He describes how, the last Saturday before Christmas, the Indians come from miles and miles around to converge on Oaxaca, "a central point," for their open market. The point of the essay is to reveal that the deep purpose of coming to market is not merely to buy and sell but to commingle. The Indians—as Lawrence sees them—delight in the give and take of barter as "an intermingling of voices, a threading together of different wills" (*MM*, 39). He tells of an exchange between himself and a couple who want to sell him a pair of huaraches, or Mexican sandals. Lawrence sniffs the sandals and declares that "they smell." The Indian couple breaks up in laughter, insisting that they do not smell. Both Lawrence and the couple know that the Indians use human excrement in tanning leather. The Indians and the Englishman bicker, both in good humor. Ultimately, he does not want shoes that smell of human excrement. But he leaves the couple (who continue to laugh at the joke on the gringo) in a spirit of appreciative tolerance. "Everything has its own smell," he grants, "you might as well quarrel with an onion for smelling like an onion" (*MM,* 41). The essay comes to an end by affirming that the market, like the huaraches, has its unique character. That character, that purpose, is to provide contact between the vendors and the buyers: "nothing but the touch, the spark of contact." For the Indians, at least, the "gulf of the other dimension" is momentarily bridged. Lawrence may remain the gringo who dislikes the smell of human excrement in his leather goods, but he has drawn as closely to these people of the other dimension, in this essay, as he can. Most important, these are people from the Oaxaca markets, not the idealized creatures of Lawrence's imagination that he affirms in the Sayula section of *The Plumed Serpent.*

In these four essays of Oaxaca, Lawrence attempts, as Ronald Walker puts it, "to mollify his antipathy toward the Indian and his sense of being alienated from Mexico" (Walker, 62). In contrast to the discontents of daily life, and their relatively immediate reflection in his letters, these essays are thoughtful and appreciative assessments of Oaxaca. To be sure, *Mornings in Mexico* contains numerous instances of the powerful animosity that Lawrence often felt for Mexico and its Indians, an animosity sometimes bred by simple prejudice and fear but more often resulting from disappointment. Disappointment because, we must not forget, Lawrence was a modern pilgrim on a spiritual quest. On the other hand, these essays also contain moments of stunning insight and delicate empathy. Typically, the insights are intermingled with the empathy, and the perspective shifts quickly from one evaluation to another. It is an intelligent imposition of a pattern to discern in *Mornings in Mexico,* as Thomas Whitaker has done, a dramatic presentation of a sustained persona who learns, step by step, to embrace the otherness of Mexico. Rather, *Mornings in Mexico* replicates Lawrence's own experience of Mexico, which was not progress toward acceptance but vacillation between deep sympathy and outright, condescending virulence. In his letters or in conversation with Frieda or friends, Lawrence could be shockingly intolerant of Mexico. Upon reflection, he could recover his intellectual and emotional balance and could therefore perceive the positive qualities of the country. The pendulum swing of attitudes resulted from Lawrence's effort to accommodate his long-held—and cherished—ideal of the New World with the mundane realities of Mexico City, Chapala, and Oaxaca. In works like *The Plumed Serpent*, Lawrence expressed the mundane realities in the early chapters, set in Mexico City, and fabricated the ideal in the later chapters set at the lake. In *Mornings in Mexico*, he remains closer to his daily experience, and as a consequence there is little idealizing of Mexico. Instead, there is the vacillation that he actually felt: both sides of his feelings and judgment.

Lawrence completed the final draft of *Quetzalcoatl—The Plumed Serpent*—in early February 1925 and fell sick with malaria immediately afterward. He wrote Brett from Oaxaca, postmarked 5 February, that he was sick in bed, that "the novel is finished," and that he was anxious to leave Oaxaca: "I hate the place" (*ML*, 831). He was finished with both his Mexican novel and his Mexican experience. As the months passed and Lawrence recovered from the illness that almost killed him, he put his Mexican experiences increasingly behind him. On 21 May Lawrence wrote from Taos that he could not even correct proof on *The Plumed Serpent* because "it smells too much of Oaxaca, which I hated so much because I was ill." He goes on to say that he thinks "of Mexico with a sort of nausea," and that he never wants "to see an Indian or an 'aboriginee' or anything in the savage line again."[15]

Within a few weeks, Lawrence had distinguished his feelings about the novel from those about Mexico. He continued adamant about Mexico. In a letter of 10 June he wrote that he would "never forgive Mexico, especially Oaxaca, for having done me in. . . . Quoth the raven: *Nevermore*. . . . Nevermore need I look on Mexico." The same letter expresses his high regard for the novel, which "lies nearer my heart than any other work of mine" (*ML*, 844). In a letter to his agent some two weeks later, he expressed similar sentiments about *The Plumed Serpent*, calling it "my most important novel so far" (*ML*, 845).

---

[15]Harry T. Moore, *The Priest of Love: A Life of D. H. Lawrence* (New York: Farrar, Straus & Giroux, 1974), 403.

D. H. Lawrence and Mexico

It was not just Mexico that Lawrence was putting behind him. It was the whole American experience. He returned to Europe after a summer of convalescence in Taos, in late September 1925, and arrived in Spotorno, Italy by 15 November. His letters from that fall comment on the tensions of America and the pleasure of being in Italy once again, even if he preferred to move further south. A letter to Brett in late November is typical: "There is something I like very much about the Mediterranean . . . after the tension of America" (*ML*, 868). Lawrence had completed his "great curve in [the] direction" of the savages, and he was content—for the time being, at least—to savor the Mediterranean.

Yet, with characteristic complexity of feeling, Lawrence looked back to America, from the perspective of Italian contentment, with nostalgia. That is his purpose (looking back) and his mood (nostalgic) in the three-page coda to *Mornings in Mexico* that he wrote in Spotorno within ten days of arriving, "A Little Moonshine with Lemon." In this vividly detailed reminiscence of what it would be like to finish a long evening in late fall at the ranch in New Mexico rather than in Italy, Lawrence cherishes the memories of the great pine trees outside his cabin, the snow-covered countryside beneath the moon, the animals that he had once nourished, the long work table inside the cabin, even the Montgomery Ward's catalog through which he might search for something for Christmas. But Lawrence does not want to go back. He also cherishes the sound of the Mediterranean as it "whispers in the distance" (*MM*, 81). It strikes him as so eternally young, while Italy is so old. This combination of youth and age appeals to—compels— Lawrence. "I give it up," he says of America, of the ranch above Taos, of the moonshine with lemon that he would drink *there* this night, instead of the vermouth or wine that he can choose *here*, in Spotorno.

We may wonder how long Lawrence would have been content on the Mediterranean had his health not failed. In the first letters from Spotorno, he was already talking of moving further south, perhaps to Capri, perhaps to Sicily. He spoke also of Greece, Turkey, Egypt, and repeatedly of the possibility of visiting Russia. As Lawrence put it so succinctly in the opening sentence of *Sea and Sardinia:* "Comes over one an absolute necessity to move." Could he have stayed away from the ranch, had he lived? Perhaps even Mexico would have appealed to him again. After repudiating Greece or Egypt or Russia, he might have continued the search for the lost life thread in Mexico, once more. And although it was not in his nature to *find* that thread, the search would have exalted and infuriated him—and us.

[10]

Lawrence, Yeats, and "the Resurrection of the Body"

PHILLIP L. MARCUS

In the final decade of Yeats's life he "discovered" Lawrence's fiction, reading *Sons and Lovers, The Rainbow,* and *Women in Love* "with excitement." *Lady Chatterley's Lover* seemed "all fire . . . , something ancient, humble and terrible." And, making a connection that would surely have horrified Lawrence, Yeats linked him with Joyce in having "almost restored to us the Eastern simplicity."[1] The frank but "noble" sexuality of *Lady Chatterley's Lover* might even have been among the forces that encouraged the earthy, sensual element in Yeats's late work; in any case, he was beyond feeling threatened by Lawrence's achievement and no doubt felt resonance with his own experience and found reinforcement of significant aspects of his own vision. In contrast, Lawrence's few remarks about Yeats are generally negative. "I have had a lot of Yeats—he is vapourish, too thin," he wrote in 1909, and in 1912 found him "awfully queer stuff . . . now— as if he wouldn't bear touching."[2] Yet they had far more in common than Lawrence saw or, perhaps, than he was willing to admit.

In *Eminent Domain*, Richard Ellmann has described vividly the edgy competitiveness and suspicion writers so often feel toward their major contemporaries.[3] Lawrence, though not discussed by Ellmann, ex-

---

[1]*The Letters of W. B. Yeats,* ed. Allan Wade (New York: Macmillan, 1955), 803, 810, 807.

[2]*The Letters of D. H. Lawrence,* vol. 1, ed. James T. Boulton (Cambridge: Cambridge University Press, 1979), 107, 488 (hereafter *CL*1). See also *Phoenix: The Posthumous Papers of D. H. Lawrence,* ed. Edward D. McDonald (New York: Viking, 1936), for a 1913 review of *Georgian Poetry: 1911–1912* in which Lawrence, defending the Georgians as love poets, says, "What is 'The Hare' but a complete love poem, with none of the hackneyed 'But a bitter blossom was born' about it, nor yet the Yeats, 'Never give all the heart'" (p. 307).

[3]Richard Ellmann, *Eminent Domain* (New York: Oxford University Press, 1967).

emplified these feelings as much as anyone. They often mask, and may alert us to, important areas of shared vision. Lawrence was witheringly scornful about Joyce, for example, but Robert Kiely has shown how profitably the two can be discussed in relation to each other.[4] The present essay is not the first study to compare Lawrence and Yeats and does not pretend to be an exhaustive examination of their relationship. It focuses, instead, upon a few key points of explicit or implied confrontation, using those points to explore surprising congruences as well as areas of divergence.[5]

In addition to the dynamics of hostility characteristic of the literary relations among the great moderns, Lawrence's feelings about Yeats were probably affected by an unsuccessful personal meeting in 1909,[6] and certainly by the fact that Yeats's early poetry and plays shared many of the concerns and especially the weaknesses of his own work to that point and thus constituted an unpleasant reminder of a stage that by 1912 he was anxious to move beyond. From that time on he may have ignored all or virtually all of Yeats's subsequent work; but a close similarity remained. Lawrence's late novella *The Escaped Cock* offers an index of that closeness: it can be read as a "rejection" of Yeats and may even have been intended as such; but it is itself intensely Yeatsian, a work Yeats himself might almost have written, and suggests how similar their visions really were, while at the same time bringing into relief essential and irreconcilable differences between them.

I

The genesis of Lawrence's novella goes back to a letter he wrote in 1914, not long after the early negative comments about Yeats, and,

[4]Robert Kiely, *Beyond Egotism* (Cambridge: Harvard University Press, 1980).

[5]Murray Roston has a chapter on Yeats and Lawrence in *Biblical Drama in England* (London: Faber & Faber, 1968), and their aesthetics are compared by Debra Somberg Journet, "W. B. Yeats, D. H. Lawrence, and Modernism" (Ph.D. diss., McGill University, 1980). Studies containing frequent comparative references include Ethel F. Cornwell, *The "Still Point"* (New Brunswick: Rutgers University Press, 1962); David J. Gordon, *D. H. Lawrence as a Literary Critic* (New Haven: Yale University Press, 1966); Sandra M. Gilbert, *Acts of Attention: The Poems of D. H. Lawrence* (Ithaca: Cornell University Press, 1972); Brian John, *Supreme Fictions* (Montreal: McGill-Queens University Press, 1974); and especially Robert Langbaum, *The Mysteries of Identity* (New York: Oxford University Press, 1977).

[6]*D. H. Lawrence: A Composite Biography*, ed. Edward Nehls, 3 vols. (Madison: University of Wisconsin Press, 1957–59), I, 129–32; Harry T. Moore, *The Priest of Love: A Life of D. H. Lawrence*, rev. ed. (New York: Farrar, Straus & Giroux, 1974), 110–11.

significantly, it is linked there with another such comment.[7] The letter was addressed to the Irish barrister Gordon Campbell and concerned a novel Campbell was writing. The topic led Lawrence into a general attack on modern literature for its egotism and incompleteness. As he urged Campbell to try to grasp "the *Complete Whole* which the Celtic symbolism made in its great time," he brought in Yeats: "We see only the *symbol* as a *subjective expression:* as an expression of ourselves. That makes us so sickly when we deal with the old symbols: like Yeats. The old symbols were each a word in a great attempt at formulating the whole history of the Soul of Man. . . . So your Ireland of you Irishmen of today is a filthy mucking-about with a part of the symbolism of a Great Statement or Vision: just as the Crucifixion of Christ is a great mucking about with part of the symbolism of a great religious Vision."

Lawrence was acute in recognizing the "subjective" element in Yeats's use of symbolism and mythology but did not see that he was using them to a considerable extent to go *beyond* the purely personal, just as Lawrence himself was urging Campbell to do. As early as 1896 Yeats had written that "emotions which seem vague or extravagant when expressed under the influence of modern literature, cease to be vague and extravagant when associated with ancient legend and mythology"[8]—because the traditional represents the enduring elements in human experience, incarnates the archetypal patterns of reality; and in the first version of *A Vision* he identified as a primary attraction of the book's elaborate symbolism that it "would leave my imagination free to create as it chose and yet make all that it created, or could create, part of the one history, and that the soul's."[9] The "great attempt at formulating the whole history of the Soul of Man" was thus recognized by him as well.

Furthermore, while Lawrence may seem to be relating the Christian and the Celtic only analogically, the remainder of the letter reveals that he saw a more organic connection. Mrs. Henry Jenner's *Christian Symbolism,* which he went on to praise highly, was undoubtedly responsible for the prominence of Christian symbolism as vehicle for the vision Lawrence was expressing in the letter, but he asserted that "the Whole of the Celtic symbolism and great Utterance of its Conception," though never yet fathomed, "must have been in accord

---

[7]*The Letters of D. H. Lawrence,* vol. 2, ed. George J. Zytaruk and James T. Boulton (Cambridge: Cambridge University Press, 1981), 246–50 (hereafter *CL* II).

[8]Yeats, "Miss Fiona Macleod as a Poet," *Bookman,* December 1896, 92.

[9]*A Critical Edition of Yeats's "A Vision" (1925),* ed. George Mills Harper and Walter Kelly Hood (London: Macmillan, 1978), xi, cited henceforth as *Vision* (1925).

with the Latin." The underlying assumption here, he pointed out, was that "all religions I think have the same inner conception, with different expressions." Yeats, who had found the concept in such sources as Madame Blavatsky and Blake, had been making the same assumption for years.[10]

Thus the advice Lawrence went on to give Campbell, though expressed primarily in "Latin" terms, established a nexus among the Christian and Celtic visions, modern literature, and Yeats. Modern writers had preferred to "end insisting on the sad plight," on the Crucifixion: "But Christianity should teach us now, that after our Crucifixion, and the darkness of the tomb, we shall rise again in the flesh, you, I, as we are today, resurrected in the bodies." In urging Campbell to "get the *greatest* truth into your novel. . . . Give us the Resurrection after the Crucifixion," he was, as it were, proleptically advising also the Yeats who in a few years would seem to be "insisting on the sad plight" when he offered his own version of Christ's death in the play *Calvary*.

Although it has been suggested that Lawrence's conception of Judas as a liberator "probably owes something" to *Calvary* as well as to Oscar Wilde, there is in fact no external evidence that Lawrence read the play, which was first published in 1921—or for that matter that he knew any of Yeats's late work.[11] On the other hand, Lawrence's strong interest in the subject may have led him at some point to seek out that text. Whether or not he was actually familiar with the play, how *might* he have read it?

The successive frustrations of Christ's encounters with Lazarus,

[10]See, for example, Yeats, *Essays and Introductions* (New York: Macmillan, 1961), 174–76. William York Tindall, *D. H. Lawrence and Susan His Cow* (New York: Columbia University Press, 1939), 138–44, suggests that Lawrence, too, took this idea from Madame Blavatsky.

[11]Leslie M. Thompson, "D. H. Lawrence and Judas," *D. H. Lawrence Review* 4 (1971), 2; no sources cited. Wilde's story "The Doer of Good" was one of Yeats's sources for *Calvary:* see Yeats, *Autobiographies* (London: Macmillan, 1966), 286–87 and 136–37; F. A. C. Wilson, *Yeats's Iconography* (1960; reprint, London: Methuen, 1969), 174–76; Liam Miller, *The Noble Drama of W. B. Yeats* (Dublin: Dolmen, 1977), 252–53. Lawrence's only certain late reference to Yeats's work was made in "On Human Destiny" (1924), in *Phoenix II: Uncollected, Unpublished, and Other Prose Works by D. H. Lawrence*, ed. Warren Roberts and Harry T. Moore (New York: Viking, 1970), 624: "You may, like Yeats, admire the simpleton, and call him God's Fool. But for me the village idiot is a cold egg." Lawrence may be alluding to Yeats's play *The Hour-Glass* (1903), which he saw in 1912 (*CL* 1, 364). The term "God's Fool" does not appear anywhere in Yeats's poetry or plays. Lindeth Vasey, Elizabeth Mansfield, Gerald M. Lacy, Keith Sagar, and Warren Roberts, all editors of the definitive edition now in progress of Lawrence's letters, kindly responded to my queries concerning references to Yeats in yet unpublished correspondence; while the incompleteness of their labors precluded unqualified generalizations, to this point none had found *any* references.

Judas, and the soldiers might have seemed the very sort of enumeration of "the smarts of the Crucifixion" of which Lawrence had been so critical in the letter to Campbell, and because the final speech by a character, used as the culmination of that sequence of frustrations, is Christ's despairing cry, "My Father, why hast Thou forsaken Me?"[12] Yeats would then have seemed, like the other modern writers, "too mean to get any further." This impression would have been reinforced by Yeats's Lazarus, who had not wanted to be resurrected, whom Christ had "dragged . . . to the light as boys drag out / A rabbit when they have dug its hole away" (p. 783). (The same sort of reluctance is shown by Christ Himself at the *beginning* of *The Escaped Cock*.) And Christ's one happy moment in the play, when the three Marys "and the rest / That live but in His love are gathered round Him / . . . and on His arm / Their lips are pressed and their tears fall" (p. 783) would have appeared to be an instance of that "divine figure on the Cross, held up to tears and love and veneration," that Lawrence found "a bit nauseating."

An interpretation that stopped at this point, though it would be understandable, given the strength of Lawrence's feelings, would scarcely have done justice to the overall vision of *Calvary,* for it ignores the lyrics that enclose the action of the play and alter totally the response to that action that Yeats hoped to produce in his readers and spectators. The desired response is suggested in Yeats's own explanatory "Notes," which introduce the antinomies of "subjective" and "objective" characteristic of his dualistic vision of experience. Men are either subjective, that is, self-oriented, or objective, defining themselves always in relation to others. The birds in the lyrics are "natural symbols of subjectivity," and the full moon that produces the heron's reflection is a figure for the totally subjective state that in *A Vision* Yeats would represent as Phase 15 of the lunar cycle. Christ, on the other hand, is the absolute type of objectivity, only happy when sacrificing Himself for others.[13] Yeats surrounds Him with "the images of those He cannot save, not only with the birds, who have served neither God nor Caesar," but also with subjective men like Lazarus and Judas, and with the Roman soldiers suggestive of "a form of objec-

[12]*The Variorum Edition of the Plays of W. B. Yeats*, ed. Russell K. Alspach, assisted by Catharine C. Alspach (New York: Macmillan, 1966), 787. Page numbers in text refer to this edition of *Calvary*.

[13]Yeats, *Variorum Plays*, 789–91; see also *Vision* (1925), 185, 186–87; and W. B. Yeats, *A Vision* (1937; reprint, New York: Macmillan, 1961), 273, cited henceforth as *Vision* (1937). In unpublished notes, Yeats explored possible subjective characteristics of Christ: see *Vision* (1925), Notes, p. 79 (note to p. 244).

tivity that lay beyond His help." The Marys, who "live but in His love," can provide Him only a brief respite from despair, and He dies feeling that "He has died in vain."

Elsewhere Yeats was to make it abundantly clear that the subjective-objective antinomy had a historical dimension, but in *Calvary* that dimension remains only implicit, emblematized by the soldiers' dance, in which they "wheel about the cross" (p. 787). This image expresses in compressed form the concept of a unique, linear, "Christian" history enclosed by a cyclical history in which the repetition of patterns seems to deny the uniqueness of any one set of individuals and events.[14] A vision of history consisting of subjective and objective eras alternating in cycles of roughly two thousand years each had occupied Yeats's imagination since the 1880s and organizes the structure of his earliest major poem, *The Wanderings of Oisin*. And from *The Wanderings* to *The Death of Cuchulain*, he was especially fascinated by those historical watersheds where one era was about to end and its opposite to begin: the warrior-bard Oisin returns to Ireland from the otherworld to find that the subjective, Celtic society of which he had been a part has given way to the Christianity of St. Patrick, which rejects all that Oisin's society had most prized; and in *The Death of Cuchulain*, Christ's life overlaps that of the "pagan" hero he will supplant, but the author, writing at the *end* of the Christian cycle, recreates the image of Cuchulain to serve as a model for a new heroic era.[15] *Calvary* also focuses upon such a moment, one that, despite Christ's despair, ushered in an era dominated by His own objective word. It is impossible to be sure whether Lawrence would have seen Yeats's meaning here, or the further implication that in his and Yeats's own time the power of that word was diminishing and a new influx from beyond was about to inaugurate a new, antithetical cycle dominated by the subjective. Yeats was not offering Christ's "plight" as an object of veneration and pity; his historical vision requires an ironic perspective.

Yeats did eventually write a play called *The Resurrection*, but in it Christ appears only briefly, a phantom with a beating heart whose proved divinity ensures a new reversal of the historical gyres. The play was published first in the *Adelphi*, in June 1927, after Lawrence

[14]As Lawrence would have recognized, "wheel about the cross" suggests the Rosicrucian symbol of the cross within a circle; he shows his familiarity with the symbol in "The Two Principles," *Phoenix II*, 228.

[15]See W. B. Yeats, *The Death of Cuchulain: Manuscript Materials*, ed. Phillip L. Marcus (Ithaca: Cornell University Press, 1982), 1–16.

had begun work on *The Escaped Cock*.[16] As Lawrence had had several pieces in the *Adelphi* earlier in 1927, it is quite possible that he did read *The Resurrection;* if so, it could only have reinforced his negative feelings about Yeats and his sense of the need for *The Escaped Cock*, as it was certainly not the resurrection "in the flesh" *he* called for.

II

Whether or not Lawrence was reading Yeats in the years after 1912, he was in any case exploring extensively the same tradition from which Yeats had drawn so many of the elements of his own vision. Rose Marie Burwell, in her survey of Lawrence's reading, notes that during those years Lawrence "began to pursue an interest in theosophy, astrology, the occult, and ancient religions," an interest that "remained a life-long one."[17] The interest was, one might add, a deep and engaged one. In 1918 he wrote to Mark Gertler: "Also I have been reading another book on *Occultism.* Do you know anybody who cares for this—magic, astrology, anything of that sort? It is very interesting, and important—though antipathetic to me. Certainly magic is a reality—not by any means the nonsense Bertie Russell says it is."[18] Apparently Lawrence did not realize that among his contemporaries no one "cared for this" more, or was more willing to assert so emphatically the reality of magic, than Yeats. Nor would Yeats have been offended by Lawrence's antipathy, which showed that he took the question seriously in a way that conventional skepticism did not. In 1892, in response to criticism of his "magical pursuits" by his father and John O'Leary, Yeats claimed that "if I had not made magic my constant study I could not have written a single word of my Blake book, nor would *The Countess Kathleen* have ever come to exist. The mystical life is the centre of all that I do and all that I think and all that I write."[19]

William York Tindall has argued convincingly that Lawrence's periodic disparaging remarks and his casualness in reference to sources

[16]For date of composition, see D. H. Lawrence, *The Escaped Cock*, ed. Gerald M. Lacy (Los Angeles: Black Sparrow Press, 1973), 137. Page numbers in text refer to this edition of the novella.

[17]Rose Marie Burwell, "A Catalogue of D. H. Lawrence's Reading from Early Childhood," *D. H. Lawrence Review* 3 (1970), 196. See also Tindall, 134; and Emile Delavenay, *D. H. Lawrence: The Man and His Work* (Carbondale: Southern Illinois University Press, 1972), 458–93.

[18]*The Letters of D. H. Lawrence*, ed. Aldous Huxley (New York: Viking, 1932), 444.

[19]Yeats, *Letters*, 210–11.

have made the nature of his interest in the occult tradition seem less passionate than it really was. Frieda Lawrence informed him that Lawrence "read and delighted in all of Mme Blavatsky's works," and Tindall demonstrates her impact and that of other Theosophists such as Annie Besant and especially James M. Pryse upon such texts as *Fantasia of the Unconscious, The Plumed Serpent,* and *Apocalypse.* Despite Lawrence's disclaimers, he found attractive elements in Hinduism and "was particularly fascinated with yoga."[20] Often the books Lawrence read were ones that were important also to Yeats: Madame Blavatsky's *The Secret Doctrine,* Frazer's *The Golden Bough,* Burnet's *Early Greek Philosophy,* the *Upanishads* and others, even such less well known texts as Balzac's "occult" novel *Seraphita.*[21] Given these common interests and sources, it was almost inevitable that the work of Yeats and Lawrence would sometimes seem very similar, and the similarities are not necessarily signs of "influence" in the conventional sense in either direction. The relationship may well be comparable to that of Yeats and Jung, whose thought seems so close, though they apparently owed nothing to each other, because it was derived from the same tradition.[22]

Furthermore, the broad lineaments of that tradition pervade European thought from the end of the eighteenth century, so that it could be a part of the general cultural inheritance of almost any writer.[23] We know, nevertheless, that at least in 1914 Lawrence had strong negative feelings specifically about Yeats's treatment of aspects of that tradition. And we can say with certainty that nearly all the major elements of the vision embodied in *Calvary* can be found also in Lawrence, in letters, fiction, poetry, essays, and "mythologies" such as the "Study of Thomas Hardy" (1914), "The Reality of Peace" (1917), "The Two Principles" (1919), and *Reflections on the Death of a Porcupine*

[20]Tindall, 133, 136–50. For an example of the disparaging remarks, see D. H. Lawrence, *Studies in Classic American Literature* (1923; reprint, Garden City: Doubleday, 1951), 121. His casualness of reference is illustrated in a 1918 letter in which he recommends Madame Blavatsky's *Isis Unveiled* "and better still the 2 vol. work whose name I forget"—that is, *The Secret Doctrine (Letters,* ed. Huxley, 480). See also Delavenay, 459–62.

[21]See Burwell, 193–324; Tindall, 97–161; *CL* II, 364, 470; Lawrence, *"Psychoanalysis and the Unconscious"* and *"Fantasia of the Unconscious,"* 1 vol. ed. (New York: Viking, 1960), 54, 56.

[22] On Yeats and Jung, see James Olney, *The Rhizome and the Flower: The Perennial Philosophy—Yeats and Jung* (Berkeley: University of California Press, 1980). Lawrence had read Jung, in whose work he found support for his ideas concerning the Magna Mater: see *The Collected Letters of D. H. Lawrence,* ed. Harry T. Moore, 2 vols. (New York: Viking, 1962), I, 565; and Hilary Simpson, *D. H. Lawrence and Feminism* (DeKalb: Northern Illinois University Press, 1982), 92–93. See also *Psychoanalysis,* 3.

[23]See M. H. Abrams, *Natural Supernaturalism* (New York: Norton, 1971).

(1925), the last of which corresponds to *A Vision* in Yeats's canon and was even published in the same year.

Lawrence regularly described experience in dualistic terms. In *Psychoanalysis and the Unconscious,* for example, he counterpoints "subjective" and "objective" planes of consciousness, using Yeats's very terms.[24] A comparable pattern pervades the following passage from *Twilight in Italy:*

> The Infinite is twofold, the Father and the Son, the Dark and the Light, the Senses and the Mind, the Soul and the Spirit, *the self and the not-self,* the Eagle and the Dove, the Tiger and the Lamb. *The consummation of Man is twofold, in the Self and in Selflessness.* By great retrogression back to the source of darkness in me, the Self, deep in the senses, I arrive at the Original, Creative Infinite. By projection forth from myself, by the elimination of my absolute sensual self, I arrive at the Ultimate Infinite, Oneness in the Spirit. They are two Infinites, twofold approach to God. And man must know both. [Emphasis added][25]

"Self" and "Selflessness" correspond to Yeats's subjective and objective states. A similar distinction appears in *The Crown* (written 1915, included with revisions in *Reflections on the Death of a Porcupine*), where the myriad opposites include "submitting to the divine grace, in suffering and self-obliteration, and . . . conquering by divine grace, as the tiger leaps on the trembling deer, in utter satisfaction of the Self, in complete fulfilment of desire."[26] In an entry in his diary for 1930, Yeats characterized the antithetical impulses as "the realisation of myself as unique and free" and "the surrender to God of all that I am." He added that "could those two impulses, one as much a part of truth as the other, be reconciled, or if one or the other could prevail, all life would cease."[27] In the same way, Lawrence referred to each impulse as a "great half-truth" and declared that if either the Lion or the Unicorn (symbols for the opposites in *The Crown*) could triumph, "there would be a great cessation from being, of the whole universe."[28] Birkin's theory of "star polarity" in *Women in Love,* stressing as its ideal a balance between the integrity of the individual and relationship with another, is one obvious fictional manifestation of such a

---

[24]Lawrence, *Psychoanalysis,* 28–29; see also *D. H. Lawrence and Italy* (New York: Viking, 1972), *Etruscan Places,* 74. This volume contains *Twilight in Italy, Sea and Sardinia,* and *Etruscan Places,* each separately paginated. I shall cite these travel books individually by volume title and page number.

[25]Lawrence, *Twilight in Italy,* 46–47.

[26]Lawrence, *Phoenix II,* 411.

[27]W. B. Yeats, *Explorations* (New York: Macmillan, 1962), 305.

[28]Lawrence, *Twilight in Italy,* 71; *Phoenix II,* 366.

vision. Significantly, his crucial encounter with Ursula in "Excurse" brings to each of them both a "perfect passing away" and an "intolerable accession into being."[29]

Lawrence's essay "The Two Principles" offers, in addition to the basic duality, a *fourfold* division comparable to the Four Faculties of Yeats's *A Vision*.[30] This essay is an excellent example of the impact of Lawrence's philosophical and occult studies. In it he refers to the *Prima Materia* and the alchemistic elements, to "the Chinese three sacred mysteries" and other "Oriental symbolism," to the Pythagoreans, to the Rosy Cross, and to Blake; and he draws heavily throughout upon Madame Blavatsky, both her cosmogony and her quasi-scientific approach. It was published in 1919, while Yeats was receiving the spirit communications that became *A Vision* and shortly before he wrote *Calvary*.[31]

In *Calvary* the antinomies have religious and historical dimensions. As Yeats observed in the same passage from the diary of 1930, "two conceptions, that of reality as a congeries of beings, that of reality as a single being, alternate in our emotion and in history. . . . I think that there are historical cycles wherein one or the other predominates, and that a cycle approaches where all shall [be] as particular and concrete as human intensity permits." To see reality as a "congeries of beings" is to identify it with the individual self in its highest form, whereas to see it in a single being is to recognize a divinity outside of, other than, us. Historically, the pre-Christian era embodied the former vision; since the birth of Christ the opposite conception has been dominant. Now the end of that cycle approaches and the era to follow will once more be a subjective one. In the seventh chapter of the "Study of Thomas Hardy" Lawrence discerns a comparable religious and historical pattern of antinomies, with the advent of Christ marking the moment of counterflux:

> The senses, sensation, sensuousness, these things which are incontrovertibly Me, these are my God, these belong to God, said Job. And he persisted, and he was right. They issue from God on the female side.
>
> But Christ came with His contradiction: That which is Not-Me, that is God. All is God, except that which I know immediately as Myself. First I must lose Myself, then I find God. Ye must be born again.

[29]Lawrence, *Women in Love*, ed. Charles L. Ross (Harmondsworth: Penguin, 1982), 396.

[30]Yeats, *Vision* (1925), 14.

[31]Lawrence, *Phoenix II*, 227–37. Tindall, 141, notes that some occult elements in the periodical versions of the essays in *Studies in Classic American Literature* were omitted when the essays were collected in volume form; see further Delavenay, 462–83.

Unto what must man be born again? Unto knowledge of his own separate existence, as in Woman he is conscious of his own incorporate existence. Man must be born unto knowledge of his own distinct identity, as in woman he was born to knowledge of his identification with the Whole. Man must be born to the knowledge, that in the whole being he is nothing, as he was born to know that in the whole being he was all.[32]

The entire chapter of the Hardy study anticipates the "Dove or Swan" section of *A Vision* and shows how close their ways of interpreting history were, even to the pervasive practice (possibly influenced in both cases by Pater) of defining the nature of eras through the visual and plastic art they produced. Thus Lawrence wrote of how

> with the Renaissance, the God of Aspiration became in accord with the God of Knowledge, and there was a great outburst of joy, and the theme was not Christ Crucified, but Christ born of Woman, the Infant Saviour and the Virgin; or of the Annunciation, the Spirit embracing the flesh in pure embrace.
> This was the perfect union of male and female, in this the hands met and clasped, and never was such a manifestation of Joy. This Joy reached its highest utterance perhaps in Botticelli, as in his *Nativity of the Saviour,* in our National Gallery.[33]

Yeats, in his discussion of the Italian Renaissance, would detect in the same artist almost the same significance, even citing the same painting:

> Had some Florentine Platonist read to Botticelli Porphyry upon the Cave of the Nymphs? for I seem to recognise it in that curious cave, with a thatched roof over the nearer entrance to make it resemble the conventional manger, in his "Nativity" in the National Gallery. . . .
> Botticelli, Crivelli, Mantegna, Da Vinci, who fall within the period, make Masaccio and his school seem heavy and common by something we may call intellectual beauty or compare perhaps to that kind of bodily beauty which Castiglione called "the spoil or monument of the victory of the soul." Intellect and emotion, *primary* curiosity and the *antithetical* dream, are for the moment one.[34]

And Lawrence, like Yeats, saw the end of the Christian cycle and the coming of a new, antithetical era as near. "Now it is time for us to leave our Christian-democratic epoch," Lawrence wrote in a letter in

---

[32]Lawrence, *Phoenix*, 453. See comparable passages in *Twilight in Italy*, 39–41, 70–74.
[33]Lawrence, *Phoenix*, 454–55. See also Gordon, 96–110.
[34]Yeats, *Vision* (1925), 202–203.

1916. In another letter he dismissed Christianity as "the has-been" and asserted that "there must be something new."[35] His own fiction reflected the transition, perhaps was intended partly to help effect it. He particularized the "message" of *The Rainbow* as "the old order is done for, toppling on top of us. . . . There must be a new Word"; and he wrote of *Women in Love* "the book frightens me: it is so end-of-the-world. But it is, it must be, the beginning of a new world too."[36] In *Sea and Sardinia* he would rejoice that "the era of love and oneness is over"; and one of the underlying assumptions of *Apocalypse* was that "Time still moves in cycles, not in a straight line. And we are at the end of the Christian cycle."[37]

For Yeats, the era to come "will be concrete in expression, establish itself by immediate experience, . . . make little of God or any exterior unity," and, "unlike Christianity which had for its first Roman teachers cobblers and weavers, . . . must find expression among those that are most subtle, . . . among the learned . . . among the rich . . . among men of rank . . . and the best of those that express it will be given power."[38] Lawrence set up the "Pagan, aristocratic, lordly, sensuous" against the "Christian, humble, spiritual, unselfish, democratic."[39] The *ideal* for each man was a combination of elements from both types of era, what Yeats called "Unity of Culture,"[40] but when faced with a choice they shared a preference for "the pagan many gods" and for subjective eras.[41]

In terms of personality, too, both saw as the ideal human condition a balance, an equilibrium, a creative tension between subjective and objective elements and impulses. "These two halves I always am . . . ," Lawrence wrote, "But I am never *myself* until they are consummated into a spark of oneness, the gleam of the Holy Ghost."[42] The Crown

---

[35]Lawrence, *CL* II, 592, 633–34.

[36]Ibid., 526; Lawrence, *Letters*, ed. Huxley, 380.

[37]Lawrence, *Sea and Sardinia*, 92; Lawrence, *Apocalypse* (1931; reprint, New York: Viking, 1966), 148.

[38]Yeats, *Vision* (1925), 214–15.

[39]Lawrence, *Phoenix II*, 410; see also "Blessed Are the Powerful," in *Phoenix II*, 436 and Yeats's poem "Blood and the Moon." On other occasions Lawrence and Yeats both defined the contrasting eras in terms borrowed from Nietzsche's *The Birth of Tragedy* (*Twilight in Italy*, 136; Yeats, *Letters*, 402–403) and Joachim of Flora (*Classic American Literature*, 89, 120, and Burwell, 253; Yeats, "The Tables of the Law," *The Secret Rose, Stories by W. B. Yeats: A Variorum Edition*, ed. Phillip L. Marcus, Warwick Gould, and Michael Sidnell [Ithaca: Cornell University Press, 1981], 153).

[40]Lawrence, *Twilight in Italy*, 73; Yeats, *Autobiographies*, 190–95, 269, 295.

[41]Lawrence, *Letters*, ed. Huxley, 612; *Explorations*, 305. "The return of the pagan gods" was anticipated by Pater in *The Renaissance* and *Imaginary Portraits*.

[42]Lawrence, *Phoenix II*, 410; see also 430–35, and *Classic American Literature*, 17: "the deepest *whole* self of man, the self in its wholeness, not idealistic halfness."

and the Rainbow were other Lawrencian symbols for this relationship between the antinomies, which he usually evoked in passages charged with poetic intensity: "It is the battle-ground and marriage-bed of the two invisible hosts. It flames up to its full strength, and is consummate, perfect, absolute, the human body. It is a revelation of God, it is the foam-burst of the two waves, it is the iris of the two eternities."[43] Yeats called this state Unity of Being, describing it in "A General Introduction for my Work," in terms very similar to Lawrence's, as "my Christ, . . . that Unity of Being Dante compared to a perfectly proportioned human body, Blake's 'Imagination,' what the Upanishads have named 'Self': nor is this unity distant and therefore intellectually understandable, but imanent, differing from man to man and age to age, taking upon itself pain and ugliness."[44] It is obvious that "Christ" here has a far different import from Christ in *Calvary:* the character in the play is committed to a vision that almost totally devaluates one side of the duality.

A natural concomitant to such conceptions was, for both Lawrence and Yeats, the divinity of man. In *Fantasia of the Unconscious* (1922), Lawrence had countered the cosmogonies of modern science with the assertion "It was life itself which threw the moon apart on the one hand, the sun on the other. . . . The moon is as dependent upon the life of individuals, for her continued existence, as each single individual is dependent upon the moon. The same with the sun. . . . Without man, beasts, butterflies, trees, toads, the sun would gutter out like a spent lamp."[45] Here man assumes the creative power traditionally assigned to God, and a dynamic of reciprocity replaces the scientific vision of an indifferent cosmos in which life plays a minor and inessential role. Yeats presumably did not know this passage, but some lines from his poem "The Tower" (written 1925–26) show him exploring a comparably humanist metaphysics:

> Death and life were not
> Till man made up the whole,
> Made lock, stock and barrel
> Out of his bitter soul,

[43]Lawrence, *Phoenix II,* 411.

[44]Yeats, *Essays and Introductions,* 518. The printed text actually reads "imminent," but "imanent" was what Yeats wrote; see Edward Callan, *Yeats on Yeats* (Portlaoise: Dolmen, 1981), 60–61.

[45]Lawrence, *Fantasia,* 206. Compare Earl Brewster's account of how Lawrence startled him by saying, "Man himself created the sun and the moon," and insisting that he meant it in a non-"subjective" sense, Nehls, II, 118–19.

Aye, sun and moon and star, all,
And further add to that
That, being dead, we rise,
Dream and so create
Translunar Paradise.[46]

A manuscript version containing the line "Men on the third day rise" made an explicit identification of man and risen Christ.[47] Lawrence was soon to do the same in his fiction.

III

In the Hardy essay, which was contemporaneous with the 1914 letter to Campbell, Lawrence called upon man to "cease, first to live in the flesh, with joy, and then, unsatisfied, to renounce and to mortify the flesh, declaring that the Spirit alone exists, that Christ He is God. . . . Does not a youth now know that . . . consummation is consummation of body and spirit, both?"[48] The same idea appears in a letter written nearly fifteen years later: "And Church doctrine teaches the resurrection of the body; and if that doesn't mean the whole man, what does it mean? And if man is whole without a woman . . . then I'm damned."[49] The context was a defense of his own story *The Escaped Cock.*

An "authorial" passage in *The Rainbow* laments that "a risen Christ has no place with us!" Two uncollected poems from the decade before the novella also adumbrate some of its major concerns. In "Resurrection of the Flesh," apparently written not long after the letter to Campbell, the speaker, anticipating Yeats's Lazarus and Judas, asks God to "show us nothing! leave us quite alone! / . . . Leave us quite alone / Within the silence, void of echoes even"; while the end of the poem—

I let the whole thing go! Still there is me!
Touch me then, touch me, touch me, I did not die!

[46]*The Variorum Edition of the Poems of W. B. Yeats*, ed. Peter Allt and Russell K. Alspach, 3d printing, with corrections (New York: Macmillan, 1973), 415.

[47]Curtis B. Bradford, *Yeats at Work* (Carbondale: Southern Illinois University Press, 1965), 95. An earlier draft has "Why could no Rabbi say / That Eternal Man / Rested the seventh day" (p. 84).

[48]Lawrence, *Phoenix*, 468–69.

[49]Lawrence, *Letters*, ed. Huxley, 786–87.

> Upon the wincingness of next to nothingness
> That I am now, Ay, lay one little touch
> To start my heart afresh!

—looks ahead to Christ's rejection of his past and movement toward self-realization in *The Escaped Cock*.[50] "Resurrection" (published 1917) depicts a Christ-like resurrected speaker ignored by hosts of war dead; but his frustration yields at the end of the poem to optimistic assertion:

> Yet is uplifted in me the pure beam
> Of immortality to kindle up
> Another spring of yet another year,
> Folded as yet: and all the fallen leaves
> Sweep on to bitter, to corrosive death
> Against me, yet they cannot make extinct
> The perfect lambent flame which still goes up,
> A tender gleam of immortality,
> To start the glory of another year,
> Another epoch in another year,
> Another triumph on the face of earth,
> Another race, another speech among
> The multitudinous people unfused,
> Unborn and unproduced, yet to be born.

In these lines, as in the novella, personal rebirth and the beginning of a new historical cycle merge.[51]

The story "Glad Ghosts" (1925) is yet another text that points toward and prepares for *The Escaped Cock*. At the center of the story is the sort of situation that Yeats explored with obsessive frequency, especially in plays such as *The Dreaming of the Bones, The Words upon the Window-Pane,* and *Purgatory:* the spirit in torment after death as the result of unresolved painful elements in its previous life. In "Glad Ghosts" the unresolved elements reflect distinctively Lawrencian concerns: "Her poor ghost, that ached, and never had a real body! It's not so easy to worship with the body. Ah, if the Church taught us *that*

---

[50]D. H. Lawrence, *The Rainbow* (1915; reprint, New York: Viking, 1961), 279–80. *The Complete Poems of D. H. Lawrence*, ed. Vivian de Sola Pinto and Warren Roberts (1964; reprint, New York: Viking, 1971), 737–38; for date of composition, see p. 1023.

[51]Lawrence, *Complete Poems*, 743–46. Compare Yeats's *The King's Threshold*, 1904 version (*Variorum Plays*): "O silver trumpets be you lifted up / And cry to the great race that is to come. / Long-throated swans among the waves of time / Sing loudly, for beyond the wall of the world / It waits and it may hear and come to us" (pp. 311–12).

sacrament: *with my body I thee worship!* that would easily make up for any honouring and obeying the woman might do. But that's why she haunts you. You ignored and disliked her body, and she was only a living ghost. Now she wails in the afterworld, like a still-wincing nerve."[52] Most of the characters in the story have been similarly guilty of exalting spirit at the expense of flesh; and one of them, Lord Lathkill, says so in terms that (like "wincing" in the passage above) echo the poem "Resurrection of the Flesh" and also refer overtly to Jesus: "I've only realised how very extraordinary it is to be a man of flesh and blood, alive. It seems so ordinary, in comparison, to be dead, and merely spirit. That seems so commonplace. But fancy having a living face, and arms, and thighs. . . . Think how ghastly for Jesus, when He was risen and wasn't touchable! How very awful, to have to say *Noli me tangere!* Ah, touch me, touch me *alive!*"[53] Both he and the narrator even experience regenerative unions with female characters, and the story ends with images of the plum tree bearing its spring blossoms unseasonably in autumn.[54]

Many of the elements of Lawrence's vision that he shared with Yeats appear in *The Plumed Serpent,* which Lawrence published in 1926, the year before he began *The Escaped Cock.* "Its theme is that of Mme Blavatsky's *Secret Doctrine:* the recovery of lost Atlantis by means of myths and symbols," Tindall has asserted.[55] Antinomies dominate the book at every level, and the cult of Quetzalcoatl and the "old gods" heralds a new subjective era destined to replace the exhausted Christian cycle.[56] In one of Don Ramón's speeches on this subject, he even includes the pre-Christian deities of Ireland: "I wish the Teutonic world would once more think in terms of Thor and Wotan, and the tree Igdrasil. And I wish the Druidic world would see, honestly, that in the mistletoe is their mystery, and that they themselves are the Tuatha De Danaan, alive, but submerged. And a new Hermes should come back to the Mediterranean, and a new Ashtaroth to Tunis; and Mithras again to Persia, and Brahma unbroken to India, and the oldest of dragons to China."[57] Yeats had anticipated this passage thirty years earlier in his apocalyptic story "Rosa Alchemica" (1896),

[52]D. H. Lawrence, *The Complete Short Stories* (New York: Viking, 1961), 692.

[53]Lawrence, *Complete Stories,* 689.

[54]For the association of plum blossoms with the resurrected deity, see "The Risen Lord," *Phoenix II,* 574.

[55]Tindall, 144; see also Gilbert, 311.

[56]Lawrence, *The Plumed Serpent* (1926; reprint, New York: Vintage, 1954), 101, 455–56, 65.

[57]Ibid., 272–73; see also Langbaum, 280.

in which Michael Robartes, like Don Ramón the founder of an occult order, says in reference to the pious Catholic Irish peasantry, "A time will come for these people also, and they will sacrifice a mullet to Artemis, or some other fish to some new divinity, unless indeed their own divinities set up once more their temples of grey stone. Their reign has never ceased, but only waned in power a little."[58] It is clear from Don Ramón's words that Lawrence had not forgotten his efforts in 1914 to persuade Gordon Campbell to "grasp . . . the *Complete Whole* which the Celtic symbolism made in its great time." In *The Plumed Serpent* again he prepared the ground for *The Escaped Cock*, in which he would take the further step of dealing directly with Christ as character and revealing the true meaning of His death and resurrection.

IV

Lawrence's decision to write the novella was probably influenced by a variety of forces, among them Middleton Murry's work on Jesus, a painting by Dorothy Brett, the Etruscan trip, an Easter display in a shop window, and V. V. Rozanov's *Solitaria*.[59] Whether *Calvary* could legitimately be added to the list is uncertain; in any case, the story can be read as both a "continuation" and an inversion of Yeats's play.

Lawrence offered an approach to his novella in the contemporary essay "The Risen Lord," where he suggested that "the great religious images are only images of our own experiences, or of our own state of mind and soul."[60] Although these words sound like the sort of approach for which Lawrence had criticized Yeats in 1914, his actual practice is comparable to Yeats's balance between the personal and the mythic. Lawrence's story begins, like *Calvary*, with a vignette describing a symbolic bird. Flocks of barnyard fowl might well carry objective associations, but the single proud cock seems more like one of Yeats's "natural symbols of subjectivity." In *The Dreaming of the Bones* (which was, like *Calvary*, one of the *Four Plays for Dancers* Yeats published in 1921), Yeats had made extensive use of the red cock's supposed power to ward off spirits and possibly associated the bird also with the beginning of a new cycle.[61] The birds in *Calvary* repre-

---

[58]Yeats, *The Secret Rose*, 139; see also pp. 170–71.

[59]Lawrence, *The Escaped Cock*, 129–41.

[60]Lawrence, *Phoenix II*, 571; see also "Resurrection," in *Phoenix*, 737–39.

[61]Wilson, 236. See also Patricia Abel and Robert Hogan, "D. H. Lawrence's Singing Birds," in *A D. H. Lawrence Miscellany*, ed. Harry T. Moore (Carbondale: Southern Illinois University Press, 1959), 204–14.

sent a subjective counterpoint to Christ's objective being: "God has not died for the white heron," who waits for "none or for a different saviour."[62] Lawrence's subjective protagonist is just that savior, and actually liberates the bird by purchasing him from the peasant, while the cock's cry seems to him a "challenge from life to death" (p. 21) and plays an important role in the development of his own decision to move from death to life.

Calvary had ended with Christ's despair on the cross. Picking up where Yeats left off, Lawrence introduces his central character "dead" in the darkness of the tomb. Darkness, in the terms of Yeats's lunar symbolism, signaled the end of one cycle, the beginning of another. *"There in the tomb the dark grows blacker,"* he would write in "The Black Tower"; in "The Statues" the Irish attain their "proper dark," and in "The Gyres" the new cycle will be disinterred "From marble of a broken sepulchre, / Or dark betwixt the polecat and the owl, / Or any rich, dark nothing. . . ."[63] For Yeats, the movement of a new phase of individual or historical development toward the fullness of self-absorption and self-realization generally parallels the waxing of the moon; Lawrence had made use of moon symbolism in similar ways in memorable scenes in *The Rainbow* and *Women in Love*. It is the sun that plays the corresponding role in *The Escaped Cock*, but there is implicit lunar symbolism as well in the encounter with the priestess of the moon-goddess Isis.[64]

The man's development from this point to the end of part I involves a series of reversals of incidents in *Calvary*. Leaving the tomb, he walks with "disgust" and "wincing feet" (p. 16) past the now motionless soldiers. Then the peasant who takes him in evokes thoughts equally appropriate to Lazarus, who had hoped to find in death an escape from Christ's power: "But the man who had died no longer wished to interfere in the soul of the man who had not died, and who could never die, save to return to earth. Let him return to earth in his own good hour, and let no one try to interfere, when the earth claims her own" (p. 23). Yeats's Christ had known only the brief moment of happiness when he was surrounded by the devoted women who *needed* him. For Lawrence's character, Madeline embodies the values he has now turned away from, and so he must reject her. He tells her that he is "no longer a lover of multitudes" (p. 24). The objective roles of "teacher" and "saviour" are dead in him, and he wants to pursue

[62]Yeats, *Variorum Plays*, 780–81, 790.
[63]Yeats, *Variorum Poems*, 636, 611, 565.
[64]On solar and lunar symbolism, see also *Fantasia*, 183–89.

his subjective development: "now I can go about my own business, into my own single life." The encounter with her shatters him as those with Lazarus and Judas had shattered Yeats's character, "a revulsion from all the life he had known came over him again, the great nausea of disillusion, and the spear-thrust through his bowels" (p. 26). When she reappears, with Mary and Joan, he literally flees them (pp. 28–29).

His view of Judas likewise inverts the corresponding scene in Yeats's play: "Now I can wait on life, and say nothing, and have no one betray me. I wanted to be greater than the limits of my hands and feet, so I brought betrayal on myself. And I know I wronged Judas, my poor Judas. . . . But Judas and the high priests delivered me from my own salvation" (p. 24). In *Calvary*, the betrayal had been an act of subjective self-assertion designed to frustrate the Christ whose "Father put all men into my hands"; here it liberates the man into his own subjective freedom. The sign that he has achieved it is precisely this delight in the state of solitude, of "pure aloneness," that had been a torment to him before his crucifixion: "For nothing is so marvellous as to be alone in the phenomenal world, which is raging and yet apart. . . . Now I will wander among the stirring of the phenomenal world, for it is the stirring of all things among themselves which leaves me purely alone" (p. 30).[65]

His subsequent hope that "perhaps one evening I shall meet a woman who can lure my risen body, yet leave me my aloneness" (p. 32) represents a further stage in the subjective personality's evolution toward Unity of Being, the condition in which all aspects of the individual are fully realized and held in a harmonious balance.[66] It is achieved in *The Escaped Cock*, as in Yeats's work, through an encounter with a figure who seems externally considered the individual's opposite but who corresponds to a latent side of the individual's own being and who thus serves "to unite us to ourselves."[67] For the man who had died, this will be the priestess of Isis: "As he watched her, he saw her soul in its aloneness, and its female difference. He said to himself: How different she is from me, how strangely different!" (p. 53). Through union with her his "resurrection" will be completed.

The climactic moment of the process involves yet another reversal of his objective life. As the priestess is chafing him with oil, he recalls how "once a woman washed my feet with tears, and wiped them with

[65]Compare Christ's "objective loneliness" in *Calvary*, *Variorum Plays*, 790.
[66]See Yeats, *Vision* (1925), 60.
[67]Ibid., 18.

her hair, and poured on precious ointment," and he feels ashamed for having "wanted them to love with dead bodies. If I had kissed Judas with live love, perhaps he would never have kissed me with death. Perhaps he loved me in the flesh, and I willed that he should love me bodilessly, with the corpse of love—." These thoughts lead him to the realization that "resurrection" means "the whole man": "I am going to be whole!" (pp. 54–56) His scars, he tells her, have become "suns" and "they are my atonement with you" (p. 58). Because Isis is a moon goddess, his union with the priestess enacts the mystical marriage of sun and moon, the hierosgamos of alchemy and the fertility rituals.[68] He has also achieved the secular and literal "atonement" of union with himself, and (as in Yeats's "A General Introduction for my Work") "Christ" and "Unity of Being" merge.

In part II of *The Escaped Cock,* Lawrence also suggests a historical reversal. As if Christ had stepped from the New Testament into the world of *The Golden Bough,* the man who had died abandons the uniqueness claimed for him by Christianity and becomes merely one among many pagan fertility deities, an Osiris linked with the rhythms of the seasons and the crops. In one sense this suggests a movement backward, into the era preceding that of Christianity; but it also looks ahead, beyond the end of the Christian cycle, to the day when the world will enter a cycle comparable to the era of the "old gods," dominated by similar subjective values. (Similarly in *St. Mawr* the New England woman encounters on the ranch "a world before and after the God of Love.")[69] The man's final promise (recalling the end of the poem "Resurrection") that he will "come again, sure as spring" (p. 60) sets up against the despair of Christ in *Calvary* an affirmation at both a universal level and a personal one.

Lawrence was aware that the fertility rituals had had both an exoteric level concerned with rainfall and crops and an esoteric level at which they involved individual transformation and regeneration. In the posthumously published *Apocalypse,* he argued that Revelation was originally "a pagan work," a description of an initiation ritual for one

[68]See Robert Graves, *The White Goddess,* enlarged ed. (New York: Farrar, Straus & Giroux, 1981), 275; C. G. Jung, *Mysterium Coniunctionis,* trans. R. F. C. Hull, 2d ed. (Princeton: Princeton University Press, 1977); Sir James Frazer, *The New Golden Bough,* ed. Theodor H. Gaster (New York: New American Library, 1959), 132. In Yeats's play *The Only Jealousy of Emer* (published in 1919), Cuchulain, who has frequently been identified as a solar deity, is tempted by but eventually rejects the goddess Fand, symbolically associated with the full moon. See also "O may the moon and sunlight seem / One inextricable beam," from "The Tower," *Variorum Poems,* 411.

[69]Lawrence, *St. Mawr and Other Stories,* ed. Brian Finney (Cambridge: Cambridge University Press, 1983), 149; *St. Mawr* was first published in 1925.

of the Mystery Cults, perhaps for the cult of Isis, and that this text had then been reworked and radically altered first by Jewish and then by Christian apologists. Their modifications were inspired by a vision antipathetic to the original: "The Jewish mind hates the mortal and terrestrial divinity of man: the Christian mind the same. Man is only postponedly divine: when he is dead and gone to glory. He *must not* achieve divinity in the flesh. So the Jewish and Christian apocalyptists abolish the mystery of the individual adventure into Hades."[70] The result was a palimpsest, and Lawrence proposed by his detailed analysis of the revised text to uncover the underlying original stratum. He approached the Gospels the same way in *The Escaped Cock;* thus for him writing the story was an act of restoration. Yet the myth was at the same time the correlative of his own personal "adventure into Hades." Lawrence, like his protagonist, had known the spear thrust through his side and the pain and regenerative ecstasy of union with "the woman of a lifetime"; he had lived against the grain of his own time, consoled by the wisdom concealed within the hackneyed, now revivified phrase, "tomorrow is another day" (p. 61).[71]

In light of Lawrence's struggles to express his personal vision of the Christ mythos, *Lady Chatterley's Lover* (1928) reveals an added dimension. The intermediate version of the novel written just before Lawrence began *The Escaped Cock* contains a lengthy house party discussion of what became the events of the novella.[72] During the discussion, the minor character Tommy Dukes calls for a historical reversal: "We've had two thousand years of *noli me tangere.* Just imagine *voli me tangere,* for a change."[73] In Connie's mind, Christ's words seem applicable to virtually the entire generation that fought in the Great War; they had died in the War and "had not yet got the body of the new life."[74] But there were some exceptions. Yearning for a "God" to open her heart to, but unable to accept Jesus because He is "too like Clifford," she sees in the gamekeeper Parkin's naked torso a body that "was of the world of the gods. . . . And she felt again there was God on earth; or gods."[75] In a passage reminiscent of Ursula's final vision in *The Rainbow,* Connie

[70]Lawrence, *Apocalypse,* 62, 109, 104; cf. also p. 110 and *Etruscan Places,* 51–52.

[71]Lawrence, *Letters,* ed. Boulton, 1, 384.

[72]Dating of the composition of *Lady Chatterley's Lover* follows Keith Sagar, *D. H. Lawrence: A Calendar of His Works* (Austin: University of Texas Press, 1979); and Michael Squires, *The Creation of "Lady Chatterley's Lover"* (Baltimore: Johns Hopkins University Press, 1983), 4–9.

[73]Lawrence, *John Thomas and Lady Jane* (1972; reprint, New York: Penguin, 1977), 66.

[74]Ibid., 68.

[75]Ibid., 41–42, 51.

discovers a source of hope for the blighted Midlands: "It could all come alive again. . . . If only that hateful pale Spirit which men had in them didn't prevent it. 'Thou hast conquered, O pale Galilean!' But there was to be a resurrection. . . . The resurrection of the body! Even the true Christian creed insisted on it." In addition to expressing Lawrence's own interpretation of Christian doctrine, this passage links Connie by way of the Swinburne allusion to the Proserpine legend, commonly interpreted allegorically as a fertility myth.[76]

Lawrence finished the third version of *Lady Chatterley's Lover* before writing Part II of *The Escaped Cock*. Given the overlapping composition of story and novel, it is not surprising that there are significant links between the story and the novel in its final form as well. Mellors's desire for aloneness, for instance, obviously corresponds to Christ's subjective turn: "Especially he did not want to come into contact with a woman again. He feared it; for he had a big wound from old contacts. He felt if he could not be alone, and if he could not be left alone, he would die. His recoil away from the outer world was complete; his last refuge was this wood; to hide himself there!"[77] Clifford, for whom "the life of the body . . . is just the life of the animals," corresponds to Christ in his objective stage.[78] Although Clifford in a sense came back from the dead, his symbolic paralysis ensures that *he* will never be able to say "I am risen!" To reverse the comparison, the man in *The Escaped Cock* is a Clifford who becomes a Mellors. "Resurrection" imagery pervades Connie's denial of Clifford's view, a denial that alludes to the historical pattern that Lawrence would suggest also in Part II of the novella: "The human body is only just coming to real life. With the Greeks it gave a lovely flicker, then Plato and Aristotle killed it, and Jesus finished it off. But now the body is coming really to life, it is really rising from the tomb. And it will be a lovely, lovely life in the lovely universe, the life of the human body."[79] While the present moment of the novel offers little cause for optimism, Connie, like the priestess of Isis, carries in her womb the seed of hope for a better world to come. At one level, then, *Lady Chatterley's Lover* can be seen as

---

[76]Ibid., 89–90. See also *The First Lady Chatterley* (London: Heinemann, 1972), 62; and *Lady Chatterley's Lover* (1928; reprint, New York: Modern Library, n.d.), 94.

[77]Lawrence, *Lady Chatterley's Lover*, 97–98.

[78]Ibid., 266. In *John Thomas and Lady Jane*, Clifford had been wounded on Christmas day (p. 58).

[79]Lawrence, *Lady Chatterley's Lover*, 266. See also James C. Cowan, "D. H. Lawrence and the Resurrection of the Body," in *D. H. Lawrence: The Man Who Lived*, ed. Robert B. Partlow, Jr., and Harry T. Moore (Carbondale: Southern Illinois University Press, 1980), 94–104.

The Escaped Cock in modern dress, playing out the archetypal drama at the next cyclical crisis point.

V

In the 1930s, after Lawrence's death, Yeats did write a "resurrection" play that corresponds, at least on one level, to Lawrence's handling of the event in *The Escaped Cock*. The first version of that play, called *The King of the Great Clock Tower*, was written in 1933 and was performed and published the following year.[80] In a contemporary letter referring to "The Four Ages of Man," Yeats noted that in the first two of those ages "the moon comes to the full—resurrection of Christ and Dionysus," then went on to link his new play with *The Resurrection*: "Both deal with that moment—the slain god, the risen god."[81] As this letter suggests, the "god" in the new play is not a specific deity, but rather an archetypal "slain god." The setting is Ireland in the days of the Tuatha Dé Danann, the "old gods" of Celtic tradition. Incarnate as a stranger, a base "Stroller" and poet, the protagonistic deity meets death at the hands of the mysterious Queen whom Yeats identified in a note as "the mother goddess."[82] The time is midnight on the last day of the year, a further indication that Yeats borrowed the scenario for the play from the ancient fertility rites. He rewrote the play as *A Full Moon in March* (published 1935), making the archetypal identities even clearer and bringing the play closer still to Lawrence's story. In the new version the Stroller has become a Swineherd, whose foulness stresses the body:

> . . . look at me, look long at these foul rags,
> At hair more foul and ragged than my rags;
> Look on my scratched foul flesh. Have I not come
> Through dust and mire. . . .[83]

—"the fury and the mire of human veins," as Yeats had put it in "Byzantium." And the Queen, like the priestess of Isis, is now unmarried, having held herself in "the winter of virginity" until the arrival of the man to whom she is destined to give herself.[84] In both versions

[80]Yeats, *Letters*, 817.
[81]Ibid., 826; see also *Vision* (1937), 245.
[82]Yeats, *Variorum Plays*, 1010.
[83]Ibid., 981.
[84]Compare Lawrence, *The Escaped Cock:* "The very flower of her womb was cool, was almost cold, like a bud in shadow of frost" (p. 39).

of the play the god figure is beheaded, the severed head sings, and the Queen kisses its lips. The opposites come together, her purity and his foulness combine into a Unity of Being, the singing of the head represents emblematically "the risen god."

However, although the pattern of the play replicates that of *The Escaped Cock*, crucial differences remain. Yeats was drawing not only upon *The Golden Bough* but also upon early Irish legend and Wilde's *Salome*, and the elements of primitive violence and perverse sexuality in the play are foreign to the spirit of Lawrence's story. More significantly, the vision of the play is *ultimately* more transcendental than Lawrence would have found acceptable: in sharp contrast to the protagonist of the story, who "rises" in fully physical manhood, Yeats's "risen god" is only a bodiless head; and F. A. C. Wilson has shown that the play can be read as a neo-Platonic allegory of the spirit's temporary descent into matter.[85] This, too, was the sort of vision that Lawrence emphatically rejected in his poem "Demiurge":

> They say that reality exists only in the spirit
> that corporal existence is a kind of death
> that pure being is bodiless
> that the idea of the form precedes the form substantial.
>
> But what nonsense it is![86]

and not the "resurrection" for which he had called so urgently in 1914.

For in the final analysis, Yeats could not do what Lawrence *had* been able to do, to "find the mortal world enough." Both had Pater's vivid, poignant sense "of the splendour of our experience and of its awful brevity." Occasionally Lawrence sounds superficially like the Yeats who haunted séance rooms and studied the tales of Irish peasants for evidences of an afterlife. In *Studies in Classic American Literature* Lawrence showed his familiarity with psychical research: "It is true, as William James and Conan Doyle and the rest allow, that a spirit can persist in the after-death."[87] Yeats himself, after years of study of the same subject, perhaps never quite achieved such certainty, yet the term "after-death" is a telling sign of Lawrence's negative attitude, and the belief is only important to him because it supports

---

[85]F. A. C. Wilson, *W. B. Yeats and Tradition* (1958; reprint, London: Methuen, 1968), 53–94.
[86]Lawrence, *Complete Poems*, 689.
[87]Lawrence, *Classic American Literature*, 84–85.

the possibility of "the evil persistence of a thwarted will, returning for vengeance on *life*" (emphasis added); he goes on to assert, "It is a certain sign of the disintegration of the psyche in a man, and much more so in a woman, when she takes to spiritualism, and table-rapping, and occult messages, or witchcraft and supernatural powers of that sort. When men want to be supernatural, be sure that something has gone wrong in their natural stuff."[88] Again, in *Fantasia of the Unconscious* he wrote, "I am sorry to say I believe in the souls of the dead. I am almost ashamed to say, that I believe the souls of the dead in some way re-enter and pervade the souls of the living: so that life is always the life of living creatures, and death is always our affair. This bit, I admit, is bordering on mysticism. I'm sorry, because I don't like mysticism. It has no trousers and no trousers seat: *n'a pas de quoi*. And I should feel so uncomfortable if I put my hand behind me and felt an absolute blank."[89] But the apologetic tone here is not Yeatsian at all.

Yeats felt the pressure of skepticism from the time of his youthful study of Darwin and Huxley to the end of his life ("What do we know but that we face / One another in this place?"); he could delight in irreverently bringing the neo-Platonic paradise of Plotinus and Porphyry into proximity with the "belly, shoulder, bum" of nymphs and satyrs copulating in the foam at the margin of the fallen world; and he shared Lawrence's attraction to the full realization of the individual in the here and now—to "man alive."[90] In the essay on Whitman, Lawrence described both "the American heroic message" and his own:

'In my Father's house are many mansions.'
'No,' said Whitman. 'Keep out of mansions. A mansion may be heaven on earth, but you might as well be dead. Strictly avoid mansions. The soul is herself when she is going on foot down the open road.'
It is the American heroic message. The soul is not to pile up defenses round herself. She is not to withdraw and seek her heavens inwardly, in mystical ecstasies. She is not to cry to some God beyond, for salvation. She is to go down the open road, as the road opens, into the unknown, keeping company with those whose soul draws them near to her, accomplishing nothing save the journey, and the works incident to the journey, in the long life-travel into the unknown, the soul in her subtle sympathies accomplishing herself by the way.[91]

[88]Ibid., 121; see also 119–20.
[89]Lawrence, *Fantasia*, 64; see also 182–83.
[90]Yeats, "The Man and the Echo," in *Variorum Poems*, 632–33; "News for the Delphic Oracle," in *Variorum Poems*, 611–12; Lawrence, *Phoenix*, 535.
[91]Lawrence, *Classic American Literature*, 186.

There is no reason to think that Yeats was familiar with this passage, which reads nevertheless as if it were the scenario for "Crazy Jane Talks with the Bishop," including implicitly even its dialogue form:

> I met the Bishop on the road
> And much said he and I.
> "Those breasts are flat and fallen now,
> Those veins must soon be dry;
> Live in a heavenly mansion,
> Not in some foul sty."
>
> "Fair and foul are near of kin,
> And fair needs foul," I cried.
> "My friends are gone, but that's a truth
> Nor grave nor bed denied,
> Learned in bodily lowliness
> And in the heart's pride.
>
> "A woman can be proud and stiff
> When on love intent;
> But Love has pitched his mansion in
> The place of excrement;
> For nothing can be sole or whole
> That has not been rent."[92]

Crazy Jane is like the personification of the Lawrencian "soul," rejecting the concept of a "heavenly mansion," salvation achieved through a withdrawal from life or a cry to some God beyond; traveling instead "down the open road" she keeps company with "friends" through contact with whom she experiences the foulness, the rending, necessary for her to "accomplish herself."

But the Bishop in this poem was no mere man of straw. No matter how often Yeats adopted the mask of Crazy Jane, he was unable to silence for long the countering internal voice urging him to "seek out reality, leave things that seem."[93] What Lawrence called "the tedious idea of 'escaping the wheel of birth'"[94] never lost its appeal to Yeats. Much of his literary career can be seen as a quest for ways of reconciling the conflicting claims of Self and Soul, "salvation" on one hand, Homer and "original sin" on the other. The continual recurrence of

---

92Yeats, *Variorum Poems*, 513.
93Yeats, "Vacillation," in *Variorum Poems*, 499–503.
94Lawrence, *Apocalypse*, 161.

their poetic debates—"Is that perhaps the sole theme?"[95]—attests to
the continuing urgency of the search. Lawrence, of course, also heard
that countering voice, but more as an external call than as an urge
from within, and thus he could and did reject it with little or no
vacillation: "Paradise is after life, and I for one am not keen on
anything that is *after* life. . . . All things that are alive are amazing.
And all things that are dead are subsidiary to the living."[96] At the end
of his exegesis of the spiritual theology of Christianity in *Apocalypse*,
he asserted that even the final destruction envisioned in Revelation
was merely evidence of "the things that the human heart secretly
yearns after." In his eyes, "what man most passionately wants is his
living wholeness and his living unison, not his own isolate salvation of
his 'soul.' Man wants his physical fulfilment first and foremost, since
now, once and once only, he is in the flesh and potent. . . . Whatever
the unborn and the dead may know, they cannot know the beauty, the
marvel of being alive in the flesh. The dead may look after the afterwards. But the magnificent here and now of life in the flesh is ours,
and ours alone, and ours only for a time." The "supreme triumph" is
"to be most vividly, most perfectly alive."[97]

George A. Panichas has noted that what particularly attracted Lawrence about the art of the Etruscan tombs was "the depiction of death
as a further sojourn in the 'living continuum.' "[98] In the poems of his
last months, where Lawrence was forced to explore the meaning of
his own imminent death, "the mystical rebirth of the soul" became,
Sandra Gilbert believes, an "article of faith" to him.[99] "The Ship of
Death" charts a "voyage of oblivion," but Lawrence simply cannot
accept this as the final vision:

> The flood subsides, and the body, like a worn sea-shell
> emerges strange and lovely.
> And the little ship wings home, faltering and lapsing
> on the pink flood,
> And the frail soul steps out, into her house again
> filling the heart with peace.[100]

so that despite oblivion the poem ends with an assertion of "peace"
achieved not beyond but within the world, resurrected body and soul
reunited to perform once more the deed of life.

[95]Yeats, *Letters*, 798.
[96]Lawrence, *Phoenix*, 534.
[97]Lawrence, *Apocalypse*, 199–200.
[98]George A. Panichas, *Adventure in Consciousness* (The Hague: Mouton, 1964), 199.
[99]Gilbert, 310; see also 311–12.
[100]Lawrence, *Complete Poems*, 720.

[11]

The Doctrine of Individuality:
D. H. Lawrence's "Metaphysic"

GEORGE J. ZYTARUK

I

D. H. Lawrence's quarrel with Christianity has already received some critical attention.[1] Like Ursula Brangwen, his fictional counterpart in *The Rainbow*, Lawrence struggled desperately during his most formative years to reconcile the teachings of Christianity with his own developing set of ethical and moral beliefs. In his expository prose, as well as in his creative works, we can see him subjecting the Christian doctrine to the severest tests of his intelligence and artistic imagination, and a detailed examination of his encounter with Christianity would show wherein he felt the religion had failed. As a shaping force in Lawrence's thinking, the importance of Christianity cannot be overestimated. From the account of Creation in *Genesis*, to the promise of salvation, and beyond that to the vision of cataclysm in *Revelation*, the Bible stimulates and engages the artist's imagination. Nevertheless, in the final analysis, Lawrence is unable to rely on the Christian faith to provide a raison d'être. It is not that he does not believe in the existence of God; it is, rather, that he admits he knows less about God than the Christian religion claims it does. In his view, "the real problem for humanity isn't whether God exists or not. God always is, and we know it. But the problem is, how to get at Him. That

---

[1]See, for example, "The Quarrel with Christianity," in Graham Hough, *The Dark Sun: A Study of D. H. Lawrence* (London: Duckworth, 1956), 240–54; and C. J. Terry, "Aspects of D. H. Lawrence's Struggle with Christianity," *Dalhousie Review* 54 (Spring 1974), 112–29. Although I strongly disagree with Hough's opinion that "Lawrence's practical recommendations for the reform of society vary between the politics of cloud-cuckoo-land and the politics of the sergeant's mess" (p. 240), I am inclined to accept the view that "to trace Lawrence's relations to Christianity genetically . . . would be to trace the whole course of his work . . . from another and more specialized point of view" (p. 240).

is the greatest problem ever set to our habit-making humanity."[2] Lawrence is convinced that modern civilizations have lost their contact with the living God and that a new way to God must be found. The way of Jesus is no longer adequate because people need more than spiritual salvation. Lawrence feels he must break with Christianity because "Jesus, the Saviour, is no longer our Way of Salvation. He *was* the Saviour, and is not. Once it was Mithras: and has not been Mithras for these many years. It never *was* Mithras for us. God sends different Saviours to different peoples at different times. Now, for the moment, there is no Saviour."[3] "I believe in God," he insists, "But I'm off on a different road."[4] Here, then, we have Lawrence's declaration of faith and his decision to look for a new way to come into touch with the timeless and the infinite, a momentous venture undertaken in the spirit of "thought adventure."

The effort of Lawrence's life, however, was more than a "thought adventure," for he tried to discover living evidence of genuine religious inspiration. His search for a vital religion eventually led him to New Mexico where, for the first time, he found something profoundly religious, "the greatest experience from the outside world"[5] that he ever felt. The New Mexican revelation had two consequences for him: it liberated him from the mechanical civilization of the present and freed him from the hold that Christianity had on his character. The writer whose youth was spent in the charred Midlands of England found the landscape of New Mexico more than "aesthetically-satisfying." He says, "To me it was much more than that. It had a splendid silent terror, and a vast far-and-wide magnificence which made it way beyond mere aesthetic appreciation."[6] Not only did New Mexico move Lawrence with its unmatched landscape; it made him feel for the first time that religious emotion for which he had long searched in many parts of the world. At last he had an understanding of genuine religious feeling, the kind that he wished to have recaptured by the human race. There, in New Mexico, he *felt* religious:

> I had looked over all the world for something that would strike *me* as religious. The simple piety of some English people, the semi-pagan mys-

[2]D. H. Lawrence, "On Being Religious," in *Phoenix: The Posthumous Papers of D. H. Lawrence*, ed. Edward D. McDonald (New York: Viking, 1936), 726. Subsequent citations in text refer to this edition.
[3]Ibid., 729.
[4]Ibid., 730.
[5]Lawrence, "New Mexico," in *Phoenix*, 142.
[6]Ibid., 143.

tery of some Catholics in southern Italy, the intensity of some Bavarian peasants, the semi-ecstasy of Buddhists or Brahmins: all this had seemed religious all right, as far as the parties concerned were involved, but it didn't involve me. I looked on at their religiousness from the outside. For it is still harder to feel religion at will than to love at will. . . . I had no permanent feeling of religion till I came to New Mexico and penetrated into the old human race experience there. It is curious that it should be in America, of all places, that a European should really experience religion, after touching the old Mediterranean and the East. It is curious that one should get a sense of living religion from the Red Indians, having failed to get it from Hindus or Sicilian Catholics or Cingalese.[7]

Lawrence insists that he is not praising "the Red Indian as he reveals himself in contact with white civilization."[8] What had survived in New Mexico of the old religion went "back far beyond the birth of Christ, beyond the pyramids, beyond Moses."[9] This ancient religion was

greater than anything we know: more starkly and nakedly religious. There is no God, no conception of a god. All is god. But it is not the pantheism we are accustomed to, which expresses itself as "God is everywhere, God is in everything." In the oldest religion, everything was alive, not supernaturally but naturally alive. . . . For the whole life-effort of man was to get his life into direct contact with the elemental life of the cosmos, mountain-life, cloud-life, thunder-life, air-life, earth-life, sun-life. . . . It is the oldest religion, a cosmic religion the same for all peoples, not broken up into specific gods or saviours or systems. It is the religion which precedes the god-concept, and is therefore greater and deeper than any god-religion.[10]

The sort of religion for which Lawrence had searched and of which, he says, he still saw traces in New Mexico is not a religion consisting of a formalized code of beliefs, nor is it merely a moral code by means of which the individual can govern his relationships with the rest of society; it does not have a personified God who rewards or punishes, and it does not promise immortality of the soul through salvation. It is, in short, a deep and profound reverence for life the sole purpose of which is to allow life to come forth. This religion includes the whole cosmos and sees man as a vital component of the circumambient universe. Such is the principle that informs Lawrence's essential meta-

[7]Ibid., 143–44.
[8]Ibid., 144.
[9]Ibid., 145.
[10]Ibid., 146–47.

physic, his doctrine of individuality, as I will attempt to demonstrate in the ensuing pages.

II

If Lawrence were to be confronted with charges of mysticism as a result of promulgating the religious ideas that I have noted above, he would not deny the accusation. If his doctrine fails to tell where life comes from and where it is going, Lawrence would feel no embarrassment. Writing in his introduction to *Fantasia of the Unconscious*, he admitted that "the first business of every faith is to declare its ignorance. I don't know where I come from—nor where I exit to. I don't know the origins of life nor the goal of death. I don't know how the two parent cells which are my biological origin became the me which I am. I don't in the least know what these two parent cells were."[11] I hope to show that Lawrence begins with a concern for the individual and develops his doctrine from that; his "metaphysic" is in effect "a theory of human relativity."[12] Because of Lawrence's recurrent use of the term "individuality," I find it convenient to call my formulation of his metaphysic "the doctrine of individuality." Although I believe this doctrine pervades all of Lawrence's work, it is formulated most explicitly in his polemical writings, and I have in consequence drawn my evidence from them rather than from the fiction and poetry.

The doctrine of individuality, stated in its briefest form, holds that

> The final aim of every living thing, creature, or being is the full achievement of itself. This accomplished, it will produce what it will produce, it will bear the fruit of its nature. Not the fruit, however, but the flower is the culmination and climax, the degree to be striven for. Not the work I shall produce, but the real Me I shall achieve, that is the consideration; of the complete Me will come the complete fruit of me, the work, the children.[13]

Lawrence believes that the achievement of individuality is at the base of every living thing and that in man and woman it is the unfolding of the self that constitutes, as it were, the purpose of the individual's life. But the self is not a definable quantity; it cannot be made into an idea,

---

[11]D. H. Lawrence, *Fantasia of the Unconscious* (New York: Thomas Seltzer, 1922), 6–7; hereafter cited as *Fantasia*.

[12]Ibid., 15.

[13]Lawrence, "Study of Thomas Hardy," in *Phoenix*, 403.

for it is of an evolving and creative nature so that no individual may know what he or she will eventually become. To try to "fix" a person's purpose in life or to try to draw up an archetype for each person to follow is, according to Lawrence, a hopeless and a futile task:

> You can't make an *idea* of the living self: hence it can never become an ideal. Thank heaven for that. There it is, an inscrutable, unfindable, vivid quick, giving us off as a life-issue. It is not *spirit*. Spirit is merely our mental consciousness, a finished essence extracted from our life-being, just as alcohol, spirits of wine, is the material, finished essence extracted from the living grape. The living self is not a spirit. You cannot postulate it. How can you postulate that which is *there?*[14]

Since the intrinsic self is an unknown quantity, how can anyone say what it will be, or what it should be?

Because too often men and women have been trying to live up to an idea of their individual selves, says Lawrence, they are more and more falling into automatism and, instead of living, they are merely going through a fixed routine. At this point Lawrence comes into conflict with many of the ideals of modern society. These ideals, Lawrence believes, are completely at odds with the achievement of individuality. Let us look with Lawrence as he examines the Christian ideal of Oneness. To become one with God is a violation of the individual self, since the very existence of all life is made possible by the myriad identities that constitute life. We must, therefore, struggle not to achieve oneness with the rest of creation but to bring to flower the individual, spontaneous self. According to Lawrence, "The highest Collectivity has for its true goal the purest individualism, pure individual spontaneity,"[15] or, more poetically, "The living self has one purpose only: to come into its own fullness of being, as a tree comes into full blossom, or a bird into spring beauty, or a tiger into lustre."[16]

The achievement of individuality, Lawrence believes, is dependent upon the establishment of a multiplicity of relationships. As in his account of the ancient Mexican religion where, Lawrence points out, people drew "strength from the mountain," so every relationship that an individual establishes must serve to nourish the development of his or her individuality. But the nature of such relationships with other beings and other living things must not be a merging or identification; the relationships must be such that they recognize the supreme

14Lawrence, "Democracy," in *Phoenix*, 712–13.
15Ibid., 702.
16Ibid., 714.

otherness of each related individuality. There should be no attempt to see the other in terms of oneself, for "where each thing is unique in itself, there can be no comparison made. . . . There is me, and there is *another being*. That is the first part of the reality. There is no comparing or estimating. There is only this strange recognition of *present otherness*."[17]

The real danger against which men and women must guard is that of making their relationships with other people and things habitual or mechanical. Thus the Christian commandment of "love thy neighbour as thyself," Lawrence contends, violates the spontaneous being. If the relationship between one individual and another is spontaneous love, Lawrence does not object; it is when love is looked upon as an ideal and has its origin in the mind that he finds it unacceptable. Lawrence believes that if we continue further in fulfilling our ideals, we eventually "break down the living integrity" of our beings and fall into sheer mechanical materialism, becoming "automatic units, determined entirely by mechanical law."[18]

It cannot be denied that each person must establish relationships with others and that these relationships in the end give each person an individual wholeness. This "wholeness" Lawrence calls the individual's "salvation." The necessity of establishing relationships with others arises because "though man is first and foremost an individual being, yet the very accomplishing of his individuality rests upon his fulfillment in social life. If you isolate an individual you deprive him of his life: if you leave him no isolation you deprive him of himself. And there it is! Life consists in the interaction between a man and his fellows, from the individual, integral love in each."[19] Nevertheless, human relationships are not enough in themselves to enable men and women to achieve their respective individualities; there still remain the relationships with the rest of the universe. In *A Propos of Lady Chatterley's Lover*, Lawrence posits three kinds of basic relationships: "First, there is the relation to the living universe. Then comes the relation of man to woman. Then comes the relation of man to man. And each is a blood-relationship, not mere spirit or mind."[20] The essay "Morality and the Novel" provides a more specific explanation of how various relationships nurture the achievement of individuality:

[17]Ibid., 715.
[18]Ibid., 717.
[19]Lawerence, "Education of the People," in *Phoenix*, 613–14.
[20]Lawrence, *A Propos of Lady Chatterley's Lover* (London: Mandrake Press, 1930), 56.

D. H. Lawrence's "Metaphysic"

If we think about it, we find that our life *consists in* this achieving of a pure relationship between ourselves and the living universe about us. This is how I "save my soul" by accomplishing a pure relationship between me and another person, me and other people, me and a nation, me and the race of men, me and the animals, me and the trees or flowers, me and the earth, me and the skies and sun and stars, me and the moon: an infinity of pure relations, big and little, like stars in the sky: that makes our eternity, for each one of us, me and the timber I am sawing, the lines of force I follow: me and the dough I knead for bread, me and the very motion with which I write, me and the bit of gold I have got. This, if we knew it, is our life and our eternity: the subtle, perfected relation between me and my whole circumambient universe.[21]

The establishment of this multiplicity of relations with the circumambient universe results in the extension of an individual's consciousness.

In order to extend human consciousness we must, at all times, distinguish between activity that is mere repetition of some "rediscovered movement" and activity that is really creative. The necessity of work in order to ensure self-preservation often has the effect of inhibiting the achievement of individuality because such work is mere imitation of life and not life itself. The development of individuality requires spontaneous activity, although for reasons of survival, "Man has almost half his nature in the material world. His spontaneous nature *just* takes precedence."[22] Work "is one of the inevitable conditions"[23] of human existence. Nevertheless: "It seems as if the great aim and purpose in human life were to bring all life into the human consciousness."[24] The great enemy of the spontaneous self Lawrence calls "idealism," meaning by the term "fixed ideas." If men and women trust too much to their minds rather than to desire, they head more and more toward fixed mechanical activity. It is a very difficult thing for a person to come into "full, spontaneous being," since human nature seems to be a balance between "spontaneous creativity" on the one hand and "mechanical-material activity" on the other. An added complication is that while spontaneous being is "subject to no law," mechanical-material existence is "subject to all the laws of the mechanical-physical world." Thus the individual ends up with almost

---

[21]Lawrence, "Morality and the Novel," in *Phoenix*, 528.
[22]Lawrence, "Democracy," 714.
[23]Lawrence, "Study of Thomas Hardy," 430.
[24]Ibid., 430–31.

half his or her nature engaged in the material world. Fortunately, however, "spontaneous nature *just* takes precedence."[25]

The pertinent question that now arises is: how do we know when we are behaving according to the "lawless" spontaneous nature and when we are indulging in "mechanical-material activity"? In answer to this question Lawrence declares his belief in the supremacy of the passional impulses as against the rational, asserting that "the only thing man has to trust to in coming to himself is his desire and his impulse." He warns that "both desire and impulse tend to fall into mechanical automatism: to fall from spontaneous reality into dead or material reality." Thus "all our education should be a guarding against this fall."[26] Men and women are "neither the created nor the creator" but "the quick of creation." The source of deep human desires is the unknown, "the primal unknown from which all creation issues." In order to become fulfilled "we *must* yield our ultimate will to the unknown impulse."

Lawrence speculates that the purpose of all creation may very well consist in the achievement of, or the striving to achieve, a multiplicity of individualities:

> It seems as though one of the conditions of life is, that life shall continually and progressively differentiate itself, almost as though this differentiation were a Purpose. Life starts crude and unspecified, a great Mass. And it proceeds to evolve out of that mass ever more distinct and definite particular forms, an ever-multiplying number of separate species and orders, as if it were working always to the production of the infinite number of perfect individuals, the individual so thorough that he should have nothing in common with any other individual.[27]

The use of the word "evolve" raises the question of whether or not Lawrence believes in evolution. Lawrence himself says in the *Fantasia of the Unconscious*, "I do not believe in evolution, but in the strangeness and rainbow-change of ever-renewed creative civilizations."[28] However, that his views of individuality are consistent with the theory of evolution is suggested by an account of the origins of life in which he describes how "what was an utter, infinite neutrality, has become evolved into still rudimentary, but positive, orders and species. So on and on till we get to naked jelly, and from naked jelly to enclosed and

[25]Lawrence, "Democracy," 714.
[26]Ibid., 714.
[27]Lawrence, "Study of Thomas Hardy," 431.
[28]Lawrence, *Fantasia*, xii.

separated jelly, from homogeneous tissue to organic tissue, on and on, from invertebrates to mammals, from mammals to man, from man to tribesman, from tribesman to me: and on and on, till, in the future, wonderful, distinct individuals, like angels, move about, each one being himself, perfect as a complete melody or a pure colour."[29] As far as the human species is concerned, Lawrence would argue that the differentiation has been affected by the development of self-consciousness, since humanity has had a tendency to fall into automatism wherein it merely repeats what has already been evolved.[30]

In *Fantasia of the Unconscious*, Lawrence's attempt at the construction of a "metaphysic" or "philosophy" that would be systematic and yet guided by "intuition,"[31] he explains that the birth of a new individual is really a union of the two bloodstreams of the male and female; he does not mean, however, that the new individual is merely a "permutation and combination of old elements, transferred through the parents."[32] Rather, says Lawrence, "the new individual, in his singleness of self, is a perfectly new whole . . . , something underived and utterly unprecedented, unique, a new soul."[33] What Lawrence wishes to stress is that in the newly formed individual the "father-germ" and the "mother-germ" do not disappear but are ever present; their union is only a balance or relationship set up by what Lawrence characteristically calls the "Holy Ghost." The new individual is a "tripartite being, the mother within him, the father within him, and the Holy Ghost."[34]

The most essential quality of individuality is really the result of a balanced relation set up in an individual between the male quality and the female quality even though the individual is, outwardly at least, distinctly male or female.[35] Individuality is achieved, not through merging of the male and female "germs," but through a mysterious and unknowable connection between them that holds them in balance, so that all "existence is dual, and surging towards a consummation."[36] That which constitutes the consummation is the relation between the two dual elements.

The duality of existence that Lawrence significantly sees as begin-

---

[29]Lawrence, "Study of Thomas Hardy," 432.
[30]Lawrence, "Democracy," 714–15.
[31]Lawrence, *Fantasia*, viii.
[32]Ibid., 23.
[33]Ibid., 23.
[34]Ibid., 24.
[35]Ibid., 25.
[36]Lawrence, *"Reflections on the Death of a Porcupine" and Other Essays* (Bloomington: University of Indiana Press, Midland Books, 1963), 211.

ning in the individual at the time of conception continues throughout childhood. At puberty, however, the maleness in the male triumphs and the femaleness in the female triumphs, and so, in the "dynamic" sense, sex is really born. It is now, after the birth of sex, that "new relationships are formed, the old ones retire from their prominence" (*Fantasia*, 145). During adolescence, more than at any previous time in one's individual life, each person feels and becomes conscious of his or her isolated existence. It is "the first hour of true individuality, the first hour of genuine, responsible solitariness" (p. 146).

With adolescence "sex comes into active being." For Lawrence, sex is not just a way of propagating the species; it is no mere biological function. For the individual it is rather "a great psychic experience, a vital experience of tremendous importance" on which "the life and very being of the individual largely depends" (p. 147). After coition "the heart craves for new activity. For new *collective* activity. That is, for a polarized connection with other beings, other men" (p. 150). Lawrence says further, "Men, being themselves made new after the act of coition, wish to make the world new. A new, passionate polarity springs up between men who are bent on the same activity, the polarity between man and woman sinks to passivity. It is now daytime, and time to forget sex, time to be busy making a new world" (pp. 150–51). Lawrence stresses that the individual's drive toward creative activity is more powerful than the drive toward sexual consummation. Having achieved the requisite sexual polarity, the individual must move "in the opposite direction." "I am sure," says Lawrence, "that the ultimate, greatest desire in men is this desire for great *purposive* activity" (p. 151). The loss of a "deep sense of purposive, creative activity" is at bottom the reason for the feeling of alienation that is now widespread. Making "sexual consummation the supreme consummation, even in [one's] *secret* soul," leads to "the beginnings of despair" (p. 152). In what is surely an appropriate description of his own role as a man and a writer, Lawrence unequivocally sets down the direction that he would urge others to take:

> Man must bravely stand by his own soul, his own responsibility as the creative vanguard of life. And he must also have the courage to go home to his woman and become a perfect answer to her deep sexual call. But he must never confuse his two issues. Primarily and supremely man is *always* the pioneer of life, adventuring onward into the unknown, alone with his own temerarious, dauntless soul. Woman for him exists only in the twilight, by the campfire, when day has departed. Evening and the night are hers. [Ibid.]

Feminist critics might well object to the prominence that Lawrence gives to the male here, but we should remember that he is speaking from his own perspective; there is no reason why a woman cannot adopt the same stance toward the relative importance of sex and purposive activity. Indeed, if the sexual revolution is to succeed, Lawrence's recognition that "purposive activity" must remain as the higher aspiration is a good starting point toward achieving equality for both sexes. It may be necessary, Lawrence observes, for man to surrender "his individuality to the great urge which is upon him. He may have to surrender his name, his fame, his fortune, his life, everything" (p. 153). Such a surrender is impossible in sex, for sex is "an individual affair, there is no superior or inferior" (ibid.). Even though individual sexual fulfillment is the necessary condition that leads ultimately to any great purposive activity in a society, the sexual passion must, nevertheless, be "subordinate" to the great purposive passion (pp. 155–56).

The repercussions that result when an individual is hurt in his sexual self, that is, when he is unfulfilled in his sexual being, are analyzed by Lawrence in his comments on the Italian novelist Giovanni Verga. In the preface to Verga's novel *Cavalleria Rusticana*, which Lawrence himself translated into English, we have Lawrence's veneration of the "purely naïve human being, in contrast to the sophisticated."[37] Verga "felt himself in some way deeply mortifed, insulted in his ultimate sexual or male self, and he enacted over and over again the drama of revenge."[38] According to Lawrence, the explanation for Verga's outlook is the fact that man is not ultimately a "reasonable creature," but a "passional phenomenon." Lawrence asks: "Is man a sweet and reasonable creature? Or is he basically a passional phenomenon? Is man a phenomenon on the face of the earth, or a rational consciousness? Is human behaviour to be reasonable, throughout the future, reasoned and rational?—or will it always display itself in strange and violent phenomena?"[39] In speaking to these questions, Lawrence propounds certain "laws," which he feels are applicable to the human phenomenon:

Man is a phenomenon on the face of the earth. But the phenomena have their laws. One of the laws of the phenomenon called a human being is that, hurt this being mortally at its sexual root, and it will recoil ultimate-

[37]Lawrence, *"Cavalleria Rusticana* by Giovanni Verga," in *Phoenix*, 243.
[38]Ibid., 244.
[39]Ibid.

ly into some form of killing. The recoil may be prompt, or delay by years or even by generations. But it will come. We may take it as a law.

We may take it as another law that the very deepest quick of a man's nature is his own pride and self-respect. The human being, weird phenomenon, may be patient for years and years under insult, insult to his very quick, his pride in his own natural being. But at last, O phenomenon, killing will come of it. All bloody revolutions are the result of the long, slow, accumulated insult to the quick of the pride in the mass of men.

A third law is that the naïve or innocent core in a man is always his vital core, and infinitely more important than his intellect or his reason. It is only from his core of unconscious naïveté that the human being is ultimately a responsible and dependable being. Break this human core of naïveté . . . and you get either a violent reaction, or, as is usual nowadays, a merely rational creature whose core of spontaneous life is dead. . . . It is one of the terrible qualities of the reason that it has no life of its own, and unless continually kept nourished or modified by the naïve life in man and woman, it becomes a purely parasitic and destructive thing. . . .

Verga, like every great artist, had sensed this.[40]

Lawrence's formulation of the three laws as they operate in the human being is founded on his belief that human reason is only one of the elements in our total makeups. To suggest that reason can or should have a separate existence from the rest of the individual is, so far as Lawrence is concerned, plain nonsense. Lawrence always identifies human will with human reason, and it is from this identification that he gets his concept of the "idea-driven" individual as opposed to the spontaneous being. The core of naivete is nothing more or less than a reliance upon passional impulse. But naivete is very intimately bound up with individual sexual fulfillment, and this fulfillment appears to be sadly lacking in today's society; the modern manifestation of frenzied mental activity is really a reaction to the hurt that men and women have suffered at their sexual roots. Lawrence believes that if we continue our mental activity in this manner, eventually this activity will recoil upon ourselves.

It must not be concluded that Lawrence does not believe in the efficacy and value of reason. He does not advocate a return to primitivism or a wholesale indulgence of the vicious appetites. What he is after, rather, is a recognition of the part in our total lives that can be said to belong legitimately to the intellect, but he does not agree that the intellect should run the whole of our existence.

[40]Ibid., 245.

D. H. Lawrence's "Metaphysic"

At least one of the ways in which the mind seems to have interfered with the health of the individual is in its mistaken relationship with the rest of the body; the mind has come to feel ashamed of the physical body. Lawrence cites the case of Jonathan Swift as an example of what can happen to a man's attitude when his intellect regards the physical body as an abomination. Lawrence does not hesitate to draw the conclusion that such an attitude on the part of Swift caused his madness. The body can become repulsive to the mind, but why should this be so? Is not the body that wherein the mind is itself contained? There ought to be no distinction between the mind and the body. Lawrence tries to put an end to the division of man into body and soul, or into flesh and spirit. For him, there exists only the one identity of the living body. The mind is to be regarded as part of the total makeup of the individual, and to say that any part is "more important than your living body, is nonsense." The emphasis must always be placed on what is alive, for there is nothing "more important than life." Lawrence "can absolutely see life nowhere but in the living." And for him "things that are alive are amazing. And all things that are dead are subsidiary to the living."[41]

In his essay "Reflections on the Death of a Porcupine," Lawrence explores his notion that life "moves in circles of power and of vividness, and each circle of life only maintains its orbit upon the subjection of some lower circle. If the lower cycles of life are not *mastered*, there can be no higher cycle" (p. 206). For Lawrence "the whole of creation is established upon the fact that one life devours another life, one cycle of existence can only come into existence through the subjugating of another cycle of existence, then what is the good of trying to pretend that it is not so?" (pp. 206–207). Lawrence's insistence that there can be no "higher" or "lower" with respect to "single individuals" or "beings," that each living thing "is itself incomparable and unique," leads him to hypothesize the "fourth dimension, of being," the state in which the triumph of individuality is of paramount significance:

1. Any creature that attains to its own fulness of being, its own *living* self, becomes unique, a nonpareil. It has its place in the fourth dimension, the heaven of existence, and there it is perfect, it is beyond comparison.
2. At the same time, every creature exists in time and space. And in time and space it exists relatively to all other existence, and can never be absolved. Its existence impinges on other existences, and it is itself impinged upon.

[41]Lawrence, "Why the Novel Matters," in *Phoenix*, 534.

And in the struggle for existence, if an effort on the part of any one type or species or order of life, can finally destroy the other species, then the destroyer is of a more vital cycle of existence than the one destroyed. (When speaking of existence we always speak in types, species, not individuals. Species exist. But even an individual dandelion has *being*.)

3. The force which we call *vitality,* and which is the determining factor in the struggle for existence, is, however, derived also from the fourth dimension. That is to say, the ultimate source of all vitality is in that other dimension, or region, where the dandelion blooms, and which men have called heaven, and which we now call the fourth dimension: which is only another way of saying that it is not to be reckoned in terms of space and time.

4. The primary way, in our existence, to get vitality, is to absorb it from living creatures lower than ourselves. It is thus transformed into a new and higher creation. (There are many ways of absorbing: devouring food is one way, love is often another. The best way is a pure relationship, which includes the *being* on each side, and which allows the transfer to take place in a living flow, enhancing the life in both beings.)

5. No creature is fully itself till it is, like the dandelion, opened in the bloom of pure relationship to the sun, the entire living cosmos. [Pp. 210–11]

The achievement of "being" is dependent upon the establishment of pure relationships with other "beings" or individualities.

Since the nature of these pure relationships is of such great importance, it deserves detailed consideration. In point 4 above, Lawrence says that there are many ways in which one species can absorb vitality from another species. Besides applying to matters of existence between different species, the prescription also covers the all important and profound relationship between man and woman, who are members of the same species. Lawrence does not, however, imply that woman is a "lower" creature than man, nor does he mean that man is a "lower" creature than woman. When he writes about "higher" and "lower" cycles of existence he is concerned with survival of *all* species in the natural world in which the struggle for existence proceeds in accordance with the Darwinian principle of "the survival of the fittest" (p. 208). The question which Lawrence now asks is, "wherein does fitness lie?" Because he thinks the question has not been answered, he answers it by placing the question in the "fourth dimension." "The clue to all existence is being," he says, and "being is *not* ideal, as Plato would have it: nor spiritual. It is a transcendent form of existence, and as much material as existence is. Only the matter suddenly enters the fourth dimension" (p. 211).

What gives the quality of *being* to a thing besides giving it existence?

For Lawrence "being" is the manifestation of the "Holy Ghost," which "wanders forth in the comparative chaos of our universe" (p. 213), seeking new incarnations. The clue to being is vitality and "vitality depends upon the clue of the Holy Ghost inside a creature, a man, a nation, a race. When the clue goes, the vitality goes" (p. 214). In achieving being, the creature, man, animal, or whatever it is must always be "moving towards a blossoming: and the most powerful is that which moves towards the as-yet-unknown blossom" (ibid.). The only way to achieve being is to yield to the Holy Ghost or the unknown which is working through creation and, having achieved one's pure individuality, to pass finally into the unknown. The "Holy Ghost" may also be looked upon as "the individual in his pure singleness, in his totality of consciousness, in his oneness of being."[42]

Lawrence regards the whole cosmos as a living creation; he is obsessed with the living nature of things (pp. 217–218). Nevertheless, he does not shun death, for he realizes that death is inevitable:

> We can never conquer death; that is folly. Death and the great dark flux of undoing, this is the inevitable half. Life feeds death, death feeds life. If life is just one point the stronger in the long run, it is only because death is inevitably the stronger in the short run of each separate existence. They are like the hare and the tortoise.
>
> It is only in understanding that we pass beyond the scope of this duality into perfection, in actual living equipoise of blood and bone and spirit. But our understanding must be dual, it must be death understood and life understood.[43]

Lawrence regards death as the "final" consummation, that unknown into which all living things eventually vanish or disappear. He does not speculate on life after death, nor does he address the type of immortality in the spirit that is inherent in the teachings of Christianity. To him death is one of the paradoxical conditions of life. Without death there could be no life. According to him, there are only two desires—"the great desire of creation and the great desire of dissolution." Neither of these desires can be denied if we as individuals are to come to our separate fulfillment, for none is the author of individual desires. Death is the condition of created life, and we have no choice but to submit to this condition. Lawrence believes that "there are ultimately only two desires, the desire of life and the desire

[42]Lawrence, *Fantasia*, 191.
[43]Lawrence, "The Reality of Peace," in *Phoenix*, 681.

of death."[44] Beyond them "is pure being, where I am absolved from desire and made perfect. This is when I am like a rose, when I balance for a space in pure adjustment and pure understanding. The timeless quality of *being* is understanding; when I understand fully, flesh and blood and bone, and mind and soul and spirit one rose of unison, then I *am*. Then I am unrelated and perfect. In true understanding I am always perfect and timeless. In my utterance of that which I have understood I am timeless as a jewel."[45] Thus understanding death is really a way of transcending death; "we only transcend death by understanding down to the last ebb the great process of death in us. We can never destroy death. We only transcend it in pure understanding."[46] The understanding of death is accomplished in the "mind"; "the first great activity of the living mind is to understand death in the mind." Death is the unknown end into which we are all gathered.

There is only one way to come to fulfillment, and that is to yield to the deep desires that are inherent in the individual man and woman. Desires come upon us from the primal unknown out of which all life comes and into which all life vanishes. "It is our business to burn, pure flame, between the two unknowns."[47] Lawrence confesses that we may "never know how it comes to pass that we have form and being," but such uncertainty should not prevent us from becoming our true selves.[48] We must learn to listen to the call of the unknown in us; we must not quarrel with any part of our nature; we must submit to the process of creation that is going on through us. And in submitting to creation we come to our own fullness:

> I am not born fulfilled. The end is not before the beginning. I am born uncreated. I am a mixed handful of life as I issue from the womb. Thenceforth I extricate myself into singleness, the slow developed singleness of manhood. And then I set out to meet the other, the unknown of womanhood. I give myself to the love that makes me join and fuse towards a universal oneness; I give myself to the hate that makes me detach myself, extricate myself vividly from the other in sharp passion; I am given up into universality of fellowship and communion, I am distinguished in keen resistance and isolation, both so utterly, so exquisitely, that I am and I am not at once; suddenly I lapse out of the duality into a sheer beauty of fulfilment. I am a rose of lovely peace.[49]

[44]Ibid., 680.
[45]Ibid.
[46]Ibid., 682.
[47]Lawrence, "Life," 696.
[48]Ibid., 696–97.
[49]Lawrence, "The Reality of Peace," 694.

D. H. Lawrence's "Metaphysic"

Such a passage also evokes Lawrence's fiction—Paul Morel extricating himself into singleness; the man who died meeting the unknown of womanhood; Ursula Brangwen and Rupert Birkin struggling to achieve the requisite balance between fusion and detachment; Aaron Sisson giving himself to the hate that makes him detach himself from the other in sharp passion; Lou Witt at the pole of extreme isolation; Connie Chatterley achieving the beauty of fulfillment and becoming a rose of lovely peace. The fiction itself, as Lawrence declared, was often the milieu in which the doctrine was first worked out, and in the final analysis where visionary creativity and discursive expression coalesce.

CONTRIBUTORS

PETER BALBERT is professor of English and codirector of American Studies at Wells College. He is the author of *D. H. Lawrence and the Psychology of Rhythm* and is at work on a second book on Lawrence, four sections of which have been published as essays. He has also written widely on modern and contemporary fiction.

MARIA DiBATTISTA, associate professor of English at Princeton University, is the author of *The Fables of Anon: Virginia Woolf's Major Novels* and is preparing a study of apocalyptic figures in the modern novel.

AVROM FLEISHMAN is professor of English at Johns Hopkins University. His books include *Conrad's Politics; A Reading of "Mansfield Park"; The English Historical Novel; Virginia Woolf; Fiction and the Ways of Knowing;* and most recently *Figures of Autobiography: The Language of Self-Writing in Victorian and Modern England.*

SANDRA M. GILBERT, professor of English at the University of California at Davis, is the author of *Acts of Attention: The Poems of D. H. Lawrence.* She also coauthored *The Madwoman in the Attic: The Woman Writer and the Nineteenth-Century Literary Imagination* and coedited *Shakespeare's Sisters: Feminist Essays on Woman Poets.*

ROBERT KIELY, Loker Professor of English and American Literature at Harvard University, has written on Lawrence in *Beyond Egotism: The Fiction of James Joyce, Virginia Woolf, and D. H. Lawrence.* He is also the author of *Robert Louis Stevenson and the Fiction of Adventure* and *The Romantic Novel in England.*

A. WALTON LITZ, Holmes Professor of English Literature at Princeton University, is the author of *Introspective Voyager: The Poetic Development of Wallace Stevens; James Joyce; Jane Austen: A Study of Her Artistic Development;* and *The Art of James Joyce.* He has also edited or coedited numerous volumes, including *Eliot in His Time; The Scribner Quarto of Modern Literature; Modern Literary Criticism, 1900–1970; The Joyce Archive;* and *Ezra Pound and Dorothy Shakespear: Their Letters, 1909–1914.*

PHILLIP L. MARCUS is professor of English at Cornell University. He has published *Yeats and the Beginning of the Irish Renaissance; Standish O'Grady; The Secret Rose, Stories by W. B. Yeats: A Variorum Edition;* and *The Death of Cuchulain: Manuscript Materials.*

MARJORIE PERLOFF is Florence Scott Professor of English and Comparative Literature at the University of Southern California. She has published *Rhyme and Meaning in the Poetry of Yeats; The Poetic Art of Robert Lowell; Frank O'Hara: Poet among Painters;* and *The Poetics of Indeterminacy: Rimbaud to Cage.* A collection of her essays, *The Dance of the Intellect: Studies in the Poetry of the Pound Tradition,* is forthcoming.

CHARLES ROSSMAN, associate professor of English at the University of Texas at Austin, is a member of the editorial board of the *D. H. Lawrence Review.* He has published many essays on Lawrence and Joyce and has edited a collection of essays on Mario Vargas Llosa.

MARK SPILKA is professor of English and comparative literature at Brown University. He is the author of *The Love Ethic of D. H. Lawrence* and a series of articles on Lawrence as well as the editor of *D. H. Lawrence: A Collection of Critical Essays.* His other books include *Dickens and Kafka* and *Virginia Woolf's Quarrel with Grieving.*

GEORGE J. ZYTARUK, professor of English and former president of Nipissing University College, Ontario, Canada, has served as president of the D. H. Lawrence Society of America. He has published *The Quest for Rananim: D. H. Lawrence's Letters to S. S. Koteliansky, 1914–1930* and *D. H. Lawrence's Response to Russian Literature.* He has coedited volume 2 of the Cambridge Edition of *The Letters of D. H. Lawrence.*

INDEX

(Names appearing in footnotes are indexed only if the reference is substantive or involves substantive citation.)

Index

Index

Library of Congress Cataloging in Publication Data
Main entry under title:

D. H. Lawrence: a centenary consideration.

   Includes index.
   1. Lawrence, D. H. (David Herbert), 1885–1930—Criticism and
interpretation—Addresses, essays, lectures.   I. Balbert, Peter, 1942–
       II. Marcus, Phillip L., 1941–
III. Title: DH Lawrence.
PR6023.A93Z544   1985   823′.912   84-45800
ISBN 0-8014-1596-9 (alk. paper)